FLORIDAE AMERICAE PROVINCIAE
Recens & exactissima descriptio
Auctore Iacobo le Moyne cui co-
gnomen de Morgues, Qui Laudô-
niertum, Altera Gallorum in eam
Prouinciam Nauigatione comitat*
est, Atque adhibitis aliquot militibus,
Ob pericula, Regionis Illius interi-
ora & Maritima diligentissime
Lustrauit, & Exactissime dimensus
est, Observata etiam singulorum
Fluminum inter se distantia, ut ipse,
met redux Carolo IX Galliarum
Regi, demonstrauit.

SEPTENTRIO

OCCIDENS · ORIENS

MERIDIES

Pars Maris Antillarum

Scala Leucarum.
Marinarum.
Itinerarium.

Le Moyne. Floridae Americae . . . descriptio. 1591.

Places in the Sun

Places in the Sun
The History and Romance of Florida Place-Names

Bertha E. Bloodworth

Alton C. Morris

A University of Florida Book

The University Presses of Florida
Gainesville/1978

Library of Congress Cataloging in Publication Data

Bloodworth, Bertha E.
  Places in the sun.

  "A University of Florida book."
  Bibliography: p.
  Includes index.
  1. Names, Geographical—Florida. 2. Florida—History, Local.
I. Morris, Alton Chester, joint author.
II. Title.
F309.B55   975.9   77–13754
ISBN 0–8130–0544–2

The University Presses of Florida is the
scholarly publishing agency for the State
University System of Florida.

Typography by Copy Grafix, Tallahassee

Printed by Storter Printing Company, Inc., Gainesville

Contents

COUNTIES

ALACHUA, Gainesville
BAKER, Macclenny
BAY, Panama City
BRADFORD, Starke
BREVARD, Titusville
BROWARD, Ft. Lauderdale
CALHOUN, Blountstown
CHARLOTTE, Punta Gorda
CITRUS, Inverness
CLAY, Green Cove Springs
COLLIER, East Naples
COLUMBIA, Lake City
DADE, Miami
DE SOTO, Arcadia
DIXIE, Cross City
DUVAL, Jacksonville
ESCAMBIA, Pensacola
FLAGLER, Bunnell
FRANKLIN, Apalachicola
GADSDEN, Quincy
GILCHRIST, Trenton
GLADES, Moorehaven
GULF, Wewahitchka
HAMILTON, Jasper
HARDEE, Wauchula
HENDRY, LaBelle
HERNANDO, Brooksville
HIGHLANDS, Sebring
HILLSBOROUGH, Tampa
HOLMES, Bonifay
INDIAN RIVER, Vero Beach
JACKSON, Marianna
JEFFERSON, Monticello
LAFAYETTE, Mayo
LAKE, Tavares
LEE, Fort Myers
LEON, Tallahassee
LEVY, Bronson
LIBERTY, Bristol
MADISON, Madison
MANATEE, Bradenton
MARION, Ocala
MARTIN, Stuart
MONROE, Key West
NASSAU, Fernandina
OKALOOSA, Crestview
OKEECHOBEE, Okeechobee
ORANGE, Orlando
OSCEOLA, Kissimmee
PALM BEACH, West Palm Beach
PASCO, Dade City
PINELLAS, Clearwater
POLK, Bartow
PUTNAM, Palatka
ST. JOHNS, St. Augustine
ST. LUCIE, Ft. Pierce
SANTA ROSA, Milton
SARASOTA, Sarasota
SEMINOLE, Sanford
SUMTER, Bushnell
SUWANNEE, Live Oak
TAYLOR, Perry
UNION, Lake Butler
VOLUSIA, DeLand
WAKULLA, Crawfordville
WALTON, DeFuniak Springs
WASHINGTON, Chipley

JEFFERSON HAMILTON NASSAU
MADISON BAKER DUVAL
SUWANNEE COLUMBIA
TAYLOR LAFAYETTE UNION CLAY ST. JOHNS
BRADFORD
GILCHRIST PUTNAM
DIXIE ALACHUA FLAGLER
LEVY MARION
VOLUSIA
CITRUS LAKE
SEMINOLE
HERNANDO SUMTER
ORANGE
PASCO OSCEOLA
HILLSBOROUGH BREVARD
POLK
PINELLAS INDIAN RIVER
MANATEE OKEECHOBEE
HARDEE ST. LUCIE
HIGHLANDS
SARASOTA DE SOTO MARTIN
GLADES
CHARLOTTE
LEE HENDRY PALM BEACH
BROWARD
COLLIER
MONROE DADE

Foreword

FRED LEWIS PATTEE in his essay "The Soul of Florida" describes Florida as a "Never-never Land," "the land of escape," "a domain beyond the rabbit-hole where romance still lingers." The men and women who came to Florida for adventure and the settlers whose roots were embedded deeply in the soil gave names to towns and villages reflecting the romance they found or the history that they made. The place-names of this state tell us what these people found here and preserve a record of the endeavors they wished to make permanent for posterity. These names display what Floridians have believed in, what sides they took in wars and politics, where they came from, what they thought was funny or beautiful or impressive, whom they admired, what natural phenomena molded their culture, and what supported their economy. The place-names of Florida presented here illuminate those spots of time that the authors have found meaningful and momentous in the development of the state.

The sources from which this information is drawn are various, some of them not wholly reliable, but an attempt has been made to winnow fact from fiction in the history of the naming of Florida's places. The unpublished and unedited Federal Writers' Project of the Works Projects Administration, which attempted in the Depression years of the 1930s an etymology of all Florida place-names, has been a source, for example. Similarly the endeavors of one hundred National Youth Administration workers who collected old settlers' stories and the folklore of the state under the supervision of one of the authors of the book have made a contribution. The Allen Morris *Florida Handbook* has been useful. For the names of Indian origin the authors are indebted principally to the manuscript dictionary of the late Clarence Simpson (edited by Mark F. Boyd and published by the Florida Geological Survey) and to the dictionary of place-names of Indian origin published by William Read in 1934. The early maps of Florida have proven useful in showing the semantic changes that have taken place as the state developed and as new names supplanted the original ones. In addition to works specifically devoted to place-names, the authors have researched many other printed materials—handbooks, histories, newspapers, documents—and have interviewed and corresponded with various officials and private citizens concerning names both old and new. The purpose of this book, then, has been to bring together in one volume an honest, comprehensive picture of Florida as unveiled in her place-names.

For purposes of presentation the authors have discussed the naming of Florida, the histories of the county names, the stories of the men and women who left a legacy to the state and whose names Floridians have wished to commemorate, the contributions that the flora and fauna and topography have made in naming the land, the cultural history that has made an impact, and certain lost names from Florida's past that should not go unremembered.

The authors wish to acknowledge their indebtedness to all those persons, past and present, who have assisted in making this book possible and to the administration of the University of Florida, which made time and financial assistance available to them in their endeavor to put together the Florida place-name story.

1

"Because They Discovered It at Easter"

THE FIRST PERMANENT NAME bestowed by the white man on the continent of North America was FLORIDA. We may with much justice assert that it is older than the name of America itself, since that name was not fully recognized and applied to the whole western hemisphere until Mercator placed it on his map in 1538; and even after that, it was seriously questioned. Before that, in 1507, the name had been proposed and had been written on a map to designate the continent of *South* America by a German scholar named Waldseemuller, who was taken in by certain letters to which the name of Amerigo Vespucci had been forged. But even as late as 1627 a demand was made for the suppression of all geographical works and maps containing the name *America*.

Meanwhile, on April 2, 1513, during the Easter season, Juan Ponce de León of Spain had bestowed on the green shores of North America the name Florida, which has never been in jeopardy, though the area it designated has several times changed in size through the years. If the Spanish had dominated in North America, there seems every reason to suppose that the entire continent would have been called Florida, for all the land they saw to the north and west of the present peninsula was regarded as a part of the Florida territory by the Spaniards.

As things happened, the name rests today where it was born—on that peninsula which Ponce de León thought was a great island, like Cuba—and it calls to the imaginative mind the mystery and wonder of those days when no man knew what lay beyond the horizon. For, as foremost place-name authority George Stewart remarks, "the meaning of a name is more than the meaning of the words composing it."

As for Florida, the meaning of the word is significant in itself. Its connotation of flowers and its remembrance of Easter speak poetry to every sensitive ear. Antonio de Herrera, historiographer to His Catholic Majesty the king of Spain, says of the discovery and naming, "Believing that land to be an island, they nam'd it Florida because it appear'd very delightful, having many pleasant groves, and it was all level; as also because they discovered it at Easter, which as has been said, the Spaniards called Pasqua de Flores, or Florida." A twentieth-century historian embroiders the story thus: "Partly in consequence of the bright spring verdure and flowery plains that met his eye, and the magnificence of the magnolia, the bay and the laurel, and partly in honor of the day, Pasqua Florida, or Palm Sunday, and reminded, probably, of its appropriateness by the profusion of the cabbage palms near the point of his landing, he gave to the country the name of Florida."

That two reasons—the beauty of the place and the time of year—could so coincide as to find their justification in a single word will ever be the delight of name fanciers. The absence of a priest on the Ponce de León expedition to tell which saint's day it was may have prevented the somewhat automatic Spanish custom of naming the place for a saint. If so, we may be grateful for that lack, and we may also be thankful that Juan Ponce was so impatient for a name that he did not wait to learn what the Indians called the land, for surely Florida was the best possible choice.

In time the English put their mark upon the word by shifting the stress from the second to the first syllable and changing the quality of the vowels (not to mention the alteration of the Spanish *r*), so that today it would sound strange to Ponce de León's ears, though to Americans it sounds like flowers still. The Floridian may well revel in the name, for few indeed must be the place-names which in a single breath both commemorate and describe.

Cool-headed realists take pleasure in disclosing that Florida was not discovered on Easter Sunday, as romantics have liked to say. But what matter as long as Easter was close enough at hand for Juan Ponce to think of it when he needed a name for the new land? Easter was in late March that year, and it was early in April when Juan Ponce and his men, edging in to the beach, first saw the woodlands of Florida. Sometime thereafter, Ponce de León went ashore and took possession; how ceremoniously we cannot know; he had no priests for mass, no government officials, no historians, but we associate ceremony with those Renaissance *conquistadores*, and we sense drama in that long-ago event, when Florida became, once and for all, the name of a New-World peninsula. There is no indication that the name has ever been questioned throughout the centuries since 1513. All the nations that claimed Florida as their own took her name along with the land, and when the territory became one of the United States of America in 1845, there was no debate, as in the case of some other territories, concerning that name.

George Stewart, in *Names on the Land*, said, "The land has been named, and the names are rooted deep. . . . Let the conqueror come, or the revolution rage; many of our names have survived both already, and may again. Though the books should be burned and the people themselves be cut off, still from the names—as from arrowheads and potsherds—the patient scholar may piece together some record of what we were."

Such a scholar would read in the place-names of Florida the names of men and women and would know that Florida had honored those who built her. He would see in the language of those names that the builders came from many places. He would see that her people had remembered events and had commemorated ideals that were dear to them, and by these he would know what kind of a people they were. He would note names on Florida's map which were the same as those of other places throughout the world, and from this he would see again that Florida had been a cosmopolitan place. He would see how Florida's place-names describe her and would know from this what things about the land her people prized most—what things they most wanted the world to know about her. He would read in the metaphor of these names the hopes her people had for the places, and the poetry that stirred in the namers' hearts. He would see some of the people's means of livelihood. He would learn that humor and whimsy played their part in the naming of places, and perhaps he would decipher some of the word play engaged in, whether or not he could trace the folk etymology and the other processes of change in the names. He would guess the religious affiliations of the people and learn something of their literary tastes. And he would see much that was mystery from an ancient past.

To us, from whom the books are not burned nor the people cut off, the names can tell all these things more clearly and completely. The names of the people on Florida's map, from Christopher Columbus to John F. Kennedy, give us, when we investigate them, about as complete a story of Florida's history since 1492 as could be written. They tell us of the Spanish discoverers and explorers (Ponce de León, de Soto); of the short-lived French regime (Ribault); of the time of the British occupation (Hillsborough, Charlotte, Turnbull); of the second Spanish occupation (Fernandez, Gomez, Gonzales); of the American territorial period (Jackson, Walton, DuVal) and the Seminole Wars (Osceola, Micanopy, Dade); of early statehood (Levy, Polk); of the Civil War (Lee, Bradford); of the Spanish-American War (Dewey); of World War I (Pershing, Samsula); and even of World War II (MacArthur), though by then the naming was nearly done.

For the most part we can tell by the names of these men where Florida's allegiance lay in the various wars. But if the books had been burned and Florida's history had really been lost, it must be admitted that there would be ample room for error in reconstructing her history from the names alone. A confusing factor would be the many names of American Revolutionary heroes and founding fathers among the Florida place-names, for these names were given retrospectively and reflect the loyalties of men who came to Florida nearly fifty years after the Revolution, during which Florida had been a loyal British colony. But those Americans who began to settle Florida in the 1820s first brought her to maturity as a homeland, and their traditions made an imprint upon her map. Even the scholar without guideposts would not be misled if he assumed from these names that Florida's people had a solid American tradition behind them as well as an inheritance from the Spanish, the French, the English, and the Indians. He would know, too, which flag flew over Florida in the tragic War between the States, and thus the names would account for all of Florida's major commitments over hundreds of years.

Besides such broad matters as national loyalties and commitments, we can see in the commemorative names on Florida's map her recognition of local enterprise and leadership—reflected in the places named for postmasters and merchants and solid citizens whose fame was purely local. We see her respect and appreciation for millionaire developers (Flagler, Plant, Collier), who opened up her wilderness and made possible her magic twentieth-century growth. We see, too, that she honored her governors and legislators in her naming, and that the colorful past of the pirates and smugglers off her coast was not blotted from the record. We see that some of her people remembered the kindness and love and beauty of women when they named lakes and towns and that they sometimes perpetuated the memory of their children in the place-names they gave.

Some of what we see in the hundreds of names commemorating people on the map of Florida is substantiated by the names which commemorate ideas and ideals (Union, Liberty, Dixie, Fellowship), showing the genuine American heritage of Floridians. And the names that directly commemorate events which occurred at the places—Matanzas and Court Martial—add to the history already told in the personal names.

In the names that commemorate places elsewhere, we read again the record of Florida as a place where men from all over the United States and from far places throughout the world have gathered. Yamato, Slavia, New Upsala, New Smyrna, Andalusia, Bohemia, Dania, Gotha, Hibernia, Switzerland—all these names and more tell of people who came from faraway places to this American peninsula seeking a better home.

Florida is a land of palms and pines and oaks and "many pleasant groves." This we read abundantly in her place-names—Palm Beach, Pinellas, Oakhurst, Cedar Keys, Cypress, and others. She is a land where oranges grow; names that say "orange" in several ways tell us so—Orange, Citrus, Naranja, Aurantia, Yalaha, Satsuma, Seville. She is a land of flowers, and her own name as well as the names of hundreds of her places record this fact—Flora, Lotus, Oleander, Magnolia Springs, Garden City, Myrtle Grove, and so on. Her names tell us, too, of the Spanish moss so characteristic of her landscape—Moss Bluff, Mossdale, Mossyhead. Those names that describe her vegetation reveal Florida as a transition spot where the temperate and tropical climates meet: Banyan, Bamboo, and Palm City, as well as Pine Level and Oak Knoll, are all within her borders.

Similarly, the names that tell of Florida's wildlife give us a picture of a place where the temperate zone and the tropics meet—Alligator Bay, Snake Creek, Mosquito Inlet, Bear Creek, Bee Ridge, Bullfrog Creek, Deer Island, Echashotee River ("Beaver House River"), Fox Point, Rabbit Island, Raccoon Key, Tiger Bay, Gopher Ridge, Loggerhead Key, Wolf Creek, Manatee, and Otter

Creek. And there are the names for the domestic animals, which do not after all describe Florida except as a place inhabited by man—Cowpen and Duroc and Stock Island being a few of them.

Many of Florida's birds, too, are listed in her place-names—for example, Cuckoo Point, Curlew, Dove Key, Duck Key, Gull Point, and Pelican Island. Like her hundreds of fish names—Devil Fish Key, Oyster Bay, Pompano, Trout Creek, and others—they corroborate the hint of her plant and animal names that Florida is a land of many waters and much coastline. The direct water names—like Bahia, Bayport, Gulf, Surfside, Broadbranch, and Lakeland—labor the point. No one would be in doubt about Florida's abundance of water, both fresh and salt, if he had only a list of her place-names.

Other place-names describe the low land (Boggy Point) and the high land (Alturas), though some names, such as Mountain Lake, exaggerate the height of the land, for Florida is nowhere truly mountainous, in spite of the extensive rolling country in some sections. Some names describe the sinkholes (Alachua) and the flat lands (Acline), and some of them (Everglades and Pahokee) tell of trackless rivers of grass found in Florida alone.

The sunshine that furnished Florida with one of her nicknames—"the Sunshine State"—has also furnished her with a number of place-names—Sun City, Sunniland, and Sunshine Beach being examples. And the Florida sand that the folk say will always bring the wanderer back if he gets it in his shoes has inspired the names of several places, such as Cape Sable, Sand Island, and Sandy Creek.

Some names, half cultural and half descriptive, tell us not only what Florida is like but what the namers thought. These names express approbation and the bragging which is characteristic of a pioneer people—Belleair, Charm, Frostproof, Safety Harbor, Winter Haven, Content Key, Buena Vista, and Zephyrhills.

Other names which tell us something of the people as well as of the land speak of the occupations and industries which arose from the natural conditions of Florida. For example, there is Brickton, telling of the brickyards which utilized the red clay of northwest Florida; there is Farmdale, representing the agricultural pursuits of the area; there are Logging River, Lumberton, and Mill City, recalling the lumber industry; there is Azucar, calling attention to the sugar industry of the section.

Some names are particularly rich in a quality which separates them from the purely commemorative and descriptive categories. A study of the cultural names on Florida's map shows many things about Floridians—inventiveness, humor, whimsy, religion, superstition, literary taste, and legend, as well as a deliberate striving toward poetry and romance, and the naturalness that creates poetry without effort.

Among Florida's place-names there are many which reflect the wish of the namers to be poetic, to connote beauty and romance. Bal Harbour, Floweree, Honey Heights, Lyrata, Solana, and Taru are characteristic. Many such names began as the names of real-estate developments in the Florida boom days and were selected for their sales appeal, but some were given in older days out of sheer pride, and all reflect the imagination of the namers and their feeling for the exotic and romantic.

A certain crude ingenuity and inventiveness are seen in the names which are reverse spellings of words significant to the places—Nolem, Ekal, Remlap, and Senyah. Names like Flomich, Talquin, Okeelanta, Pennsuco, and Sanlando demonstrate ingenuity too, in their combinations of syllables from two or more words which together tell a great deal about the place designated. The linguistic trait called "blending" is a characteristic of some of these names—Tamiami and Indialantic, for example. Language mixture sometimes takes place—as in Indrio and Belleview—while some of the names of this nature, like Belmar, take their syllables from words in the same language.

Another way that Florida's people have played with words to make names is by shortening older names—Okaloo (from Okaloosa), Withla and Lacoochee (from Withlacoochee), and Wannee (from Suwannee), for example. Sometimes they have simply constructed a euphonious word by changing the ending of an "unpoetic" one which means much to the community—as exemplified in Phosphoria (from the phosphate mined in the area). They have exhibited humor and playfulness in names like Teen Jay for a station on the "T. 'n' J.," an early railroad connecting Tampa and Jacksonville, and they have strung together initial letters of a phrase to make a name—as in Kicco (Kissimmee Island Cattle Company). In many cases they have simply let the names "happen," and places have been called what came naturally to the inhabitants—Cuke, Spuds, Hen Scratch, and Pin Hook, for instance. Names like Peghorn, Two Egg, and Norum came about because of incidents which intrigued or amused the namers, and a name like the Devil's Millhopper reflects the superstition and imagination of the folk. Yankeetown was a name given in derision and accepted in defiance, and Crackertown was the name that answered it. Some names are bluntly eloquent of their era—Telegraph Creek, Neon, Texaco—and may be the poetry of another age.

Floridians have taken names from other languages and have "made sense" of them in their own language. On the basis of what the foreign names *sounded* like to them, they have made Key West from the Spanish *Cayo Hueso* ("Bone Key") and Black Creek from the Spanish *Blanco* (or "white") River. And for all we can tell, the Indians' Suwannee and Sampala may go beyond mere corruption and be folk etymologies for the Spaniards' *San Juan* and *San Pablo*. For names they did not change but still could not understand, Floridians have invented derivations—"My! Am I?" for Miami and "He's stiff and ugly" for Estiffanulga.

In doing all these things, Floridians have followed the habit of place-namers all over America, but their namings have been distinctly Floridian because all such processes, being a sort of folklore, follow the culture in which they take place.

Floridians have honored the historical past of their state by giving Spanish names, sometimes ignorantly and incorrectly, and Indian names, sometimes with little significance except their Indian sound. They have misspelled names and so changed them that their origin is lost to the eye (e.g., Waukeenah for *Joachina*). By a strange and complicated process, they have derived Jupiter from the lost Indian *Hoe Bay* and Charlotte from the ancient *Calos*. They have translated some names and let others stand as they were. They have made linguistic mistakes like adding the superfluous "River" to Indian names that already contained the word, such as Choctawhatchee River—*hatchee* being the Seminole-Creek word for "river" or "creek." They have made many mistakes, but they have made many happy choices too, and they have retained enough from the past and added enough of both the present and the past to the list of place-names to give the whole a particularly Floridian flavor. The mistakes and fumbling of a people are an index of its culture too, and the "mistaken" names are as interesting and valuable a part of our heritage as any.

But cultural names tell of more than fancy and folkways. They tell of religion and reading as well. In Florida a long parade of saints' names—among them St. John, Santa Rosa, and St. Augustine—recalls the Roman Catholic religion of Florida's first white settlers. One name (Iola) hints at the religion of her Indian people. St. George's Island is a record of faith left by the British. And biblical names all over the map (Salem, Shiloh, Sharon) proclaim the sturdy protestantism of the American settlers.

As for literature, the place-names of Florida reflect the reading habits of an English-speaking people. Classical mythology and legend have given her a sizeable group of place-names—Jupiter, Juno, Mars, Neptune, Marathon, Electra. Names from English authors—among them Kipling (Mandalay), Shakespeare (Romeo and Juliette [sic]), and George DuMaurier (Trilby)—dot the Florida map. And American writers—Longfellow (Minnehaha Lake and Nokomis) and Edgar Rice Burroughs (Tarzan)—have furnished names for Florida places. Fairy tales (Golden Egg) and the *Arabian Nights* (Aladdin) were a part of the background of the namers, too.

So people have demonstrated in naming Florida places what they cherish and believe in, what some of their limitations were, and most abundantly what their limitations were *not* and how wide their horizons were. These names—commemorative, descriptive, and cultural— have told a story and painted a picture amazingly detailed. Not the least attractive of the details is the mystery that lingers still in names of ancient vintage—Wakulla, Ocala, Sarasota—telling of a past we cannot penetrate. The native American who roamed the Florida swamps and hills before the white man came is remembered still as long as these names endure. They, as well as the names the later Indians gave and the ones the white man made from their language, are an aspect of the glamour of Florida. Strangers repeat with wonder and fascination the strange syllables of Miccosukee, Chattahoochee, Wewahitchka, and Kanapaha. That in literal translation these exotic syllables are frequently rather prosaic descriptive tags matters little, and the white man has fallen into the habit of romanticizing the English translations when necessary to preserve his illusion. For Florida is above all else a land of romance.

Land of Romance, indeed, is one of the epithets popularly applied to the state. Others are *Land of Flowers, Never Never Land, Birthplace of a Nation, Empire of the Sun, Land of Promise,* and *Land of the Second Chance.* These epithets and the place-names scattered over the entire state repeat in many ways the romance and reawakening expressed in the name that Ponce de León gave the land. It is a place of strange and many-splendored names, telling a story exceedingly varied and difficult to grasp in its full meaning.

Florida as revealed in her place-names is a land with a polyglot heritage and a lively history—a land of work and industry and a land of vacation and play—a haven for wanderers the world over—a land of beauty and plainness—a land of tradition and imagination—a land of yesterday and tomorrow. Her place-names have abundantly lived up to the romantic beginning that Ponce de León made when he gave the name with a double meaning to the New World peninsula nearly five centuries ago. In the discussion that follows, the reader will find details of how the land was named and see the ingenuity of those who had a part in the naming.

2

The Pageant of the County Names

THE ESTABLISHMENT and official naming of Florida's sixty-seven counties extended over a period of 104 years, from 1821 to 1925, but the names themselves recall a story more than four centuries long. Some of them, indeed, suggest a time before the white man's New World romance began, but that suggestion is dim and only fitfully illuminated by the wavering light of conjecture. Let the names tell first the story the white man knows.

 COUNTY NAMES THAT COMMEMORATE

EARLY EXPLORERS AND LEADERS

Most of the county names commemorate men who took part in Florida's history since 1513 or who have been important to her people in some way during those centuries. Discussing these names in order of historical associations, though not in the order of their bestowal, we first encounter COLUMBIA COUNTY, named for Christopher Columbus, who, though he was cheated of the honor due him when the New World he discovered was named for a man who never saw it, lives on in "Columbia," which poets apply to that world and which men have generously attached to its rivers, cities, lakes, motion-picture theaters, hotels, streets, counties, business establishments, and almost anything nameable. The naming of Columbia County in Florida is one of the many belated tributes to Isabella's ill-treated admiral. The county was established and named on February 4, 1832, the sixteenth county of the United

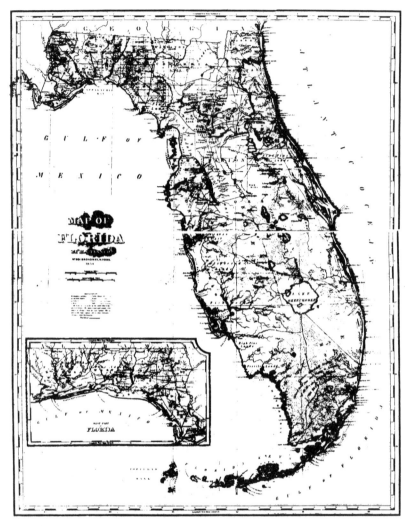

H.S. Tanner, Map of Florida, 1850.

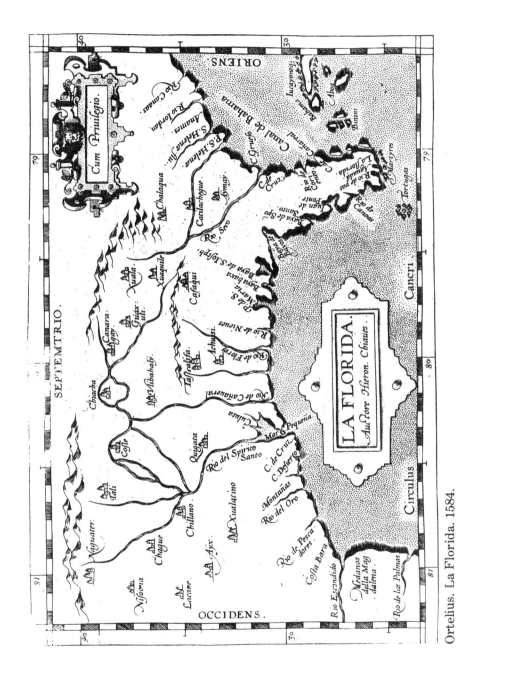

Ortelius. La Florida. 1584.

States Territory of Florida, when the fearful voyage of the *Niña*, the *Pinta*, and the *Santa Maria* was 340 years past. Though Christopher Columbus himself did not set foot on her shore, his discovery of the New World gives him a rightful place among the company which gathers when Florida's county names are called.

Juan Ponce de León, though perhaps not the first European to sail to Florida, is called its discoverer because he bestowed upon it a lasting name and claimed the land for his king. It would be strange indeed if Floridians had failed to honor him as they filled their map with names. His name is liberally used, not only for places but for hotels, theaters, streets, and a host of other things. Appropriately, the county which was named for him is the one in which the capital of the state is located—LEON COUNTY. He himself would hardly recognize the name as his own, for its American pronunciation not only changes the quality of both vowels, but shifts the accent, so that the Spanish "lay-óhn" is now the American "leé-un." Even Floridians are frequently surprised to learn that the name honors Ponce de León, for they are accustomed to using his name in full, as doubtless he himself was. The usual—and correct—habit of Floridians when they shorten it is to say "Ponce" (which they pronounce "pahnts"), as was shown in their custom of referring affectionately to St. Augustine's famous Ponce de Leon Hotel (now no longer a hotel) as "the Ponce," never "the Leon." *De León* was, after all, only a distinguishing phrase added to Juan Ponce's family name to indicate the family's place of origin or residence—the province of León in Spain. But the men who named the county overlooked this fact, and "Leon" was the name they chose in honor of Juan Ponce de León. Leon County, despite its preeminence in rank and in historical associations, is not the oldest of Florida's counties. It was established and named in 1824, along with four other counties, after five had already been established during the years 1821, 1822, and 1823.

Twenty-six years after Ponce de León added the name of Florida to the world map, another Spaniard sailed to that green land and spent the winter of 1539–40 within a few miles of what is now Tallahassee, celebrating with his band of soldiers and priests the first Christmas ever known in what became the United States. That man was Hernando de Soto (sometimes Ferdinando or Fernando de Soto), and Florida honors him today with two of her county names—HERNANDO and DE SOTO. The first was named for him in 1850, and the second in 1887.

One gentleman of the sixteenth century who enters rather dubiously the assembly of those men evoked by Florida's county names is His Catholic Majesty Charles I of Spain, who as Charles V was also Holy Roman Emperor. For many years, it was believed that CHARLOTTE COUNTY was named for him by his Spanish countrymen, although there was no direct evidence of it.

Charlotte County was created and named by the Florida legislature in 1921. However, it is safe to say that nobody at all was in the minds of the solons, for the county got its name from *Charlotte Harbor* (one time *Charlotte Bay*), on which it borders. That name had been on the Florida map since the British regime (1763–83), but one must look 200 years before that time to find the whole truth. On the map of the artist Le Moyne, who recorded in pictures the French Huguenot expedition of Jean Ribault to Florida in 1562, there appeared the name *Calos* to designate the southern part of the peninsula of Florida. At the time of the coming of the Europeans, a powerful tribe of Indians called the *Calusa* controlled all of Florida south of Tampa Bay; and it seems obvious that Le Moyne's *Calos* referred to the kingdom of these Indians. The Spanish, however, sometimes corrupted the name to *Carlos*, and on their maps there appeared for what is now Charlotte Harbor the name *Bahia de Carlos* ("Bay of Charles"). Because of this corruption, there grew a notion in the Spanish mind that the name of the Indians came from Spanish *Carlos*. Fontaneda, a sixteenth-century Spaniard who lived captive among the Calusa for a while, said that *Calusa* meant "a fierce people," and he probably was right. But Solís de Merás says, "This Cacique [chief] was called Carlos because his father was so-called, and his father gave himself that name, because the Christian captives he had, told him that the Emperor Charles was the greatest King of the Christians."

This is how Charles V enters the scene. That *Carlos* was really a white man's corruption of the native *Calusa* (or whatever it might have been in the local Indian tongue, for the early Europeans were hopelessly inept at transcribing the Indian names) is of some moment in arriving at the ultimate truth; but the fact does not deny His Catholic Majesty a place in the Florida sun, for a name means what its users intend for it to mean, and for a long while in the course of its evolution the name of Charlotte Harbor stood for Charles V.

When the English took over Florida, they did not stop at simply translating the Spanish *Carlos* to the English *Charles*, but went a step further and feminized it to *Charlotte*. It is altogether likely that the English seized this opportunity to honor the queen of George III, then ruling England. Throughout the British colonial world in the mid-eighteenth century "Charlotte" place-names were appearing for this reason: Charlotte, North Carolina; Charlottesville, Virginia; and Charlottetown, Prince Edward Island, Canada, are examples. Charlotte Harbor in Florida was then called *Charlotte Bay* and variations thereon, and appears in Jedediah Morse's *American Gazetteer* of 1797 as *Charlotte Haven*. It apparently was first given the name "Charlotte" by Bernard Romans on his 1774 map.

And so this name came down from the aboriginal past, evolving and shifting through error and chance until it became the name of a county. We could simply call the county name a transfer, since it came from that of a harbor; we could go back one step and say it commemorates Charlotte of England; we could go back still further and say that it honors Charles V, Holy Roman Emperor; or we could go back to what is for us its ultimate beginning and call it commemorative of a vanished tribe of Indians. It seems justifiable to take all these steps and admit the Calusa, Charles V, and Charlotte to the company of those commemorated in the county names of Florida.

No men of the seventeenth century are honored in the names of Florida counties. During this century the Spaniards continued their attempts to colonize the peninsula, and today its map still carries names bestowed by them; but later Floridians, when the counties were named, did not see fit to single out any of these Spaniards for recognition. The next phase of the Florida romance as it is hinted at in the county names is the period of the English occupation, 1763–83. After long fighting, Florida was the ransom paid by Spain to the British for the return of Havana in 1763. England held the peninsula uneasily, harassed by both the Americans (for this was the American Revolutionary period) and the Spaniards, until she returned it to Spain in 1783 in exchange for the Bahamas.

One county name (in addition to Charlotte)—that of HILLSBOROUGH COUNTY—stands as a monument to these twenty years of British possession. Writers on the subject say that Willis Hill, second Viscount Hillsborough, received a large grant of land in Florida while the British crown had the power to bestow it and was much interested in the development of the territory. He became secretary of state for the colonies the year before Bernard Romans' exploration of Florida's west coast, and it was on Romans' 1774 map that his name first appeared, on *Hillsborough Bay*. Though place-name literature unanimously states that the county was named for Lord Hillsborough, it actually was named for Hillsborough Bay and the other topographic features which had retained his name since the English occupation. For these features the spelling of the name is now *Hillsboro*—as apparently it once was for the county name. It is so shown on Rand-McNally maps of 1893, 1903, and 1913, but the map of 1923 shows it as *Hillsborough*, as it has remained ever since and as the United States Geographic Board lists it. Strangely, on the 1893 map Hillsboro Bay appears as *Hillsborough Bay*, though the river and county are shown as *Hillsboro*. But no matter how confusing the changes seem or how illogical the present official variations in spelling are, Hillsborough is a name which gained a solid footing in Florida during the British period and has spread extensively over the peninsula. The county which bears the name was formed in 1834.

Though Florida was a "loyal" colony and served as a haven for nearly 10,000 British patriots who fled the United States during the Revolution, several of her counties, named after she had given her allegiance to another flag, honor American Revolutionary militarists and statesmen. WASHINGTON COUNTY was created and named for George Washington in 1824, three years after the Spanish cession of Florida to the United States. SUMTER COUNTY, named in 1835, honors Thomas Sumter, patriot and last surviving general officer of the Revolutionary army. Prominent in the southern campaign of the war, General Sumter was a native of South Carolina, and the county named for him was settled largely by emigrants from that state. JEFFERSON COUNTY was named for Thomas Jefferson, writer of the American Declaration of Independence and third president of the United States, early in 1827, six months after the great man had died on Independence Day of 1826. Benjamin Franklin, that versatile builder of America, is commemorated in the name of FRANKLIN COUNTY, created in 1832. And the romantic "Swamp Fox" of the Revolution, dashing General Francis Marion, is there; MARION COUNTY, settled largely by emigrants from his native South Carolina, was established and named in his honor in 1844.

The memory of one great foreigner—Marie Joseph Paul Yves Roch Gilbert du Motier, the Marquis de Lafayette of France, who stands tall among the American Revolutionary group—is evoked by the name of the thirty-third county, LAFAYETTE COUNTY, established in 1856, eleven years after Florida achieved statehood. Lafayette's connection with the American Revolution is well known, but it may be instructive to mention that he had a more direct connection with Florida in that the United States Congress granted him in 1824 a township of land (23,040 acres) in the Florida territory, just east of Tallahassee. Though he never came to Florida, he took an interest in the territory (dreaming of a slave-free colony that would be a bit of old France, with vineyards and the culture of silkworms as the chief industries) and sent French settlers to it. The marquis had met Richard Keith Call, Florida's territorial delegate in Congress, and had been greatly impressed. Florida's territorial legislature sent the Frenchman an invitation to make Florida his home. In 1832, a small colony of Norman peasants, led by a few of Lafayette's friends, settled on his Florida land, but disease and climate defeated them, and the colony died. Although Lafayette himself died in 1834 without ever seeing his land, the township he chose near Tallahassee remained in the possession of his heirs until it was sold in 1855. Even today, Tallahasseeans refer to a certain area to the east of the city as the "Lafayette Community."

Alexander Hamilton, George Washington's brilliant secretary of the treasury, joined the honored group of early Americans when HAMILTON COUNTY was named for him in 1827, at the same time that MADISON COUNTY was named to honor James Madison, fourth president of the young nation (1809–17). The latter county, next-door neighbor to Jefferson, was settled largely by Virginia colonists—hence the name in honor of a great Virginian.

INDIAN HERITAGE

An exciting chapter in the long Florida story concerns the wars against the Seminole Indians. According to the superintendent of the Seminole Agency (Bureau of Indian Affairs), the only treaties the United States entered into with the Seminoles were those of 1823 and 1833. Not all Seminoles agreed to the provisions of these treaties, and not all went west. A considerable number still reside in the state, and have never yet surrendered to the government of the white man. Though some factions of this proud nation are technically still at war with us, the actual fighting was finished in the days before Florida's statehood. Six counties of the state have names reflecting that critical period of Florida history.

The first American war against the Seminoles took place before Florida was "American"—i.e., during the turbulent second Spanish occupation, when British, Spanish, Americans, runaway slaves, Indians, and pirates made the Florida story a tangled tale too long for telling here. The Americans' part in the struggle was not always an honorable one, but treachery and violence seemed the order of the day in Florida, and by 1818 it was apparent that Spain could not keep order there. The United States, having high-handedly ousted the pirates and occupied Fernandina, sent General Andrew Jackson (or closed her eyes to his going, for some say General Jackson took the mission upon himself) to quell the Seminoles, who constantly harassed the Americans who had settled in Florida. He campaigned against the Indians and the outlaw Negroes from the Suwannee River to Pensacola and provoked protests from both Great Britain and Spain. But Spain had begun to realize that she could not hope to hold "the Floridas" (East and West) against the spreading Americans, and in 1819 a treaty was negotiated by which Spain ceded them to the United States, though Spain did not ratify the treaty for almost two years and it was not proclaimed until February 22, 1821. Jackson, appointed both as commissioner to receive the lands from Spain and as their governor until a permanent civil government could be established, chose to accept the transfer of West Florida in person, while his adjutant, Colonel Robert Butler, acted for him in East Florida.

As things turned out, East Florida was transferred first. On July 10, 1821, the Spanish and American flags were raised together over the historic old Castillo de San Marcos in St. Augustine, and the Spanish flag was then lowered and the Spanish garrison marched out.

In West Florida dilatory Spanish officials delayed arrangements at Pensacola while Jackson, determined not to enter the town until he could come as governor, fumed on the outskirts. He sent his wife, Rachel, on into the city, where she took up residence in a house across the Plaza from Government House and waited until the transfer could be made in circumstances of sufficient dignity to satisfy her husband. Arrangements were completed by July 17, and on that day General Jackson and his escort rode into

Pensacola to the beat of a military band, passed between Spanish and American guards drawn up in the square, and entered Government House, where the formal transfer took place.

The general was in full dress. His uniform was resplendent with nine bands of glittering gold braid, each one topped by a large gold button, and his heavy golden epaulets gleamed in the Florida sun. As he reached the square, he raised his low, cockaded hat to Rachel, who watched from the upper gallery of their house, and "How solemn was his countenance when he dismounted from his horse," she later wrote to a friend. The ceremonies were brief but impressive. The Spanish guard in front of the governor's house was called to attention and marched away. American soldiers took their places. General Jackson, accompanied by the Spanish Governor Cavalla, walked back across the Plaza to his own house when the brief official visit was over. As Señor Cavalla reappeared, the Spanish flag came slowly down and the American flag went up (wrote Rachel), "full one hundred feet." The Spanish troops followed their departing governor, the band broke into "The Star-Spangled Banner," and cannons boomed. Pensacola's people, most of them Spanish, watched in silence. "Many burst into tears," wrote Rachel Jackson. "I have never seen so many pale faces." Apparently frontier America's "Old Hickory" had matched the sophisticated Spaniards splendor for splendor on that significant day in Florida's history and helped give to their loss a touch of high tragedy and to America's gain more than a touch of dignity.

He did not govern Florida long. He resigned his commission in November of that same year and returned to The Hermitage, tired and ready to rest, though much was ahead of him (including eight years as president of the United States) before he was to be permitted to retire from public life. Almost as if by some design (Fate sometimes exhibits a keen sense of the dramatic), Jackson died in 1845, the year of Florida's statehood, and his death occasioned an immediate adjournment of the new General Assembly, which had just convened for the first time when news came of the general's death. Members of both houses wore crepe armbands for sixty days in his memory. Thus Andrew Jackson's figure looms large and long in Florida's history, from Spanish times to statehood. So it is not surprising that "American Florida" should early honor him by naming a county after him. Jackson himself had named the first two counties (Escambia and St. Johns), which he proclaimed by ordinance four days after he accepted West Florida from the Spanish. Wisely, he had called them by names already well established in Florida and, so far as we know, had had no thought of perpetuating his own name upon the map. But the very next county to be named in the new United States territory was JACKSON COUNTY, created on August 12, 1822.

DUVAL COUNTY, created at the same time as Jackson County, was named for William P. DuVal, first civil governor of Florida and, before that, first judge of the superior court in the territory. Governor DuVal, a courageous and determined man, democratic and full of humor, and said to be the original of Washington Irving's Ralph Ringwood, held the governorship from 1822 until 1834 and was notably successful in his dealings with the Indians, who caused no serious trouble during his governorship. It is told that Tiger Tail, chief of the Tallahassee Indians, furnished the governor's wife with game and taught the DuVal children woodcraft.

But during the first year after DuVal's administration, the Second Seminole War broke out, brought on by the federal government's order to the Seminoles, despite their protests, to move to lands west of the Mississippi. January 1, 1836, was the date set for emigration to begin, and on December 28, 1835, the rebellious Seminoles struck. Led by the famous Osceola, who had dramatically flung his knife and pinned the white man's treaty to the council table when he was asked to sign (or so the legend goes), a band of them murdered General Wiley Thompson, Indian agent, and his lieutenant as they walked outside Fort King, near the present Ocala. The same day another band under Chief Alligator surprised a detachment of United States troops under the command of Major Francis L. Dade. Only 4 of the 110 soldiers of Dade's command survived the battle and the massacre that followed, now famous in Florida annals as the Dade Massacre. Today two counties of Florida recall this double blow of the Seminoles—one of them named for the storied Osceola and the other for the ill-fated Dade. DADE COUNTY was established on February 4, 1836, little more than a month after Dade fell, but it was not until 1887, when time had glamourized the noble enemy, that the name of OSCEOLA COUNTY was given to Florida's forty-first county.

As far as the county names of Florida are concerned, those now under discussion have no meaning except as a reminder of the men for whom they are called and the part those men played in the history of Florida. Thus the name of Osceola County means only that Florida remembers an Indian leader who wove a bloody thread into the fabric of the state's history, and this is quite enough. The meaning of Osceola's name itself is hardly relevant, but because of the interest in Indian name meanings, we yield to the tendency to explain them. Many persons believe that *Osceola* means "the rising sun," and indeed one authority states this meaning as a fact, saying that *Asseola* was doubtless the original and true name, that *asse* or *hasse* in the Seminole tongue means "the sun," and that this with the affix *ola* or *ho-ho-lar* would mean "the rising sun." However, the weight of written authority, from 1837 on, indicates that *Osceola*, "or *Asi-yahola*," is derived from the Creek *asi* ("leaves"), specifically referring to the leaves of the yaupon (*Ilex vomitoria*), from which the "black drink" was prepared, and *yaholo* ("singer"), alluding to the cry uttered by the serving attendant when this beverage was being ceremonially distributed. Thus "Singer at the Black Drink" (had Osceola performed this function at tribal rituals?) appears to be the correct interpretation—and one every bit as interesting to the white man's ear as "Rising Sun."

Osceola was not a chief, but he was a natural and powerful leader—considered the most important Seminole warrior of the time. His mother was a Creek of the Red Stick tribe; his father was rumored to be an English trader named Powell, but the artist George Catlin, who painted Osceola during his imprisonment at Fort Moultrie, believed he was a full-blooded Indian. The Fort Moultrie imprisonment came at the end of the Seminole hero's life. He had been seized, with seventy warriors, near St. Augustine, in October 1837, and—though they say he came bearing the white flag of peace—was sent to Fort Moultrie at Charleston, South Carolina, where he died the following January. His grave there is marked simply

OSCEOLA

Patriot and Warrior

Jan. 30th, 1838.

A number of attempts have been made to obtain transfer of his remains to Florida. In 1950 the Florida Legislature petitioned South Carolina to exhume the body and return Osceola to his native state, but South Carolina refused. The next year Florida tried to take its case to President Harry S. Truman, and then appealed to the United Nations, on the ground that the Seminoles, having never surrendered to the United States, were a separate nation. In this appeal the Seminole Nation joined the state of Florida. But South Carolina won every legal skirmish. In October of 1976 a less legal sort of attempt was in the news, when an Associated Press story reported that a "welded-shut steel box" supposedly containing the bones of Osceola had been presented to the Ocala (Florida) Chamber of Commerce by officials of Context Development Corporation, owner of nearby Rainbow Springs. The steel box had been delivered to Context, according to the report, by Miamian Otis Shriver, who claimed he had stolen its contents from the chief's grave at Fort Moultrie in 1966. But to still the alarm aroused by rumors of the 1966 grave robbery, the National Parks Service had excavated the South Carolina grave in 1968 and found a skeleton which it proclaimed to be the body of Osceola; and the skeleton, accepted as the remains of his ancestor by Joe Dan Osceola, great-great-grandson of the warrior chief, had been reinterred in the same grave. Shriver scoffed. At any rate, legal difficulties have persuaded the Ocala Chamber of Commerce to return the steel box to Context without either opening or X-raying it. No further information has been released.

No matter where Osceola's bones lie, his name is prominent on Florida's map, where one county, at least two villages, and a national forest bear it. A monument to him near Ocala stands on the site where the Seminoles held council with territorial officers. But his greatest monument is the name of Osceola County—and a fine and tragic figure he makes in that gathering we imagine as the county names are called.

Other memories of the Seminole Wars are preserved in the county names Gadsden, Putnam, and Taylor. James Gadsden, as aide-de-camp to General Jackson, took part in the 1818 campaign against the Seminoles, and Florida named GADSDEN COUNTY, her fifth county, for him in 1823, before he achieved prominence as an American diplomat and before he played his role in events leading to the Second Seminole War. This role was the negotiation of the Treaty of Payne's Landing, by which Indian chiefs, signing near Ocala in 1832, agreed to examine the lands proposed for them west of the Mississippi and, if satisfied, to emigrate to them with their people. In 1849, Florida gave the name of PUTNAM to her twenty-eighth county, to honor Benjamin A. Putnam, a prominent St. Augustine lawyer who had been an officer in the Second Seminole War—or so one story goes. Others say that it is General Israel Putnam who is honored—a man who was one of the great American commanders in the Revolutionary War, having left his plowing when he heard news of the battle of Lexington. The last Seminole War hero commemorated in the roll call of Florida county names is Zachary Taylor, who defeated the Indians in the decisive battle of Okeechobee and received the brevet of brigadier general and, in 1838, the chief command of Florida. He was, of course, subsequently president of the United States (1849–50), and it was on December 23, 1856, that TAYLOR COUNTY was established and named in his honor.

SEMINOLE COUNTY recognizes with its name the entire nation of Indians who played so dramatic a role in the territorial history of Florida and who still today are a part of her culture. The immigrant tribes who began to come to Florida in the early eighteenth century formed the great Seminole Nation, which eventually absorbed the remnants, if any, of the native tribes. The Seminoles are chiefly Creek and Hitchiti in origin, with Creek predominating, so that most Indian place-names of Florida are traceable to the Creek language. The Seminoles' name is thought to mean "wild men" or "separatists" (corrupted from Creek *Ishti semoli*, "wild men"); they were so called because they were runaways from their own tribes. (The Creeks are said to have first applied the name to those Oconee who settled in Alachua territory rather than return to the Lower Creeks after they assisted Oglethorpe in his 1740 attack on St. Augustine.) It has also been suggested that *Seminole* is an Indian corruption of the Spanish word *cimarron*, which means "wild" or "unruly" and was applied to runaway slaves or beasts. (The Seminoles have no "r" sound in their language and usually substituted the "l" sound. This substitution, plus metathesis, would account for the corruption, but perhaps most authorities incline to the first theory—i.e., the Creek origin.) In any case, Seminole County was created and named for these Indians in 1913.

STATESMEN

But people other than Indians and Indian fighters were involved in Florida's territorial years. Some of these others who were important to Florida's history during that period are remembered, too, in the county names.

MONROE COUNTY was named for James Monroe, who was president of the United States when Spain ceded to her the Floridas and an outlet to the Pacific in return for recognition of the Texas boundary and the payment of $5 million to American citizens for claims against Spain. Official transfer of the Floridas had not taken place, but the treaty had been ratified when Monroe began his second term as president in 1821; and Florida was an important theme of his inaugural address. "To the acquisition of Florida too much importance cannot be attached," he said. "It secures to the United States a territory important in itself, and whose importance is much increased by its bearing on many of the highest interests of the Union. It opens to several of the neighboring states a free passage to the ocean. . . . It secures us against all future annoyance from powerful Indian tribes. It gives us several excellent harbors in the Gulf of Mexico for ships of war of the largest size. It covers by its position in the Gulf the Mississippi and other great waters within our extended limits and thereby enables the United States to afford complete protection to the vast and very valuable productions of our whole Western country, which finds a market through these streams." The county named in President Monroe's honor was created three years later, while he was still in office.

In the same year, WALTON COUNTY was established and named for Colonel George Walton, who at that time was serving as secretary of the territory of Florida. He had, at the time of Florida's acquisition by the United States, been an aide to General Jackson and had served as secretary of West Florida. When Jackson resigned his commission as military governor in 1821 and returned to Tennessee, Walton remained to govern West Florida until the expiration of Jackson's nominal term in June of 1822 and then, under Florida's first civil governor, William P. DuVal, acted as secretary of the entire territory until 1826. Colonel Walton was the son of another George Walton, who had been governor of Georgia and a signer of the Declaration of Independence—and he was the father of a daughter called Octavia, who is credited with naming Tallahassee, established as Florida's capital in 1824.

Later in the territorial period, before the Seminole wars were settled, another great American gave his name to a Florida county. John C. Calhoun, United States senator from South Carolina and former vice-president of the nation, then at the height of his popularity as the champion of the doctrine of states' rights, was honored when CALHOUN COUNTY was created on January 26, 1838. This naming was prophetic of Florida's position in the great civil struggle that was to come, for John C. Calhoun, who died in 1850, was a prime mover of the forces which Florida, under statehood, joined. He died fighting Henry Clay's slavery compromise of 1850.

That was Florida's next step through history: a step into statehood. The first day of her statehood was the first day of the administration of James K. Polk as president of the United States, and Florida's thirty-ninth county—POLK COUNTY—remembers him. Strangely, Florida does not honor with any name the president who signed the bill for her admission on the last day of his term—President John Tyler.

Though Polk County did not come into being until 1861 and its naming was retrospective, the naming of LEVY COUNTY to honor David Levy Yulee, territorial delegate to Congress from Florida (1841–45) and United States senator from Florida at the beginning of her statehood, was a quick and spontaneous recognition of a man who meant much to the young state and who would mean much more, for his service to Florida had just begun. Levy County was formed and named on March 10, 1845, seven days after Florida's admission had climaxed the long debate in which David Levy Yulee, as David Levy, had participated so actively. Levy added *Yulee*, his grandfather's name, which his father had dropped in favor of *Levy*, to his own in 1845, and other places and buildings in Florida have since been given that name to honor him; but the name of Levy County is Florida's first salute to her first senator. More than that, it stands as justification of a dream cherished by Moses Levy, David's father, who, five centuries after his ancestors had been expelled from the Hispanic peninsula because they were Jews, raced by ship from Charleston to East Florida in 1821 to be there when Spain transferred the territory to the United States, for he had learned that all who were there on the day of transfer would, *ipso facto*, become American citizens. He lost his race because his ship was becalmed, but in recognition of his intention, expressed a year before in Philadelphia, to change his nationality, he was given a certificate of citizenship on March 23, 1822. Later, when the legality of the certificate was questioned, he was issued a second one in 1831. When David—a minor at the time of the first certificate and so automatically sharing in its effect, but a man of twenty-two at the time of the second and thus unaffected by it—sought to represent the territory of Florida in Congress in 1841, the question of his citizenship became an issue, an issue decided in his favor. So the handsome and brilliant David Levy, later David Levy Yulee, descendant of Jews who had wandered the world in search of sanctuary, wove the scarlet and somber threads of Hebraic story into the Florida tapestry. He lived out his life as servant and developer of the state, and it is altogether fitting that Levy County on Florida's map should pay tribute to him.

Another county, renamed in 1855, honors a distinguished North Carolinian who came to Florida two years after statehood and entered actively into her government. Theodore W. Brevard served as comptroller of Florida from 1853 to 1861, and the county then named *St. Lucie* was renamed BREVARD COUNTY in his honor.

A statesman rather curiously represented in Florida county names is Henry Clay, whose connection with the state's history was such that it could almost be said that Florida honored him in spite of it rather than because of it. Clay was arch-enemy of Andrew Jackson and led a movement in the United States House of Representatives to censure the general for his campaign against the Seminoles in 1818. In other ways as well he opposed Andrew Jackson all his life. Further, Clay's famous slavery compromise of 1850, though it postponed the conflict, in the long run worked against the interests of the slave-holding South and brought on the bloody war at the end of which Florida shared the bitterness of defeat with her neighbors. But in 1858, this end was not known, and in that year Henry Clay, the Great Compromiser, was recognized in the South—whose interests he had ignored in tariff matters as well—by having CLAY COUNTY named for him.

More likely candidates for Florida names were James McNair Baker, Robert E. Lee, and Richard Bradford. Baker, Lee, and Bradford counties remember these three men, who were citizens of the Confederate States of America, under whose flag Florida fought. Florida was the third state to secede from the Union, and her capital was the only one never taken by federal forces. So, in the naming of her counties, Floridians did not forget the men who championed the lost Confederate cause. BAKER COUNTY, named in 1861, honors the man who served first as Judge of the Fourth Judicial District of Florida and then as Confederate States senator from Florida; LEE COUNTY, created in 1887, commemorates the commander-in-chief of all the Confederate forces; and BRADFORD COUNTY, renamed on December 6, 1861, stands as a monument to the first Florida officer killed in the Civil War. Captain Richard Bradford fell in the battle of Santa Rosa Island on October 9, 1861, and his state did not long delay in honoring his memory. The county which bears his name had been established three years earlier with the name of *New River County*, but embattled Floridians found it sweet and fitting in the bitter days of 1861 to give it a hero's name instead. These three counties—Baker, Lee, and Bradford—tell the story of a lost cause and of a fifth flag which flew over Florida for a little while.

The story of Reconstruction is forgotten in Florida county names. One name remembers, however, the time when Florida had emerged from the long ordeal and was gathering the reins of statehood into her hands once more. PASCO COUNTY, created on June 2, 1887, was named for Samuel Pasco of Monticello, at that time speaker of the Florida House of Representatives and later United States senator from Florida. Pasco had served as chairman of the Florida Constitutional Convention of 1885, which revised the "carpetbag" constitution of 1868 so as to give the state government back to the people.

SETTLERS AND DEVELOPERS

In the story of a state, more than heroes and statesmen and more than military and political affairs leave their imprint upon the land. There are always the "settlers"—the men who came there to live and who, by virtue of living and prospering there, are a part of the fiber which makes the state strong. Often, place-names remember such men, as do the names of some Florida counties—those of Hendry and Holmes counties certainly, and possibly that of Volusia County.

HENDRY COUNTY was named in 1923 for Captain Francis Asbury Hendry, a pre–Civil War state legislator and Confederate captain, who built up a colossal South Florida cattle empire in the post–Civil War decades. Captain Hendry settled in Fort Myers in 1868, established contacts with the Cuban market, and developed ranges south of the Caloosahatchee River, where cattle had never grazed before. He built wharves and pens, and as early as 1876 had fenced in a tract of 25,000 acres where he planned to improve the grasses for fattening stock for market. Other cattlemen exceeded his efforts later, but Hendry was the first pioneer cattle king in Florida. The cattle industry not only has become a source of wealth and prosperity for Florida, but long ago it furnished the name "Crackers," which native Floridians are often called. The name was suggested, it is said, by the skill with which early Florida cowboys cracked their long whips when they rounded up the cattle. Hendry had come to Florida before the Civil War, had served in both the higher and the lower branches of the state legislature, and had voted against secession, but, when overruled by the majority, had accepted a captain's commission and served the Confederacy throughout the war. Despite these early activities, it was as a pioneer cattle king that Floridians chose to honor him when they named Hendry County. The name of Hendry County fittingly honors a man so significantly connected with the development, history, and folklore of the state.

HOLMES COUNTY was created and named much earlier—on January 8, 1848. It was named for *Holmes Creek*, the county's eastern boundary, which in turn was named for *Holmes Valley*, which received its name, according to most opinions, from Thomas J. Holmes, who settled in that vicinity from North Carolina about 1830 or 1834, and who shared, however obscurely, in the early history of American Florida. Little is known about this man, and it seems more by chance than by design that he is honored by a Florida county name. But others say that Holmes Valley got its name from a half-breed Indian who fell victim to one of Andrew Jackson's raids in 1818, and indeed there is evidence of the existence of an Indian with such a name in that very area. Whoever Holmes may be, he seems destined to sit in the shadow of Florida's history.

The same is true of the mysterious Mr. Volus or M. Veluche who, it is said, was honored when VOLUSIA COUNTY was named in 1854. Apparently, the origin of the name rests on tradition alone, and all that is certain now is that the county was named for *Volusia Landing*—a settlement within its limits on the St. Johns River, near Lake George—presumably because the name was pleasing to the ear. According to tradition, *Volusia Landing* was named for an early settler. The WPA unpublished study quotes the *Magazine of History* for August 1908 as saying that the place was named for "one Volus, an English settler." Pleasant Daniel Gold, a local historian, reveals the tradition that a Frenchman or Belgian named *Veluche* ("pronounced 'Voolooshay,' " says Gold) owned a trading post there at one time. However, Gold points out that there is no record either in the Spanish, territorial, or county titles of any land being owned at any time in that vicinity or anywhere in the county under the name Veluche or any name resembling it. The name *Volusia* is mentioned first in history when Governor Richard Keith Call made the landing his headquarters in his campaign against the Seminoles in 1836. Today a road sign reading "Volusia" stands on the Volusia County side of the St. Johns River opposite Lake County's Astor. The occasional assumption that Volusia is an Indian name is very doubtful, since the letter *v* is rare in transcriptions of words from any Indian tongue, and no extant compilation of Florida Indian words and names contains the word Volusia or any other word beginning with the *v* sound. The weight of evidence, if evidence it can be called, supports the placing of Volusia among those county names which presumably remember early settlers.

Looming large in the Florida story are the developers—the millionaires who poured their dollars into carving civilization out of jungle in the late nineteenth and early twentieth centuries. Despite its distinction as the state earliest settled, Florida long remained a wilderness through vast stretches of the peninsula. Population centered in the northern part, where reclamation and trailblazing were relatively unnecessary. Poor transportation facilities, brought about by the trackless Everglades and the generally difficult topography, had prevented full penetration and settlement of Florida as a whole. After the Civil War, the collapse and disorganization of the state's program of internal improvement intensified the problem. Government demoralization and impoverishment brought on by the Civil War left development necessarily in the hands of private entrepreneurs. The state's sale of four million acres of land to Philadelphia capitalist Hamilton Disston in 1881 opened the doors. Though Disston's reclamation ventures were not financially successful, they made it possible for other capitalists to profit by his beginning.

The greatest of all the developers in the imagination of most Floridians is Henry Morrison Flagler, the man who, as one historian has pointed out, lived two lives successively in the span of years in which most men live one. The first life he devoted to amassing an enormous fortune; the second he dedicated to the spending of that fortune to create a new world in the wilds of subtropical Florida. Other capitalists invested in Florida for their own profit; Flagler, it is said, was pursuing an ideal. His string of palatial hotels from St. Augustine to Palm Beach, his railroad system spanning the entire eastern coast of the peninsula, and his crown-ing achievement—the unbelievable overseas railway from the toe of the peninsula to Key West—are as romantic as any part of the Florida story. Though Flagler's overseas railroad was later lost in a tropical hurricane and has now been replaced by an overseas highway, it blazed a daring trail through heartbreaking hard-ships; and a year and four months before he died on May 20, 1913, his dreams were made real when he rode into Key West in his private railway car. Florida remembers Flagler in many ways in her place-names; one of these is the name of FLAGLER COUNTY, created in 1917.

COLLIER COUNTY, created in 1923, is another county named for a developer. Barron G. Collier, a large-scale landowner in the region and a former Tennesseean, had become wealthy in the advertising brokerage business and invested his money in Florida develop-ment. Collier's investments came later than Flagler's; and though they were not such idealistic or uncharted adventures as Flagler's, they were significant in opening up the undeveloped areas of the state.

GOVERNORS

Four counties bear the names of men who have served as gover-nors of the state during the twentieth century—Broward, Gil-christ, Hardee, and Martin. BROWARD COUNTY—named for Napo-leon Bonaparte Broward, governor from 1905 to 1909—was created in 1915. It commemorates one of the most colorful political figures Florida has had, as well as one of the most influential. Broward was a native Floridian, born of humble parents in Duval County in 1857, and grew up under almost unbelievable hardships during Reconstruction years. Orphaned before he was twelve, he held one odd job after another until in manhood he became a joint owner of steamboats plying, with passengers and mail, between Mayport and Palatka. He served as sheriff of Duval County and later as a member of the state legislature. In 1896, for profit as well as a romantic desire to aid the cause of human freedom, he became captain of the *Three Friends*, the famous filibustering steamer which ran the blockade to Cuba with arms and munitions for the Cuban insurgents. To save the primary election law and to safe-guard the freedom of Florida's people to govern themselves, he announced his candidacy for the governorship of Florida and won in 1904. So influential and beneficial was Broward as governor of Florida that the years of his administration and those following, when his policies were continued, have become known in Florida annals as "the Broward era." It is noted for the reforming of the educational systems of the state, both higher and lower, and for the beginning of the gigantic task of draining the Everglades. For these two accomplishments and more, Florida honors Napoleon Bonaparte Broward, native son, who gave her tremendous impetus toward status and maturity among the states. The name of Broward County stands as partial recognition of his contribution. Broward died in 1910, just after his election as United States senator from Florida, and did not live to know of this gesture of appreciation.

Albert W. Gilchrist followed Broward as governor. He served from 1909 to 1913. He was not a Broward supporter, but nonetheless "Browardism" continued during his administration; reclamation of the Everglades proceeded, and there was little change in state policy under Gilchrist. It was during his term that the commission form of government for towns and cities was introduced into the body of state laws. In 1925, a year before his death, a new Florida county was created and named GILCHRIST COUNTY in his honor.

HARDEE COUNTY was created in 1921, when Cary A. Hardee was governor of Florida. It was, as so many other counties have been, created by the splitting of another county, De Soto, which was divided into five counties. Agitation in favor of division of the tremendous county had been going on since the early twentieth century, and it was intended that the portion now forming Hardee County should be named *Seminole*. But long before the division controversy could be settled another Florida county had been given that name. Other names were suggested, such as *Cherokee* (apparently for its picturesqueness as an Indian word), *Goolsby* (for a pioneer resident), and *Wauchula* (the name of the town that became the county seat). But when the division act was finally introduced, the name of the current governor was chosen. Cary Hardee, another native son, lived thirty-seven years to enjoy the honor accorded him. He died in 1958 at Live Oak in Suwannee County, where he was a lawyer and a bank president.

Succeeding Cary Hardee as governor was John W. Martin, a native of Marion County. Martin's inauguration year, 1925, was the year when the fabulous Florida land boom, which had been gathering momentum since the reclamation of the Everglades began, peaked and exploded, plunging Florida into depression four years ahead of the rest of the nation. In the last year of his administration occurred the most disastrous of a series of tropical hurricanes that had harassed southern Florida for six years. This one laid waste the heart of the vegetable kingdom around Lake Okeechobee and drowned about 2,400 people. It drowned, also, the seemingly endless bickering about flood control which had occupied so much of Martin's energy; and his successor, Doyle G. Carleton, was able to accomplish, with federal aid, what Martin had sought in vain to achieve—the control of the water level of Lake Okeechobee. Martin's heartbreaking administration is commemorated in the name of MARTIN COUNTY, established in 1925.

Martin County was the last of the county names commemorating people. Whether there will be others we cannot know. Article VIII, Section 1, of the Constitution of Florida provides that "counties may be created, abolished or changed by law"; and there is, of course, always the possibility that a county name will be changed, as has happened in the past; but after all these years we may with some safety assume that the naming is ended. The men—and the queen—who are remembered in Florida's county names tell a story more than four hundred years long—of discovery and exploration in a new world, of wars and heartbreaking hardships, of peace and prosperity, of confusion and purpose, of ideals and realities, of Florida under five flags.

IDEALS AND ORIGINS

The names of places may commemorate things other than men and women. Three county names of Florida commemorate directly the ideas and ideals of their founders. LIBERTY COUNTY was created in 1855, when Florida was still in the pride of her early statehood, and in 1921 UNION COUNTY was established, adding another primary American ideal to Florida's place-name roster. But as if to remind men of other dreams that she had fought for, Florida also named DIXIE COUNTY that year—a name that suggests all that the South stood for in its struggle against the North. Thus Florida county names commemorate national and regional ideals as well as the people who upheld those ideals.

Place-names often commemorate other places too, as does the

name of Florida's NASSAU COUNTY. Actually, the county, created in 1824, was named for the *Nassau River*, which had been so named by the British during their occupation of Florida. Many emigrants from the Bahamas came to this section during the British occupation, and it is reasonable to assume that they named the Nassau River after the principal town of the Bahamas. The names of Nassau Sound and the town of Nassauville also remained from that period, and when the county was created, the name came naturally as a local tradition. In its ultimate commemoration of the British Nassau, it also commemorates the English era in Florida's history.

🏵 COUNTY NAMES THAT DESCRIBE 🏵

The story that Florida's county names tell is not merely a narrative of events in her history and of people who took part in those events; in the names of her counties, one can find an amazingly detailed description of the state as well. They tell us something of her flora and fauna and indirectly reveal her climate and other natural features.

The county with the oldest of these descriptive names is PINELLAS COUNTY. According to tradition, the name *Pinellas* was inherited from the early Spanish explorers, who called the peninsula which forms the county *Punta Pinal*, meaning "pine grove point." *Pinal* is the obsolete form of modern *pinar*, meaning "grove of pines." The steps by which *Pinellas* evolved from this beginning are not definitely known, but it is easy to construct more than one plausible explanation. The plural of *pinal* is *pinales*, which, considering the vagaries of those who wrote names on the map as flags over Florida changed, is a natural basis for the change to *Pinellas* by two routes: mispronunciation and consequent misspelling, or misspelling and consequent mispronunciation. The name which is the immediate ancestor of Pinellas County seems to be *Point Pinellas*, which was written on maps to designate a place on the tip of the peninsula, sometimes shown simply as *Pinellas*, before the county was created in 1911. The pine is a prominent tree in Florida, and it is appropriate that one of the state's major place-names should publish that fact.

Another tree of Florida that is even more symbolic of the state to many people is the palm. A descriptive county name which recognizes this fact is that of PALM BEACH COUNTY, which equally well reveals Florida as a place of beaches. The county was named for the city of Palm Beach, which existed before the county's creation in 1909, and was, of course, a name descriptive of the surroundings.

To show how significant the orange and its relatives are in Florida, the state has two counties named for the citrus trees which abundantly grow there—ORANGE COUNTY, so named in 1845, and CITRUS COUNTY, established in 1887.

The recognition of the pine, the palm, and the orange in place-names of such major importance is very fitting, for these trees have been some of Florida's greatest treasures. Evidence of the state's regard for them is also seen in the large number of other place-names derived from them, to be discussed later.

The sole representative of Florida's fauna among her county names is that of MANATEE COUNTY. This county, created in 1855, was named for the manatee, or sea cow, which is found in the waters off the county's coast, as well as elsewhere in Florida's coastal waters. Perhaps it is appropriate that the manatee is the only Florida animal among the county names (though some might choose the alligator), for it is said that the manatee is found nowhere else in the United States. The name is from the Spanish *manati*, meaning "sea cow."

The hints in the flora and fauna descriptive names that Florida is a place of many waters are confirmed in the names of six counties that tell of waters both fresh and salt. GULF COUNTY, created in 1925, was so named because it borders on the Gulf of Mexico. BAY COUNTY, named in 1913, borders on St. Andrews Bay, for which it was named. INDIAN RIVER COUNTY, which was established in 1925, received its name from the *Indian River* (actually a coastal lagoon), which lies along its edge. In 1887, LAKE COUNTY was created and named for the many lakes within its borders. OKEECHOBEE COUNTY, created in 1917, was named for *Lake Okeechobee*, the second largest body of fresh water wholly within the boundaries of the United States. This name is from the Hitchiti Indian tongue, composed of *oki* ("water"), and *chubi* ("big"). It is the latest of a series of Indian descriptive names to be attached to the lake, all of them meaning in various Indian tongues "big water." The county seat of Okeechobee County is also named *Okeechobee*. Another "water" name for a Florida county is OKALOOSA, which could be from the Choctaw *oka* ("water"), plus *lusa* ("black"), but may be from the Chatot dialect, which was similar. The name is thought to have referred originally to what is now the *Blackwater River*.

Other descriptive county names tell us a little about Florida's terrain, ALACHUA COUNTY being one of them. When the county was established in 1824, the designation "Alachua" had already been attached to the vicinity for a very long time. Maps since 1715 show it in various forms (for example, *Allachua, Lachua, Au-lot-che-wau, A-lach-uh-wuh,* and *A-lotch-uh-way*), and there is some suggestion that the name is much older than the first map on which it is recorded and, perhaps, is of Timucuan origin. There is little agreement about the name's exact source, but most authorities do agree that it refers to the numerous sinkholes in the area. For example, the following passage in the journal of a Spanish officer who traversed the region in 1716 states: "I left the said site and camped at a place they call Aquilachua this day I marched five leagues. In this day's march, no creeks were encountered but there are good springs of water, and the first named Usichua, the other Usiparachua, and another Afanochua." Pointing out that anyone familiar with the area could not doubt that the springs without effluent streams were sinkholes, he concludes that the *chua* which terminated all of their names might well be the Timucuan name for "sink." Since the Timucua had been exterminated by 1710, and the immigrant Creeks did not settle in the area until about 1740, this theory seems more plausible than the one which suggests that "Alachua" is a derivative of the Seminole-Creek *luchuwa,* meaning "jug," applied by the Indians to a large chasm near the present Gainesville. For "Allachua" was on a 1715 map, long before the Creeks were on the spot. In either case, the name describes the terrain. When Alachua County was created, its naming was a natural acceptance of a fitting heritage.

Two other Florida county names are of a descriptive nature—HIGHLANDS COUNTY, created in 1921, which tells in its name of the area's high lands, and GLADES COUNTY, located in the heart of the Everglades. The name of Glades County (also created in 1921) is perhaps the most distinctive descriptive name of all, for it is an abbreviation of *Everglades,* a topographical term which was invented in Florida to designate a Florida phenomenon and is used to describe no other area in the world. *Glade* has evidently been used by Americans since 1744 to designate a moist, swampy area. The earliest known use of *Ever Glades* was in 1823, in *Observations Upon the Floridas* by Charles Blacker Vignoles. Vignoles also used the terms *Eternal Glades, The Glade, The Great Glade*—and one time *The Never Glade*—all applied to the region of subtropical lowland, usually flooded with water and covered with tall grass, which covered mile upon mile of southern Florida and probably was never penetrated by the white man before the mid-nineteenth century. Since he used *The Never Glade* only once and *Ever Glades* several times, we may assume that the first term was a misprint and that the more logical second one was his real choice. It was apparently formed on the pattern of *evergreen*, with *ever* signifying "interminable" or "going on forever," and is today firmly established and securely attached to Florida. So the name of Glades County is uniquely Floridian as a shortened form of an exclusively Floridian topographical term.

❀ CULTURAL COUNTY NAMES ❀

Place-names grow out of the cultural background of the namers and often tell of their religion, their literary tastes, their humor, and their folklore. The county names of Florida are principally commemorative or descriptive, but there are three names which are religious in background. All three of them tell of the religion of the first white settlers of Florida—the Roman Catholic Spaniards, who habitually took place-names from the saints' calendar. ST. JOHNS COUNTY was one of the first two counties established in Florida, ordered by Andrew Jackson immediately after the delivery of Florida to the United States in 1821. The name he gave it was already well established in Florida, having earlier been bestowed by the Spanish upon the *St. Johns River* (they called it *Rio de San Juan*, of course, and the English had translated the name into their own language) after a mission on its banks named for St. John the Baptist. SANTA ROSA COUNTY was named in 1842 for *Santa Rosa Island*, named by the Spanish for Santa Rosa of Viterbo, Italy, saint of the Roman Catholic Church. The name of the village of *Santa Rosa* is also a part of this name cluster. ST. LUCIE COUNTY bears a name which ultimately honors St. Lucy of Syracuse (Spanish *Santa Lucia*); it was first bestowed in Florida by the Spaniards in 1565, when they built a fort by the name of *Santa Lucia* near Cape Canaveral. The name was associated with several natural features and was part of the Florida heritage when it was bestowed, in its English form, upon a county created in 1844. It lasted there only until 1855, when the land it designated became

Brevard County instead, but in 1905 the large area was subdivided, and one piece of it became the present St. Lucie County.

Some of the place-names of Florida are such an ancient inheritance that their original significance is lost. Even of some of the county names, all of which have been assigned since 1821, this is true. For several counties of Florida were given names that had lingered upon natural features within their boundaries for hundreds of years. One of these names is that of ESCAMBIA COUNTY, which was named by Andrew Jackson when he proclaimed the first two counties. He named it from the *Escambia River* (shown as "River Escambe" on the Romans map of 1774 and as "River Scambia" on the Gauld Chart of 1780), but how the river was named nobody knows. Attempts have been made to connect it with the Spanish *cambiar* ("to exchange"), on the theory that it may have been applied to a trading or bartering place, but this is pure conjecture, and the chances are that it is derived from a name in one of the lost Indian dialects. San Cosmo y San Damian de Escambe (or Scambe) was an Indian village in Apalachee during the mission period. It is probable that the prefixed *e* in *Escambia* and some of its earlier forms resulted from the Spanish pronunciation of the initial letter *s* as "es" when it precedes a consonant. (Note the Spanish *espiritu* for spirit, *espiral* for spiral, *esposa* for spouse, *esfera* for sphere, *escriba* for scribe, *esbelto* for svelte, etc.) *Escambia Bay* is a part of this name cluster too, and there is a small settlement named *Escambia* within the county (established about 1884).

The name of WAKULLA COUNTY is another of the names whose original meaning is lost. The name was given to the county when it was created in 1843, but *Wakulla* had already been applied to the *Wakulla River*, *Wakulla Springs*, and perhaps to the village of *Wakulla* (though *Wakulla Beach* probably came into existence later). Although the origin of the name is a mystery, there is no justification for the popular belief that the word itself means "mystery." *Wakulla* is a corruption of *Guacara*, which was the Spanish phonetic spelling of an aboriginal Indian name. *Wakulla* developed because of the later Seminoles' pronunciation of *Guacara*, Spanish *gua* being equivalent to Creek *wa* and *cara* being pronounced *kala* by the Creeks because they have no *r* sound in their language—thus *Wakala*. The name was probably a Timucuan word in the beginning, and perhaps its meaning will never be known. *Kala* signified a "spring of water" in some Indian dialects, but whether it meant that in the tongue of the lost Florida aborigines we cannot say. A mission called *San Juan de Guacara* was situated on the bank of the Suwannee River during the seventeenth century, and both the Suwannee and the Wakulla are characterized by large springs. Similarities between Wakulla and Ocala, both as names and as places, should also be noted.

The third mystery name—that of SUWANNEE COUNTY—may have come from the name of the Spanish mission mentioned above: *San Juan de Guacara*. The county was named in 1858 for the *Suwannee River*, which flows through it on its way to the Gulf of Mexico, and the name has been used extensively in Florida (for example, there are the villages of *Suwannee* within Suwannee County and *Suwannee Valley* in Columbia County, as well as other places and features bearing the name). Many meanings have been imagined for it, and the folk have even invented an Indian princess to be the river's namesake, but a more convincing conjecture rests on the name of the Spanish mission. Captain Bernard Romans' map of 1774 shows the river as "River St. Juan de Guacara vulgo [i.e., commonly called] little Seguana," and there is convincing logic in the theory that *Seguana* is a Spanish transliteration of an Indian attempt to pronounce *San Juan*, with the "wa" sound spelled *gua*, as we should expect. It is easy to see how *Suwannee* might have grown from this beginning. There is a *Seguana* (or perhaps it is *Sequana*) on the sixteenth-century Le Moyne map of Florida, apparently labelling a river flowing into the Atlantic Ocean (*not* the Gulf of Mexico). Could this be the St. Johns River (*Rio de San Juan*)? The "*San Juan* equals *Seguana* equals *Suwannee*" theory, espoused by more than one respectable cartographer and/or historian since the eighteenth century, is countered by another theory which seems equally convincing to some: There is a village named *Suwannee* in Gwinnett County, Georgia, which stands on the site of a former Cherokee town called *Suwani*. The Cherokees claim that the name of their town was of Creek origin. If this is true, the derivation of *Suwannee* must be from the Creek *suwani*, meaning "echo." And good echoes are indeed a feature of the high-banked Suwannee. But the matter is not settled—and Suwannee remains one of Florida's mystery names.

The name of SARASOTA COUNTY, given in 1921, is the most mysterious of all. It is probably a Calusa Indian name, though Spanish derivations have been attempted and a Spanish lady named "Sara de Sota" has been invented for a namesake, but no meaning for it has ever been established. It is an old name, having designated part of the shore line in the area for a long time; and astonishing variations on the name appeared on maps published during the eighteenth and nineteenth centuries—*Puerto de Saxasote, Porte Sarasota, Boca Sarasota, Sara Zota, Port Sarasote, Boca Quarasote,* and *Sarazola* being but a few. It had long become fixed as *Sarasota* for *Sarasota Bay* by the time the county was named. The town of *Sarasota,* now the county seat, had been established around 1880, growing out of a settlement begun by William Whitaker in 1843, across the bay from an abandoned fishing camp and Indian trading station which had been called *Saraxola* when Whitaker arrived in the area.

And so in the sixty-seven county names and the name of the state itself much of the history of Florida can be read. In them one sees something of the kind of place she is. Through them, also, one learns a little about the culture of the earliest white settlers and finds that she has a distant past he can scarcely hope to penetrate. In the following pages many other place-names of Florida will be called on to fill in details of the story and the picture discovered through these sixty-eight names.

3

Florida Remembers

THE COMMEMORATIVE IMPULSE of man is nowhere more apparent than it is in the names he bestows. To perpetuate the memory of people, ideas and ideals, events, and places is one of the prime forces behind the selection of names everywhere. The Florida place-names which sprang from the commemorative impulse are a large part of the total number, as the state name and its county names have already indicated.

❀ NAMES COMMEMORATING PEOPLE ❀

The practice of naming places after people is an ancient and honorable one. Sometimes such names are given in a conscious attempt to do honor to great persons and incidentally to reflect glory upon the places named. Sometimes they are bestowed by people who seek to perpetuate their own names, sometimes by those who wish to make a gesture of affection to a spouse or child or friend, sometimes by citizens who want to thank a community leader or developer. Sometimes personal names are even accidentally given to places; they attach themselves, without plan or design, to an area or a settlement because a certain man owns the land or runs the store where settlers meet. Thus the crossroads where Tom Smith has a general store becomes known as "Tom's" or "Smith's Corner," and as a town grows about it the name may linger out of habit, even after the man himself is gone and forgotten.

Floridians have been liberal practitioners of the commemorative method of naming. The category of places named after people is the largest of all, with the possible exception of descriptive names. Literally thousands of places and natural features in Florida bear the names of men, women, or children, either famous or obscure. It is probable that some of those about whom we know nothing have the most interesting stories of all; for, though from one point of view it may seem that personal place-names are the least imaginative, it is nonetheless true that such names, when investigated, reveal a great deal that is colorful and important in the history of the state and its people.

THE SPANISH

Because the Spaniards first wrote the name of Florida into history, it is fitting that they head the parade of men whose names now dot the map of the state. Already it has been noted that Floridians have liberally used the name of Juan Ponce de León, the discoverer, to designate natural features, buildings, institutions, business establishments, and political subdivisions. Some of the better-known places bearing his name (besides Leon County) include PONCE DE LEON BAY, off the coast of Monroe County, and PONCE DE LEON SPRINGS, a large spring in Volusia County which, legend has it, was visited by Ponce de León himself in 1513. According to legend, the discoverer and his men were fleeing, with stolen treasure, from the Indians when they chanced upon this deep spring, into which they threw the heavy chest of gold and silver. There it has lain for centuries, though it is claimed that treasure hunters a few years ago almost succeeded in raising it before it fell into a fissure where it cannot now be seen. The name of Ponce de León, however, was not given to this site until 1885. It had been called *Garden Springs* after its purchase in 1854 by Thomas Stark of South Carolina "for the consideration of 50 Negro women." The post office today is called DE LEON SPRINGS. It was originally named in 1882 for Hernando de Soto, but the United States Post Office Department (now called the U. S. Postal Service) refused to recognize the name because it was a duplicate. A town established in Holmes County in 1875, PONCE DE LEON, is named for the Florida discoverer, and Polk County has a DE LEON SPRINGS.

Hernando de Soto, mentioned earlier, is commemorated by DE SOTO BEACH in Brevard County, DE SOTO CITY in Highlands County, FORT DE SOTO in Hillsborough County, and HERNANDO and

HERNANDO JUNCTION in Citrus County. These names are recent, having been given in the late nineteenth and early twentieth centuries. This predilection for the names of Spanish *conquistadores*, who roamed Florida's shores and forests when she offered mystery and danger, is likewise shown in the name of CORTEZ, a fishing village in Sarasota Bay in Manatee County, though the colorful and cruel Hernando Cortez, for whom the village is named, had no direct connection with the Florida story.

Later Spaniards whose names are on Florida's map include Don Domingo Fernandez, who received a land grant from Spain in 1785, during the second Spanish period. FERNANDINA BEACH (formerly just *Fernandina*), a town which claims to be the second oldest settlement in the United States, bears his name. It is on Amelia Island in Nassau County and is the county seat. On this island, then called *Guale*, Menéndez, who had founded St. Augustine two years before, built a fort in 1567; and since that time, according to local tradition, there has been continuous white settlement. Little is now known about the Don Domingo Fernandez who received this land as a grant in 1785, and some historians deny that the name of the city honors him. They believe that King Ferdinand V of Spain—the same Ferdinand after whom Columbus named Cuba in 1492 (for Cuba was Fernandina then)—is the man commemorated here. There seems to be no evidence to support this claim, however. The name most likely honors the eighteenth-century Don Domingo.

On Pelican Island, between the Halifax River and the sea, is a settlement called PONCE PARK (Volusia County). The assumption is easily made that here once again Floridians have honored the ubiquitous Juan Ponce de León, but records show a Spanish royal order of 1790 granting the land on the peninsula to a man named Antonio Ponce. The place has been known by other names, among them "Bob's Bluff" (and who Bob was we do not know), but in 1866 a General Babcock, who purchased land there with a settlement in view, named the post office Ponce Park in honor of the Spanish grantee of 1790.

GONZALEZ, in Escambia County, was established in about 1800 by Don Manuel Gonzalez, another Spaniard of the second occupation. It was at first "Gonzalia," the name of Don Manuel's ranch, where Andrew Jackson was once entertained.

An intriguing figure in the procession of Spaniards is Don Fernando de la Maza Arredondo. In 1817, just four years before Spain ceded the Floridas to the United States, the king of Spain granted to Don Fernando 289,645 $^5/_7$ acres of land in the territory of Alachua. Now every abstract of title to lands in the city of Gainesville in Alachua County and to much of the land to the south and west of the city begins with papers concerning that royal grant made in 1817 to "Don Fernando de la Maza Arredondo and Son, Merchants, of the City of Havana, Island of Cuba." Alachua County's ARREDONDO, a little settlement which was named for him, is now scarcely a town. It was established in 1890 and stands as the only place-name to remember him. When the names of Gainesville streets gave way to numbers in 1950, the only other place-name reminder of the Spanish don disappeared: ARREDONDO STREET, which is now Northwest and Southwest Third Street. As late as 1957 the Cuban heirs of Don Fernando de la Maza Arredondo enlivened the conversations of Alachua County with a threat to lay claim to their ancestor's lands, but the threat was a nine days' wonder, and no more has been heard from their attorney. The little station of Arredondo remains the only public memorial to this late Spanish grantee.

GOMEZ, in Marion County, commemorates Eusobie N. Gomez, who received a land grant of 12,000 acres from the king of Spain in 1815 and about whom we know nothing more than this.

DELESPINE, in Brevard County, preserves the name of another Spanish grantee about whom nothing is now known but that he was granted 42,000 acres in this vicinity by the king of Spain.

YNIESTRA, in Escambia County, bears a Spanish name too, but the family after whom it was named were "Americans"—Spaniards who cast their fortune with Florida as a United States territory when His Catholic Majesty's flag no longer waved over Florida. The town of Yniestra was established about 1840 and named for the family who owned land and a brickyard there.

YBOR CITY, the Latin quarter of Tampa, in Hillsborough County, bears the name of another American Spaniard—Vicente Martinez Ybor. His name was originally Vicente Martinez y Bor, *Bor* being the surname of the feminine side of the family, added, according to Spanish custom, as a courteous distinction to the surname of the male. The last part of the name was contracted to "Ybor," though in Spanish the "y Bor" simply meant "and Bor." "Ybor" became the name in America of this pioneer cigar manufacturer who was born in 1820 in Valencia, Spain. He manufactured cigars in Havana, Cuba, in 1856, and eventually came to the vicinity of

Tampa to escape the revolutionary unrest in Cuba, bringing with him and attracting to the place many other Cubans of like disposition. In 1885 he established a town on his property and gave it his American name. Tampa has grown to encompass Ybor City, but the place still retains its "foreign" flavor, preserving Spanish customs and language to so marked a degree that many of its people speak English with difficulty and some not at all.

PINEDA, in Brevard County, was named in 1891 by a Spaniard of that name, according to oral report, but there are no records of him. The place itself is hardly more than a plane beacon light, a store, and a gas station.

The names of other Spaniards appear randomly on minor topographic features and sometimes as names of city streets. For example, MAURA ROAD in Pensacola commemorates a Spanish family who received a grant from Spain during the second Spanish occupation. Descendants of Francisco Maura, who came to America to claim the grant, still live in Florida, but the Maura grant has long since been lost to them.

And so the Spaniards in Florida's history—those who found her first as well as those who became involved with her later—are not forgotten in the names of her places.

THE FRENCH

The French regime in Florida was very brief and very disastrous. The names the French gave to the land were immediately changed by the Spanish and have, for the most part, been lost. Like the early Spaniards, the French did not give their personal names to places, and it was left to later men to honor them in this fashion. Only one of that sixteenth-century company—the ill-fated Jean Ribault, who claimed Florida for France in 1562—has been so honored. In memory of him a stream in Duval County, flowing into the Trout River, is called the RIBAULT RIVER. Also in Duval County is the RIBAULT REFUGE STATE PARK. Other Ribault names dot the area for minor features—a small bay in the mouth of the St. Johns, a real-estate subdivision, a lake, a street—and a Jacksonville school bears this Frenchman's name, while a large department store has named its elegant restaurant for him ("The Ribault Room"). The name of the Ribault River ("Not Sixmile Creek," says the U. S. Geographic Board) was adopted by the commissioners of Duval County on April 1, 1926, and other Ribault names were even more recently given—appropriately in the area where Jean Ribault and his Huguenots landed in 1562.

Later Frenchmen commemorated in Florida place-names include Louis de Buade, Comte de Frontenac, seventeenth-century French governor of Canada, for whom Canadian settlers named FRONTENAC, in Brevard County; Marie Joseph Paul Yves Roch Gilbert du Motier, Marquis de Lafayette, the namesake of LAFA-YETTE COUNTY; and Prince Achille Murat, nephew of Napoleon, for whom MURAT JUNCTION, in Taylor County, was named. Murat came to America in 1821, later married Catherine Willis Gray, a great-niece of George Washington, and lived in the Tallahassee area until his death in 1847. He was a director of the Union Bank at Tallahassee, was later a county judge, and wrote several books on American customs and government.

THE INDIANS

When the Indians named places, they usually named them for something which occurred there or for some feature of the land-scape. Their purpose, apparently, was simply to identify the places for themselves; they thought little of honoring persons or of ex-pressing ideals or of casting glamour upon the places, as white men often do. Thus the place-names of Florida which commemo-rate Indian men or Indian tribes were bestowed upon the places by white men.

The long-gone Timucua Indians, who inhabited Florida when the white man found it but who had been exterminated by 1710, are remembered in the name of UCETA, a Hillsborough County settlement dating only from 1926, but taking its name from that of a Timucuan chief encountered by de Soto in 1539 in the Indian village at the head of Tampa Bay, and by Pánfilo de Narváez in 1528. Narváez had become enraged at Cacique Uceta ("Ucita," as some spell it) for showing insufficient respect to the Spaniards and had ordered the chief's nose cut off and had set dogs on his old mother; so it is small wonder that when de Soto came in 1539 Uceta and his people abandoned their village at the Spaniards' approach. Uceta would be amazed to find himself a participant in our imaginary pageant after more than four centuries.

Another Timucuan place-name is that given to TOMOKA CREEK, in Volusia County. This stream was called the *Rio de Timucas* by the Spaniards in the early eighteenth century, for on its banks

lived the last of the few Timucua who survived the English-insti-
gated Creek raids of that time. *Tomoka* is an English corruption
of their name. TOMOKA STATE PARK, also in Volusia County, commemorates these tragic people, too.

TEQUESTA, in Palm Beach County, remembers in its name
another vanished people—the Tekesta or Tequesta Indians who
formerly inhabited the shores of Biscayne Bay, which was once
called *Tequesta* because of them. A reported TEKESTA near Miami
(which cannot now be located on a state map) was on the site of
a Spanish Jesuit mission abandoned after an Indian massacre
of Jesuits in 1571.

CHACALA, the name of a pond on the southeastern margin of
Payne's Prairie, in Alachua County, is thought to recall the name
of a chief called *Chikilli* who related a Creek migration legend
to General Oglethorpe in 1735. The spelling "Chichill" on a map
of 1837 suggests this origin. PAYNE'S PRAIRIE itself, a fifty-square-
mile basin south of Gainesville, is usually said to have been named
for an Oconee-Seminole who was chief of the Alachua settlements
in 1812. He was known to the whites, who killed him in that year,
as "King Payne." (It is only fair to say that King Payne has a rival
for this honor, a white man who will be discussed under "Other
Americans" commemorated in Florida place-names.) LITTLE
PAYNE'S CREEK, in Polk County, is also said to take its name from
this chief.

Between Jackson, Holmes, and Washington counties flows
HOLMES CREEK, which gave its name to Holmes County and which
may have been named for a half-breed Red Stick chief whom the
whites called *Holmes*. He was killed by one of General Jackson's
raiding parties after the general's high-handed occupation of
Pensacola in 1818. Holmes had fled to Florida with his band after
the Treaty of Fort Jackson, and his name appeared on the Williams map of 1827 for the stream which still bears his name.

BLOUNTSTOWN, county seat of Calhoun County, was named to
honor John Blount, a native chief of the Seminoles who accompanied the exploring delegation of Seminoles to the new Indian
territory west of the Mississippi when the band agreed in 1832 to
go there. Blount had been given this Anglo-American name, it is
said, because he had much in common with William Blount,
appointed superintendent of Indian Affairs by President Washington in 1790.

TIGER TAIL ISLAND, near Homosassa in Citrus County, bears the name of a Seminole chief called *Tiger Tail*, who had his tribal headquarters there. MICCO, established in Brevard County by Frank Smith in 1877, is more doubtfully named for a particular Indian chief. The word itself means "chief" in the Creek language, and it formed a part of the names of several Seminole chiefs, among them three of the fifteen who signed the Treaty of Payne's Landing in 1832, agreeing to relinquish their lands in Florida and emigrate westward to the country of the Creeks: Mico-Noha, Holat-a-Micco, and Hitch-it-i-Mico.

Other place-names which may or may not have honored individual Indians are TUSCAWILLA, designating a railroad station in Alachua County, and MATTLACHA PASS, a strip of water in Charlotte Harbor, off the coast of Lee County. The former is translated "beloved warrior" if it is corrupted from the Choctaw (*Tashka-Wulla*) and "warrior plunderer" if from the Chickasaw (*Tashka-weli*), while legend furnishes the inevitable Indian princess, this one a daughter of Chief Micanopy, as a namesake. The truth of this matter is not known, but certainly a person seems to be indicated by the name *Tuscawilla*, which is an old one in the Alachua territory, having been applied by white men to a lake and to an adjacent town site occupied by the earliest Seminoles. William Bartram, who traveled this territory in the late eighteenth century, called it *Cuscawilla*, and Charles Vignoles (1823) called it *Taskawilla*. This name, too, changed in 1950 with the renaming of Gainesville street names, when TUSCAWILLA STREET became Tenth Avenue.

The "Mattlacha" in Mattlacha Pass may be an Indian corruption of *Matanza*, which was the name Ponce de León gave to Pine Island in 1513 (the pass is just east of Pine Island); but it is more likely that the name is derived from the Creek *imala* or *emathla*, meaning "leader," and *lako* or *thlako*, meaning "big." Some Seminole chiefs used the title "Big Warrior."

A number of Seminole chiefs involved in the long war of 1835–42 have been remembered in the names of Florida places. Osceola, for whom a county was named, is further honored by the names of two Florida villages—OSCEOLA PARK, in Broward County, and OSCEOLA, in Seminole County. EMATHLA, in Marion County, preserves the memory of Charley Emathla, a signer of the Treaty of Payne's Landing who was slain by warriors of Osceola in 1835 because of that signing. ARIPEKA, established in Pasco County in 1883, remembers another signer of that treaty, a Miccosukee chief also known as "Sam Jones the fisherman," whose Indian name appears in many variations, among them *Ar-pi-ucki, Arpeika, Apiaka, Apeiaka, Appiaca,* and the one that falls easiest from English-speaking tongues, *Aripeka.* Appropriately, for a place named after "Sam Jones the fisherman," Aripeka is a fishing settlement.

MICANOPY, a village in Alachua County which was the first point of settlement in the Arredondo grant (in 1817), is named after Mico-an-opa (also written as *Mico-Noha, Mikanope, Micanopy,* and *Micanope*), nephew and matrilineal successor of King Payne to the chieftainship of the Alachua Seminoles. The name is really a title, meaning "head chief" or "chief of chiefs," from Hitchiti *Miko* ("chief"), plus *Naba* ("above"). Before this chief's accession he was known as *Sint-chakke,* said to mean "Pond Frequenter." Micanopy, who was "head chief" at the outbreak of the Seminole War and who was one of the fifteen signers of the Treaty of Payne's Landing, presents a rather ludicrous appearance when we hear the legend that he was so fat and lazy that his warriors carried him by force to the battle sites. The name Micanopy was given to the present town in 1834; it had previously been called *Wanton,* for Edward M. Wanton, an early settler who was a manager of Arredondo's land grant. There had been a town by one name or another on the approximate site for years before the white man came; it is said to have been the capital of the Timucua Indians as well as of the later Seminoles, and is on all counts the oldest settlement in Alachua County. MICANOPY JUNCTION (also in Alachua County) commemorates the same chief who, in contradiction to the report of his fat laziness, is said to have personally slain Major Francis L. Dade in the famous 1835 massacre that opened the long Seminole War.

HICKS' ISLAND, in Lake Tsala Apopka in Citrus County, is named for the Miccosukee chief Tokose Emathla, another Payne's Landing signer, known to the whites as "John Hicks." Hicks was one-time head chief of the Seminoles, appointed by Governor DuVal when the governor deposed Neamathla, who in turn had deposed Micanopy at the instigation of the whites. But by 1832 Micanopy had regained the position, and in that year Hicks died.

Holatter Micco ("Alligator Chief"), the famous Billy Bowlegs, one of the most active of the war-chiefs, is remembered in the name of BOWLEGS CREEK in Polk County. Columbia County's TUSTENUGEE perpetuates the memory of the crafty and dangerous

Halpatter Tustenugee, "The Alligator Warrior." He, with Mica-nopy and Jumper, was a leader of the band who perpetrated the Dade Massacre. A lake in Putnam County and a station in Pasco County are called CHIPCO after the Seminole chief Chipco who fought beside Osceola. And the name of CLOUD LAKE, a man-made lake excavated by Kenyon Riddle for a real estate development in Palm Beach County in the 1940s, commemorates the Seminole chief of the 1840s known as "The Cloud" (*Ta-Ho-Loo-Chee* or *Yaholochee*), who bitterly hated the whites.

In addition to honoring their individual Seminole enemies, Floridians have sprinkled their map with the names of whole tribes of Indians who have inhabited the state during its history. We have already mentioned the ancient Timucua, commemorated in the names of Tomoka Creek and Tomoka State Park. Other tribes and clans whose names are attached to Florida places in-clude the Apalachee people, or the Apalachicola, with whom the Spanish came in contact in northern Florida in the seventeenth century. The APALACHICOLA RIVER, a confluence at the state line of the Flint and Chattahoochee rivers, flows into the Gulf of Mexico through APALACHICOLA BAY off the coast of Franklin County, whose county seat was named APALACHICOLA in 1831. APALACHEE BAY, off Wakulla County, is another reminder of this group of Lower Creek Indians.

The Chatot were a warlike tribe living west of the Apalachicola River; and through a confusion of their name with that of the Choctaw (a distinct though similar tribe), the CHOCTAWHATCHEE RIVER, forming the boundary of Washington and Walton counties, is named for them, as are CHOCTAWHATCHEE BAY in the southern part of Okaloosa and Walton counties and the CHOCTAWHATCHEE NATIONAL FOREST across the southern part of Okaloosa, Santa Rosa, and Walton counties. The last two are, of course, transfer names from the river, for *hatchee* is the word for "river," and *Choctawhatchee* means "river of the Choctaw" (or *Chatot* by original intention), and thus are only indirectly named for the Indians themselves. Such earlier spellings as *Chatto Hatcha* on the Romans map of 1774 are indications of the intention of this name.

PENSACOLA (Escambia County) preserves the name of another native tribe; the city was established and named by the Spanish in their first colonial period for the Indians they called *Panzacola*.

The bay on which the city is situated is called PENSACOLA BAY, and WEST PENSACOLA is a later town belonging to this cluster.

The Indians of the native southern Florida tribe, the Calusa, are commemorated in the name of the CALOOSAHATCHEE RIVER, flowing into CHARLOTTE HARBOR, which also is named for them in the complicated way described for Charlotte County. CALOOSA LAKE, in Polk County, is also reminiscent of the Calusa, though that name is of recent application.

The EUCHEE VALLEY, EUCHEE CREEK, and the village of EUCHEE-ANA in Walton County are named for the Yuchi, a tribe of Indians from Tennessee who immigrated in the early seventeenth century to the lands along the Choctawhatchee.

The Seminoles, besides being the namesake of Seminole County, are also recognized in the name of a Pinellas County village called SEMINOLE, a Bay County one called SEMINOLE HILLS, and a Lake County spring called SEMINOLE SPRING, as well as in other miscellaneous names in Florida. Among names which recall separate Seminole tribes is MICCOSUKEE, a village in Leon County, where there is also MICCOSUKEE LAKE.

On the Apalachicola River, in Liberty County, is a place called ESTIFFANULGA. Its name may commemorate a group of red men also, for it is thought to be a corruption of an Indian word meaning "Spaniard Clan." *Isfanalgi* (*ispani*, "Spaniard," and *algi*, "clan") is suggested as the Creek original. It may, of course, have reference to Spaniards if the suggested etymology is correct at all.

"Foreign" Indians—i.e., Indians who never lived in Florida—have left names in Florida too, as shown in the names of the stations called MATOAKA (Manatee County), KOMOKO (Alachua County), and GERONIMO (Santa Rosa County). Such names were recently bestowed, sometimes by persons with a romantic interest in the American Indian, sometimes by Florida settlers who came from regions once inhabited by these Indians. *Matoaka*, authorities tell us, was the real name of the famous Pocahontas, daughter of Powhatan. And it is reported that Komoka was an Indian chief who lived in Michigan and that when a Michigan lumber company (the Cummer-Diggins Company) established itself in Florida, it remembered him in the name of one of its stations, misspelled *Komoko*. *Geronimo* was the name of the famous Apache chief who died in 1909, eleven years before the Florida town was established. Geronimo was imprisoned for a short time by the United States

Government at Fort Pickens, on Florida's Santa Rosa Island, after his capture in 1886.

THE BRITISH

The "oldest" British name on the Florida map, though not the earliest to be placed there, is that of Jonathan Dickinson, a seventeenth-century Pennsylvania Quaker whose ship foundered on the southern Florida coast in 1696. He and twenty-four other Quakers were then escorted by Indians on a difficult and harrowing walk that took them the entire length of wild Florida and finally, somehow, back to Philadelphia. Now Floridians have commemorated Dickinson and his adventure in the name of JONATHAN DICKINSON STATE PARK, a few miles south of Stuart, in Martin County, near where the ship foundered. But this is a twentieth-century naming; the names of many other Britons were attached to the land long before Jonathan Dickinson was honored.

Florida was a part of the British Empire for twenty years (1763–83), as some of her place-names still remind us. But thirty years before the Union Jack waved legally over Florida, the names of English men and women began to be sprinkled over the northeastern area. When James Oglethorpe established the colony of Georgia in 1733, he promptly built a chain of forts along the coast to the very gates of St. Augustine. He honored Princess Amelia, daughter of King George II, then ruling England, by renaming in 1733 the ancient island of *Guale* (which the Spaniards had called *Santa Maria*) AMELIA ISLAND. The island, a part of Florida's Nassau County, still bears her name, as do the AMELIA RIVER and AMELIA CITY, also in Nassau County.

Amelia's father is remembered by many "George" names that Oglethorpe gave in this same period, including Duval County's FORT GEORGE ISLAND; the town that has grown up upon it, FORT GEORGE; and FORT GEORGE INLET, off its coast. England's long habit of crowning men named George has confused this matter somewhat, and there are those who say that George III is the man honored here, for a fort was built on Gage Hill by the last British governor of Florida, Peter Chester, in 1772, when George III was England's sovereign. Oglethorpe's fort was first, however, and there is no doubt that *his* king was the original King George of the island. Actually, Oglethorpe originally named the island "St. George," presumably after the patron saint of England, but by association with the "Fort George" he built upon it, it gradually came to be known as Fort George Island.

George III, however, was almost certainly the man for whom LAKE GEORGE, an expansion of the St. Johns River farther down the peninsula, was named. This George's queen, Charlotte, lives in the name of Charlotte Harbor and its offspring, as has been pointed out earlier.

Other Britishers of the English occupation period who are remembered still on Florida's map include an Irish statesman, two lawless adventurers, a chief justice, a viscount who was granted lands in Florida by George III, two lords of the admiralty, and a Scots adventurer. LAKE BERESFORD, in Volusia County, was so named by the English, according to the Federal Writers' Project unpublished dictionary, "for Lord Beresford," an English admiral. This is highly unlikely, since the first Baron Beresford, British admiral, was not born until sixty-three years after the English had relinquished Florida, and was a popular hero (though not yet an admiral) a hundred years afterward. If indeed the English named this Florida lake during their Florida occupation, they may have named it for John Beresford, an Irish statesman who was nearing the height of his power at that time. The town of BERESFORD, near the lake, was named in 1874 for the lake. Curiously enough, this was the time when Lord Beresford, the admiral, was prominent in England as a sportsman and personal friend of the Prince of Wales. We may assume at least that the name *Beresford* honors a Britisher, and its location in an area where the British did establish residence during their ownership lends support to the supposition that the name dates from that period.

An unscrupulous adventurer named William Augustus Bowles, who served in the British army during the American Revolution but who deserted and lived among the Creek Indians, is commemorated by a place-name in Volusia County also. Bowles served as agent for a group of loyalists in the Bahamas who tried to establish a contraband trade with the Florida Indians during the second Spanish occupation. A small settlement in Volusia County is called BOWLES, proving that glamour without honor is glamour still, and William Augustus Bowles makes a picturesque figure as he walks in the Florida pageant.

Another one of the lawless ruffians active in Florida during the last months of the British occupation and labelled the "Banditti" by the outgoing British governor was William McGirt, for whom

McGIRTS CREEK in Duval County is named. McGirt, who had deserted from the American army and had then been commissioned by the British to organize the East Florida Rangers using British refugees, turned outlaw when the war was over and led a gang which specialized in stealing the property of East Florida residents who were attempting to gather their possessions and leave Florida. The naming of McGirts Creek is said to commemorate his exploit in escaping from a posse by swimming his horse across the creek.

A bewigged and berobed English justice is honored in the name of DRAYTON ISLAND, in Lake George. This island, on which stood the mission of San Antonio de Anacape during the first Spanish period, was named for Chief Justice Drayton during the twenty-year English occupation.

The Englishman most liberally commemorated in the place-names of Florida is Willis Hill, second Viscount Hillsborough. When Florida was returned to Spain, the name of *Hillsborough* lingered on the HILLSBOROUGH RIVER (now officially the HILLSBORO RIVER), which empties into HILLSBORO BAY; and later, for these natural features, Americans named HILLSBOROUGH COUNTY in 1834. Now there is in that county a railroad station named HILLSBOROUGH; in Palm Beach County there is HILLSBOROUGH CANAL; and in Broward County there are HILLSBORO INLET, HILLSBORO LIGHTHOUSE, and HILLSBORO BEACH. Properly speaking, not all of these names intentionally honor the English earl, for after the War of 1812 Americans were not given to direct English naming; but because he had left his name in Florida fifty years before the Americans acquired her and because it was a pleasant name, they continued to sprinkle it over the face of their map.

Lord Hillsborough's brother-in-law, John Perceval, second earl of Egmont, is reportedly the namesake of EGMONT KEY, an island which guards the entrance to Tampa Bay. It has been fortified by the Spanish, the British, and the Americans but is now largely deserted, except for a small Coast Guard station. Egmont is said to have been a land agent in Florida at the time the island was named, but he was also first lord of the admiralty briefly (1763–66) during the British occupation of Florida. One of his younger sons, Spencer Perceval, became prime minister of England.

The HALIFAX RIVER, in Flagler and Volusia counties, was given that name during the British occupation, presumably in honor of George Montagu Dunk, second earl of Halifax, who was prominent as first lord of the admiralty, among other things, during that time.

TURNBULL, a railroad station in Brevard County, commemorates Dr. Andrew Turnbull, the Scot who established New Smyrna, a few miles to the north, in 1768. Turnbull, at the southern end of TURNBULL HAMMOCK, was established in about 1887. TURNBULL CREEK, in St. Johns County, also remembers this strange and cruel man who brought a colony of Minorcans and Greeks to Florida and deserted them. His adventure inspired Stephen Vincent Benét's twentieth-century Florida novel, *Spanish Bayonet*.

The name of ORMOND, a city in Volusia County, honors an Englishman who received a grant of land from the Spanish government and came here from the Bahamas during the second Spanish occupation, settling at a place then called *Damietta Mosquito*. Captain James Ormond, the grantee, was killed by a runaway slave around 1815. Sixty years later a colony from New Britain, Connecticut, settled at the place and called it *New Britain*; but later residents, looking into local history, changed the name to Ormond. Just across the river is its sister city, ORMOND BEACH, famous as the winter home of the late John D. Rockefeller.

An Englishman of the Victorian period has the distinction of being the only literary man after whom a Florida place is named. John Ruskin, author and critic, was honored ten years after his death when RUSKIN, a town established in Hillsborough County as a socialist colony in 1910, was named for him because of his interest in socialism.

PIRATES

The folklore of Florida abounds in legends of buried treasure and of desperate outlaws lurking in the recesses of her irregular coast. Especially in the lawless era of the eighteenth and early nineteenth centuries, international rivalries made Florida a confusing no-man's land where anything could happen, and certainly there was a goodly measure of skullduggery along her crooked coast; but by and large the pirate stories her people tell are unverifiable. Those who have investigated the history of piracy say that the great stream of it passed Florida by in favor of more profitable operations in the West Indies. Nonetheless, there are place-names in Florida that ring like pieces of eight, to commemorate pirates real and imagined.

Ironically, one of the best known of the pirates' names on her map is probably not a pirate's name at all. Gasparilla, or "Little Gaspar," is supposed to have been a renegade Spanish naval officer who settled at Charlotte Harbor in about 1783 and lived as veritable king of the pirates, creating terror along the Gulf coast with his cruelties. The name of GASPARILLA ISLAND off the coast of Charlotte County and of the settlement of GASPARILLA upon the island are, naturally enough, said to commemorate him. There are also LITTLE GASPARILLA PASS and GASPARILLA SOUND in the same vicinity. Gasparilla's favorite wife is said to be commemorated in the name of USEPPA ISLAND, off the coast of Lee County. Legend has it that this storied pirate, whom Floridians now celebrate each year in the famous Gasparilla Festival at Tampa, took unto himself numerous wives (captured Spanish princesses, Mexican maidens, etc.) whom he set up on CAPTIVA ISLAND, whose name speaks for itself. Things went well, apparently, until the advent of a particularly beautiful captive named Joseffa. Joseffa, because she was his favorite, aroused the anger of the ordinary wives, and Gasparilla restored tranquillity by setting her up in solitary splendor on an island a few miles away. The spelling of the name eventually followed local pronunciation, and Joseffa's island, after passing through several changes, became Useppa Island. Thus, Floridians say, a glamourous pirate and his lady have left their names on the map.

However, the name of Gasparilla was on the map before the storied pirate is supposed to have made his appearance. Old Spanish and English charts show it usually referring to GASPARILLA KEY and LITTLE GASPARILLA KEY, as it still does today. In 1772 Bernard Romans, charting the Gulf coast, indicated *Boca Gasparilla* ("Gasparilla Mouth"). So it seems that someone before the pirate's appearance left the name on Florida's map. A clue appears in certain maritime reports of the mid-nineteenth century: The *American Coast Pilot* for 1842 mentions a channel, or inlet, in "Carlos Bay" (now Charlotte Harbor) called "Friar Gaspar"; the Spanish chart book for 1862 published in Madrid names "The inlet of Friar Gaspar or Gasparillo . . . to the north of the northern point of Gasparilla Key." Thus Friar Gaspar apparently is the man commemorated, a far cry from the fierce and swashbuckling pirate Gaspar. History informs us that Menéndez established a mission on Charlotte Harbor in 1567. Four of the priests who worked in this region in later years were named Gaspar. Several ancient Spanish well-heads have been found on Little Gasparilla Key; perhaps a mission was located there. It seems credible, given all these hints, that the name *Gaspar* or *Gasparilla* first came to Charlotte Harbor borne by a devoted friar or priest whose story is still buried in the records of some ancient order.

Nevertheless Floridians devote three days of gaiety and fun each year to a mythical buccaneer who sails boldly into Tampa Bay and captures the city with the greatest of ease. Gasparilla was invented, apparently, by a colorful character called Johnny Gomez, who lived on Panther Key from 1876 until 1900, when he drowned while mullet-fishing at the age of 119. Assisted by a lively imagination, some probable actual experience with pirates on the Cuban coast, a fondness for the Havana rum that men traded for his stories, and the interesting name of *Gasparilla* handily attached to several nearby landmarks, he simply made the pirate up. The officials of the old Charlotte and Northern Railroad were so pleased with Johnny's stories and so convinced by them—after all, there was the name on the map!—that they put into their railroad folder the story of Gasparilla the pirate and Johnny Gomez his "brother-in-law." The printed pamphlet became the outstanding "authority" for the legend of the fierce Gasparilla and has been extensively cited in other works—proving the power of the printed word. But there is no other authority in America. And so the roistering buccaneer enters the Florida historical pageant by a very dubious route—as perhaps a buccaneer should—and the humble and devout Friar Gaspar, who belongs there, goes unheralded. What this exposé does to USEPPA ISLAND and CAPTIVA ISLAND is a problem, but there apparently exist no alternative explanations for these names.

Two other places presumably named for pirates include BLACK CAESAR'S KEY, off Dade County, which is said to have been a hiding place of the notorious Negro outlaw Black Caesar, and TAVERNIER CREEK, at the lower end of Key Largo (off Monroe County), named for the Frenchman Tavernier, lieutenant to the famous old pirate Jean LaFitte. TAVERNIER KEY and the settlement of TAVERNIER upon it derive their names in turn from the creek. Black Caesar and Tavernier were presumably "real" pirates, though neither of them is as well known to Floridians as the pirate they invented. Whether real or imaginary, these pirates are rightfully commemorated in Florida place-names, so that an exciting part of her past may not be lost from her map.

A CZECH AND A PORTUGUESE

Another distinguished foreigner who lives on in Florida place-names is Thomas Garrique Masaryk, philosopher and statesman and first president of Czechoslovakia. Masaryk, who died in 1937, was honored by this naming while he was still living. In 1924 Joseph Joseak, with some fifty Czech families from Pennsylvania, New York, and neighboring states, established MASARYKTOWN in Hernando County as an agricultural colony for people of Czechoslovakia. Today not only the name but the customs of the place are reminiscent of the Old World origin of these people, some of whom—especially the older residents—still use the Czech language; and two flags, American and Czechoslovakian, stand at the Masaryk Memorial Library.

TAVARES, in Lake County, was named in 1882 for Lopez Para y Tavares, "a grandee of Portugal" who was an ancestor of Alexander St. Clair-Abrams, founder of the settlement.

AMERICANS

Florida has only a little more than a century and a half under the Stars and Stripes and a little more than four years under the flag of the Confederacy to balance against her 308 years of subordination to the Old World, but these 150-odd years have seen her greatest development. She was still a wilderness when the United States received her from Spain, with much of her lands not only unsettled but unexplored. Most of her cities and all of her counties have been established since then, and many of her natural features have received their names or have been renamed during the American period. Thus it is that Americans honored by Florida place-names outnumber others ten to one.

American Revolutionary Heroes.—Though Florida was a loyal British colony during the American Revolution, her later citizens have honored in her place-names several of the American Revolutionary heroes, as we have already seen in the names of Sumter, Marion, and Washington counties. POINT WASHINGTON, now in Walton County but formerly in Washington County, and WASHINGTON, a hamlet in the present Washington County, got their names from the county that was named in honor of the commander-in-chief of American Revolutionary forces. And in Sumter County the town of SUMTERVILLE is a tribute to that same General Thomas Sumter for whom the county is named.

FORT PICKENS, on Santa Rosa Island in Escambia County, was

named, as it neared completion in 1833, for Brigadier General Andrew Pickens of the South Carolina state troops in the Revolution. FORT PICKENS STATE PARK, recently added to the National Register of Historic Places, is its present designation. The town of JASPER, in Hamilton County, was renamed in 1850 to honor the Revolutionary hero Sergeant William Jasper, who rescued the American flag during the British assault on Fort Sullivan (now Fort Moultrie) in 1776. Before 1850, Jasper had been informally called "Mico Town," a name of Indian origin. MOULTRIE, in St. Johns County, honors the famous General William Moultrie, whose most direct connection with Florida history is that he was commander of the unsuccessful expedition for the invasion of Florida in 1776. The nearby MOULTRIE JUNCTION is an echo of the original honor.

National Statesmen.—National figures of the first seventy years of the nation's history are definitely on the map in Florida. Men who helped to mold the nation during these years are represented, as we have seen, in the county names of Franklin, Jefferson, Hamilton, Madison, Taylor, Monroe, Gadsden, Polk, Clay, Calhoun, Washington, and Jackson. Some of these men, as well as others prominent in the young nation, are commemorated also in the names of towns and natural features scattered over the peninsula. The county seat of Madison County is named MADISON, though the naming was accidental rather than deliberate, for the place was called *Newton* until the continual arrival of mail addressed to "Madison C. H.," signifying the courthouse or county seat of Madison County, pressured residents into the habit of referring to their town as "Madison Court House." The "C. H." was dropped after the Civil War.

The body of water called LAKE MONROE in Seminole County was called *Valdez* under the Spanish occupation, but when Florida was purchased from Spain by the United States the name was changed to honor the president then in office, James Monroe. The nearby settlement called LAKE MONROE, started in 1886, took the name of the lake.

QUINCY, county seat of Gadsden County, was named for the president who succeeded Monroe—John Quincy Adams, who was elected in 1824, the year after Gadsden County was created. The use of Adams's middle name rather than his last was a widespread place-naming habit (as, for example, Quincy, Illinois), since it is the most distinguishing part of his name.

POINSETT LAKE, in Brevard County, honors the memory of Joel

Poinsett of South Carolina, United States minister to Mexico, the man after whom the poinsettia, one of Florida's winter flowers, is also named.

POLK CITY and POLK LAKE, both in Polk County, derived their names indirectly (through the county name) from James K. Polk, who became United States president at the same time Florida became a state.

BROOKSVILLE, in Hernando County, commemorates the Honorable Preston Brooks, congressman from South Carolina, who in 1856 broke a gutta percha cane over the head of Senator Charles Sumner of Massachusetts and left him unconscious on the floor of the Senate Chamber. For this impetuous act—occasioned by Sumner's public denunciation of Brooks's uncle, Senator A. P. Butler of South Carolina, during a heated debate on the Kansas-Nebraska Bill—Brooks received a number of gold-headed canes and gold-handled whips from admirers, vehement denunciations from his enemies, and had a town in Florida named for him. EAST BROOKSVILLE, in Hernando County too, also bears his name. Brooksville had its beginning as a village in the fifteen-year period between statehood and secession (1845–60), when many settlers from South Carolina came to Florida.

The intensely sectional character of Florida during the decade of the 1860s is revealed in the fact that her place-names do not purposely commemorate national figures of this era, though many honor men who cast their lots with the new, short-lived Confederate States of America. These will be discussed in a separate section, but it can be noted here that such men as Abraham Lincoln, Ulysses S. Grant, and William Tecumseh Sherman do not appear in Florida's pageant of names. The first "yankee" name to appear among the national figures after the cleavage of the sixties is that of General Henry Sanford, former United States minister to Belgium, who was personally responsible for the fact that his name is on Florida's map. In 1871, Sanford bought 12,000 acres in what is now Seminole County for the purpose of building a city. He named the new town after himself, and today SANFORD is the county seat of Seminole County. Later, WEST SANFORD was derived from it.

The Republican president whose term of office was cut to less than four months by a bullet from the gun of disappointed office-seeker Charles Guiteau (1881) is honored in the naming of GARFIELD, established in about 1893 in Volusia County and named for James

A. Garfield. The fact that a Republican president was so honored in a state consistently Democratic since the Civil War may be indicative of the cosmopolitan character which Florida, as a haven for people from all sections of the country, was beginning to assume. Another Republican president, William Howard Taft, is honored by the name of a town called TAFT, in Orange County. This name was given to the town at the conclusion of a long campaign conducted in the *Saturday Evening Post* while President Taft was in office.

Democrat Grover Cleveland had a town named for him in Charlotte County in 1886, the year after his first inauguration. A Georgia man, Dr. A. E. Holleyman, who had bought and developed extensive property on the Peace River, named the town CLEVELAND. Perhaps the president's Florida vacation during that time prompted the naming. Two of Cleveland's cabinet members are also on Florida's map: BAYARD, in Duval County, honors Thomas Francis Bayard, secretary of state in Cleveland's 1885–89 administration and the first United States ambassador to Britain's Court of St. James in the 1893–97 administration; and LAMONT, in Jefferson County, commemorates Daniel Scott Lamont, secretary of war during Cleveland's second administration.

Other national figures of the twentieth century are rare in Florida place-names, but the Democratic Franklin D. Roosevelt, president during the Great Depression, is remembered in the name of CAMP ROOSEVELT, built in Marion County as a part of one of the job-giving public works projects of his first administration.

The name of the late President John Fitzgerald Kennedy temporarily designated a unique Florida place after President Lyndon Johnson's 1963 renaming of Cape Canaveral (Brevard County) to CAPE KENNEDY. The name rested uneasily on the cape until 1973, when in response to the insistent demand of the people the ancient Spanish name was restored. The name of KENNEDY SPACE CENTER continues to commemorate him (see chapter 4).

Florida Statesmen.—The names of men who helped to build the government of Florida from territorial days far into statehood are many upon her map. Eleven of her sixty-seven counties bear the names of such men, from her first military governor, Jackson, on through Walton, Duval, Levy, Brevard, Baker, Pasco, Broward, Gilchrist, Hardee, and Martin, all of whom have been discussed.

Andrew Jackson is further commemorated in the name of one of Florida's principal cities, JACKSONVILLE, county seat of Duval

County, and its adjacent areas JACKSONVILLE BEACH and SOUTH JACKSONVILLE. Jacksonville, referred to as "a place called the Cowford" in the territorial act of 1822 which added Jackson and Duval counties to Escambia and St. Johns, was renamed Jacksonville in that very year. The "Cowford" was a translation of the Indian name for the place—*Waca Pilatka*, "place where the cows cross." ("Ford" is actually a mistranslation of *pilatka*. The more accurate word is "ferry." The river is much too deep to ford at Jacksonville. So the name implies a cattle crossing by swimming or ferriage, not by wading.) The Indians had never seen cows until the Spaniards brought them, and their word for them—*Waca* or *Wakka*—is a variant of the Spanish *vaca*. At this point on the St. Johns River, apparently, there has always been a crossing of some kind. The Spanish called the place the Ferry of St. Nicholas, but the Americans went back to a translation of the Indian descriptive name until a sense of new dignity moved them to change it to Jacksonville. JACKSON LAKE, in Highlands County, is also thought to honor Andrew Jackson, as is LAKE JACKSON in Leon County.

WORTHINGTON SPRINGS, in Bradford County, is said to be named for W. G. D. Worthington, who was secretary and acting governor of East Florida under Jackson. Another story is that it was named for Samuel Worthington, who settled there in the 1820s. The post office is called WORTHINGTON.

FORT WALTON BEACH, in Okaloosa County, was named for the same George Walton who gave his name to WALTON COUNTY. And another Jackson man is remembered in the name of the Union County seat, LAKE BUTLER; he is Colonel Robert Butler, who formally received East Florida from Spain on July 10, 1821, in St. Augustine.

Florida's indefatigable territorial delegate, first senator, and railroad promoter, the colorful David Levy Yulee, discussed as the namesake of LEVY COUNTY, appears again in the names of Lake County's YALE LAKE (a victim of careless spelling apparently, for in 1856 it was shown as *Lake Yulee*), a town in Nassau County named YULEE in 1852, and a YULEE established in Alachua County in 1878. Alachua County also has a LAKE LEVY.

BALDWIN, in Duval County, honors Dr. A. S. Baldwin, who served in the Florida legislature in antebellum days and was a prominent surgeon in the Confederate army during the Civil War. Dr. Baldwin was a leading figure in the building of the first railroad into Jacksonville, and this nearby railroad junction, first called *Thigpen*, was named in his honor in 1860.

Although several stories are current concerning the naming of STARKE, in Bradford County, the most convincing one is that it was named for Florida Governor Madison Starke Perry, who held the office from 1857 to 1861. Governor Perry was a native of South Carolina, and his mother was a member of the prominent Starke family of that state. The *Bradford County Herald*, in a seventy-fifth anniversary edition on November 12, 1954, said, "Since the earliest residents of the little village included more people from South Carolina than any other state it is not surprising that the town was called Starke, in honor of Madison Starke Perry, Governor of Florida from 1857 to 1861." Further evidence pointing to the authenticity of this version of the naming is that the year of Starke's founding was 1857, which was also the year of Governor M. S. Perry's inauguration. He was the governor who signed the papers completing Florida's secession from the Union, on January 11, 1861.

MILTON, county seat of Santa Rosa County, may or may not be named in honor of a Florida governor. John Milton governed Florida from 1861 to 1865 and took his own life on April 1, 1865, knowing that the Confederacy had lost. In his last message to the legislature he had said, "Death would be preferable to reunion." Some say the town was named for him, while others say the name honors Milton Amos, a pioneer resident, and still others that the name was once *Milltown* and honors no man at all. At any rate the place is older than the name, having been established as a trading post during territorial days. In those rougher times, it is said that it was called *Scratch Ankle* or *Hardscrabble*, names whose loss might well be regretted by the connoisseur of colorful names.

Suwannee County's McALPIN was named by railroad officials for D. M. McAlpin, a personal friend who had represented the county in the legislature in the 1870s and was also editor of the *Florida Bulletin*.

The memory of Governor William D. Bloxham (1881–85) is perpetuated in the name of BLOXHAM, a town in Leon County. And the governor who succeeded him, Edward A. Perry, is honored by the name of the county seat of Taylor County, PERRY, which was known as *Rosehead* when the first post office was established there in 1869.

PASCO is named for its county, whose name, as has been seen, honors another nineteenth-century Florida statesman, Samuel Pasco, while GILCHRIST, in Charlotte County, is named for the twentieth-century governor Albert H. Gilchrist (1909–13), after whom Gilchrist County is also named.

Dr. John L. Crawford, Wakulla County physician and public figure, appointed secretary of state by Governor Bloxham in 1880, is the man commemorated in the name of the town where he lived, CRAWFORDVILLE, county seat of Wakulla County. The little place was named for him in 1866 when it became the county seat and while he was state senator from Wakulla County; it had formerly been called *Shell Point*, which still exists as the name of a nearby "shore dinner" spot.

Seminole War Heroes.—Florida's history as a United States territory is deeply stained with the bloody years of the Seminole War (1835–42) and its preliminary struggles. Her map, as we have seen, is dotted with the names of Seminole chiefs who fought in that war, but the Americans who finally crushed them are there in far greater numbers. Dade, Putnam, Gadsden, and Taylor counties commemorate four of the heroes—one who died at the beginning of the major conflict, one who was a prominent Florida lawyer in peacetime, and two who acquired national prominence after the war was over. Other names honoring the massacred Dade are FORT DADE, in Hillsborough County, and DADE CITY, in Pasco County. The Honorable Mr. Putnam is further memorialized in the name of PUTNAM HALL, in the county named for him.

Other Indian fighters remembered on Florida's map are numerous. General Duncan L. Clinch is honored by FORT CLINCH, in Nassau County; Colonel William Davenport is remembered by Polk County's DAVENPORT (a transfer name from *Fort Davenport*, an army post once located nearby); and Brigadier General Abraham Eustis is commemorated by LAKE EUSTIS, EUSTIS, and EUSTIS TRANSFER in Lake County, though some say that the naming of the town of Eustis, which was later than that of the lake, was for the general's son, a Civil War soldier, engineer, and college professor.

Other Seminole War heroes whose names are on the Florida map include Dr. John S. Gatlin, assistant surgeon, slain by Indians in 1835, for whom FORT GATLIN and the village called GATLIN, in Orange County, were named; General Edmund Pendleton Gaines, remembered in the name of Alachua County's GAINESVILLE; Major

William W. Harlee, honored by FORT HARLEE, in Bradford County; Colonel William Selby Harney, for whom HARNEY, in Hillsborough County, and LAKE HARNEY, in Volusia and Orange counties, were named; and Major William Lauderdale, honored in the name of FORT LAUDERDALE, in Broward County. Colonel William McRae is commemorated by FORT MCRAE, a village on an island in the Gulf of Mexico off Escambia County; Captain William Seton Maitland, by LAKE MAITLAND and the town of MAITLAND, in Orange County; and Major Richard Barnes Mason, by the village of FORT MASON, in Lake County.

Furthermore, "a captain Merritt of Seminole war fame" is said to be the namesake of MERRITT ISLAND (Brevard County) and the community thereon called MERRITT, though considerable uncertainty surrounds this version of the naming; another is that the island was named for a Spanish grantee of the first decade of the nineteenth century.

Other military men from the Seminole War years who left their names on the Florida map include a Georgia volunteer named Newnan, commemorated by NEWNAN'S LAKE and by the ghost town NEWNANSVILLE, former county seat of Alachua County; Orlando Reeves, a sentinel slain by Indians in 1835, honored by Orange County's ORLANDO, where a street named *Rosalind* is both an outgrowth and a perpetuation of the false idea that the city was named for the Orlando of Shakespeare's *As You Like It*; and Lieutenant Colonel Benjamin Kendrick Pierce, namesake of FORT PIERCE, county seat of St. Lucie County, and its offspring FORT PIERCE INLET.

Colonel Alexander R. Thompson, killed at the battle of Lake Okeechobee, is remembered by FORT THOMPSON, in Hendry County; a man named White, whose first name is unrecorded, by FORT WHITE, named for a Seminole War fort, in Columbia County; Colonel Joseph M. White, United States territorial delegate, by FORT WHITE, in Escambia County; Captain Edward S. Winder by WINDER LAKE, in Brevard County; and General William Jenkins Worth, whose brilliant strategy in the Seminole War helped to bring it to a conclusion and who went on to distinction in the Mexican War, by LAKE WORTH (both a lake and a town), in Palm Beach County. FORT MELLON PARK in Sanford (Seminole County) is named in memory of Captain Charles Mellon, killed there in action against the Seminoles. FORT COOPER LAKE, in Citrus County, memorializes Major Mark Anthony Cooper, who commanded the First Georgia Battalion of Volunteers. The fort they built and defended there in 1836 has recently been excavated.

A few of these etymologies are cloaked in doubt because of the meager and vague information given in the available sources, but the length of the list shows the prominence of the Seminole Wars in the background of Florida.

Civil War Heroes.—Just as Florida's territorial years were torn by war, so her years of early statehood were disrupted by the Civil War. Only sixteen years after her admission to the Union she withdrew from it, the third of the southern states to secede, and became a member of the Confederate States of America. The record of Florida's devotion to the cause of the Confederacy may be read in her commemorative place-names, for none of them honors a northern hero, while several recall a man in gray. As already mentioned, the most illustrious of all Confederate heroes, Robert E. Lee, is honored by the name of Lee County, created in 1887, while Bradford County, so renamed on December 6, 1861, commemorates the first Florida officer killed in the war. LEE, in Madison County, is another reminder of the honored leader of the Confederate forces; it was named for him in 1882, when the first post office was established there. Other place-names that memorialize Confederate heroes are ARCHER (Alachua County), for General James J. Archer; BARTOW (Polk County), for General Francis Bartow, first general officer of either side to die in battle; CAMP JOHNSTON (Duval County), for General Joseph E. Johnston; GRACE-VILLE (Jackson County), for Captain N. D. Grace; and INGLIS (Levy County), for Captain John S. English. EARLETON (Alachua County) was named in about 1875 for Confederate General Elias Earle, who lived there. It is instructive to note that most of these places had been settled before the Civil War and had other names, which were changed in deference to the heroes. Bartow, for instance, had been known as "Pease Creek."

The men who fought the war were not all uniformed men. Statesmen and editors and others were also prominent. Some of these who are remembered in the place-names have been discussed under "Florida Statesmen," and it may be appropriate to mention here that ARNO, in Alachua County, commemorates the Honorable George Arnow, editor of *The Cotton States* during the war.

Actually the number of place-names honoring Confederate

heroes is comparatively small in Florida. The young state seemed to hurry past this dark era and fix her mind on what was to come. For Florida had ahead of her a phenomenal period of development, and her potential was seen by many men of vision who began to emerge in the latter part of the nineteenth century.

Developers and Promoters.—Northern capitalists who spent their money to develop and promote Florida as a tourist's paradise, a vacationland *par excellence*, have left their names upon the map of the state. The most magnificent of them all, Henry M. Flagler, was honored when Flagler County was created in 1917. FLAGLER BEACH, in that county, was also named for him at the request of a homesteader whose brother had been a personal friend of Flagler's. Both of these names were given after Flagler's death; it was his own modesty that prevented the naming of the city of Miami for him while he was still alive. One of Miami's important thoroughfares, however, is FLAGLER STREET.

In Flagler County there is a lake named LAKE DISSTON, which must have been named to honor Hamilton Disston, the Philadelphia capitalist who bought and attempted to reclaim and develop four million acres of Florida land in the 1880s. Lake Disston has been on maps since the late 1800s. The DISSTON CITY which appears upon Florida maps of the 1890s and early 1900s in what is now Pinellas County was almost certainly named for him, but that city is now gone from the land (at least as a separate municipality). A St. Petersburg station named DISSTON PLAZA is listed in the zip code directory of the United States Postal Service.

Another capitalist-developer commemorated by a county name is Barron G. Collier, advertising executive after whom Collier County was named when it was established in 1923. COLLIER CITY, a town in that county, honors him also.

Henry B. Plant, a railroad titan second only to Flagler in the release of Florida from isolation, has not been honored with a county name, but a thriving city in Hillsborough County, PLANT CITY, was named for him in 1885 at the insistence of its founder, J. T. Evans, who was aware that only the building of Plant's railroad through this section made its development possible.

Other place-names of Florida evoking the memory of wealthy Americans who helped make Florida what she is today are ASTOR and ASTOR PARK (Lake County), for the Wall Street magnate William Astor; and DELAND, DELAND JUNCTION, and DELAND LANDING (Volusia County), for Henry A. DeLand, a New York

baking powder manufacturer who, with John B. Stetson, Philadelphia hat manufacturer, laid the foundation for the city of
Deland in 1876. The university there, originally established as an
academy by Mr. DeLand and called by his name, was later named,
at DeLand's request, STETSON UNIVERSITY for Mr. Stetson, who
had given the institution financial assistance.

The name of PENNEY FARMS, a community in Clay County,
reminds us of J. C. Penney, chain-store magnate who established
the place for retired ministers and gospel workers, in memory
of his minister father and his mother. And DAVIS ISLANDS, in
Hillsborough County, is named for David P. Davis, a Floridian
who, during the Florida "boom" days, 1921–25, conceived the
idea of building a town on these two islands which were formerly
called *Grassy* and *Big*. He pumped sand out of Tampa Bay to
create his city. A phenomenally successful development, the
islands are now a part of the city of Tampa—and the man their
name commemorates was drowned at sea in 1926. MUNYON'S
ISLAND, in Lake Worth (Palm Beach County), bears the name of
a wealthy Dr. Munyon, who lived on it and grew oranges and
papayas, using the latter fruit in the manufacture of medicine.

George E. Sebring, pottery manufacturer of Sebring, Ohio,
dreamed in the early twentieth century of creating in Florida a
community patterned on the ancient Egyptian city of Heliopolis,
with a central park representing the sun and the streets its rays.
He purchased land in what is now Highlands County, and construction began in 1912. Today this dream city, SEBRING, is the
county seat of Highlands County.

During the land boom of the 1920s, Roger W. Babson, well-
known statistician, purchased 400 acres of land which included
the site of a town formerly known as "Crooked Lake," in Polk
County, and the name of the place was subsequently changed to
BABSON PARK.

Other wealthy promoters have left their names on Florida's
map, but for the most part the capitalists gave descriptive or
picturesque names to their developments; and only a few, like
the spectacular Flagler and Plant, have captured Floridian hearts
and imaginations enough to warrant their commemoration in
place-names given by others. Some names which formerly remembered such men have even been changed by later citizens; for
example, the name OLDSMAR was once attached to a community
established in Pinellas County in 1916 by the Reolds Farm Com-

pany, headed by R. E. Olds, Michigan automobile manufacturer. The name—apparently a compound of Mr. Olds's name with the Spanish word for "sea"—has since been changed to TAMPA SHORES.

Other Americans.—Famous Americans who appear in Florida's assemblage of place-names include her own Dr. John Gorrie, inventor of the first practical machine to produce artificial ice. Dr. Gorrie invented the machine to cool the rooms of yellow fever patients in Apalachicola in 1845. Today his statue stands in Statuary Hall in the Capitol at Washington, and in GORRIE SQUARE in Apalachicola stands a monument erected to his memory by the Southern Ice Association. His name is perpetuated on Florida's map by the name of DOCTOR GORRIE BRIDGE across East Bay from Apalachicola to Eastpoint, in Franklin County.

When Floridians speak the name of the town of BUCKINGHAM, in Lee County, they honor Buckingham Smith, nineteenth-century Florida historian, for whom the town's first postmaster, Edward M. Williams, named the place. BURBANK, in Marion County, and AUDUBON, in Brevard County, were named to honor, respectively, Luther Burbank, noted horticulturist, and John James Audubon, famous naturalist. Audubon traveled in Florida in 1832, studying bird and animal life.

Nineteenth-century military men are remembered in the names of Fort Meade, in Polk County, and Fort Myers, in Lee County. The man whom FORT MEADE and its offspring WEST FORT MEADE commemorate is Lieutenant George G. Meade. He was with a group making a topographical survey of the area in 1852, and was assigned by his commanding officer to the job of finding the site of old Fort Clinch, which had been built in 1849 but not maintained. Meade accomplished the difficult feat before the day was over, to the intense satisfaction of his commander, a General Twiggs, who is reported to have exclaimed, "Here shall be Fort Meade!" The names of FORT MYERS and its adjacent town EAST FORT MYERS were derived from the name of Colonel Abraham Charles Myers and apparently bestowed by the same man who named Fort Meade. General David E. Twiggs, later Myers' father-in-law, assigned the name to the fort, which developed into a city in the later years of the nineteenth century and became the county seat of Lee County.

A nineteenth-century commodore in the United States Navy, Lewis Warrington, is recalled in the name of Escambia County's WARRINGTON, established during the 1840s when much of the

United States Navy Yard was under construction at Pensacola. In 1929 the village was evacuated to make way for new construction, but in its nearby relocation on the banks of Bayou Grande it retained the name of Warrington. A hero of the Spanish-American War, Admiral George Dewey, is commemorated in the name of DEWEY, a station in Hillsborough County named by railroad officials to honor the hero of the battle of Manila Bay.

However, the custom of naming places for military heroes does not flourish as it once did, for loyal though Florida has been in all United States wars since the Civil War, her place-names do not call forth many individual heroes of these later wars. It is true, of course, that the heyday of place-naming is past when an area becomes highly developed, all principal features have been named, and few new towns are being established, so that new place-names of any classification are fewer in later years. Nevertheless, to remember World War I Florida has a little place called PERSHING in Taylor County, named in about 1920 for General John Joseph Pershing, commander-in-chief of American forces in that war—the man who made the historic remark at Paris's Arch of Triumph, "Lafayette, we are here." A stream near the town is called the PERSHING RIVER. SAMSULA, in Volusia County, was renamed during World War I to honor Lloyd Samsula, a soldier from that district. Samsula superseded a Captain Briggs who used to ship oranges from this point and for whom the place had been called *Briggsville.* As for the men who fought in World War II, tributes to them are hard to find on Florida's map, though it is certain that many smaller features and memorials have been named for individuals among them—for example, MacARTHUR CAUSEWAY in Miami Beach (Dade County), named for General Douglas MacArthur.

By far the greatest number of towns bearing the names of individuals in Florida were named for men whose fame did not spread beyond the local area—settlers and builders and solid citizens who were important where they lived. The postmaster of a town—often influential in getting the post office established, and important to the town in other ways—was frequently honored by having the town named for him. In some cases he assigned the name himself. The group of United States postmasters in the Florida parade of names is large.

Among them one of the most picturesque figures is Colonel Henry T. Titus, who came to Florida after the Civil War and settled at TITUSVILLE (Brevard County) in 1867. Colonel Titus was a colorful character, a bitter foe of the famous John Brown, and a leader in the Kansas Crusade of 1855–56, with many desperate conflicts behind him. As autocrat and postmaster of the place where he settled, then called *Sand Point*, he gave it his own name instead. Legend has it that Colonel Titus and a friend, Captain Clark Rice, played a game of dominoes in 1873 to decide the name of the town. It was to be Riceville if Captain Rice won and Titusville if Colonel Titus won—and Colonel Titus's luck held.

Some other Florida towns named for their postmasters are ALLANTON (Bay County), for Andrew Allen, first postmaster (1890); BOND (Madison County), for William J. Bond, store owner and first postmaster (1897); BRANDON (Hillsborough County), for J. W. Brandon (1884); CAMPBELL (Osceola County), for A. S. Campbell, also an orange grower (1884); COLEMAN (Sumter County), for B. F. Coleman, a physician, orange grower, farmer, and first postmaster (1882); EBB (Madison County), for Albert W. Edwards, whose nickname was "Ebb," first postmaster (1904); GRUBBS (Holmes County), for Henry Grubbs (n.d.); HAGUE (Alachua County), for A. Hague, also an enterprising citizen (1883); HAROLD (Santa Rosa County), for the son of the postmaster (1912); JANNEY (Levy County), for Louis Janney (about 1900); JAY (Santa Rosa County), for the first initial of J. T. Dowling, also a store owner (1902); MANNVILLE (Putnam County), for W. H. Mann (1883); MARTIN (Marion County), for Colonel Martin, owner of the land grant and first postmaster (1883); PORT RICHEY (Pasco County), for A. M. Richey (1883); REDDICK (Marion County), for first postmaster (1882); SEFFNER (Hillsborough County), for E. P. Seffner, first postmaster (1884); SIMMONS (Taylor County), for Thomas Simmons (1845); and SPARR (Marion County), for M. S. Sparr (1883).

Railroad men are another group represented fairly heavily in Florida place-names. Since the building of railroads through unsettled country necessitated the establishment and naming of stations, railroad men did a great deal of place-naming themselves. They gave all kinds of names; some of them were their own names or the names of other railroad men. In other cases the people of a community newly liberated from isolation bestowed upon it the name of a railroad official or worker prominent in that liberation. For example, BUSHNELL, in Sumter County, was named to honor the young chief engineer of the surveying crew who laid the railroad right-of-way in 1884. CALLAHAN, in Nassau County, was named for a contractor of the old Transit Railway. Washington County's CHIPLEY bears the name of Colonel William D. Chipley, the chief railroad promoter in West Florida, whose Jacksonville, Pensacola, and Mobile Railroad was completed in 1883. Colonel Chipley also served as mayor of Pensacola and is given much credit for that city's development. CLEWISTON and WEST CLEWISTON (Hendry County) were named for A. C. Clewis, the Tampa banker who financed the extension of the Atlantic Coast Line Railroad through this point in 1922.

When a post office was established at a little place in Lake County in 1884, it was named CONANT to commemorate Sherman Conant, general manager of the Florida Southern Railway at that time; but now all that is left of Conant, which once boasted a luxury hotel, a private school, and several expensive homes, is a little cemetery containing three gravestones, around which Highway 441/27 makes a sudden curve. The name of DEFUNIAK SPRINGS (first called *Lake DeFuniak*), county seat of Walton County, honors Colonel Fred DeFuniak of Louisville, Kentucky, a prominent Louisville and Nashville Railroad official. Supposedly, DUNNELLON, in Marion County, was named to honor an early railroad promoter named J. R. Dunn (notwithstanding the Scottish ring of the name). HAINES CITY, in Polk County, was renamed after railroad official Colonel Henry Haines in about 1887, it is said, in order to induce the company to stop its trains there— and the strategy worked.

Other railroad men's names on Florida's map include LUTZ (Hillsborough County), for C. E. Lutz, railroad official; O'BRIEN (Suwannee County), for an official of the Savannah, Florida, and Western Railroad; RANDS (Seminole County), for a railroad official; STARR (Suwannee County), for an engineer on the L. O. P. & G. Railway; STEELE CITY (Jackson County), for A. B. Steele, builder of the Atlanta and St. Andrews Bay Railway in 1895; WAGNER (Seminole County), for one of the railroad's oldest employees (the place was named by the railroad in the first decade of the twentieth century); and WHITNEY (Lake County), for a Seaboard Air Line official.

Some places were named to honor men who in some way promoted or influenced the establishment or development of the place although they themselves did not live there. CARYVILLE (Washington County), formerly "Half Moon Bluff," was renamed in 1884, upon the advent of the Pensacola and Apalachicola Railroad, for R. M. Carey, Pensacola businessman; COREYTOWN (Pinellas County) was indirectly named for the Pinellas County Commissioner for whom COREY CAUSEWAY was named. Coreytown is at the eastern end of Corey Causeway at St. Petersburg Beach. EATONVILLE (Orange County) was named in 1883 for Captain Joshua C. Eaton, retired paymaster of the navy and first mayor of nearby Maitland; Eatonville was settled by Negroes, who were induced by Mayor Eaton and other Maitland citizens to move from their former section at Lake Lily, known as "St. Johns Hole," to this place. GALT CITY, in Santa Rosa County, was established about 1885 and named for the Galt family of Louisville, Kentucky, by the surveyor, Galt Chiplet. The once-famous GANDY BRIDGE across Tampa Bay (Hillsborough County) was named for the engineer who built it. Another Negro settlement, GIFFORD (Indian River County), was named for F. Charles Gifford, prominent resident of nearby Vero Beach.

Among the hundreds of other interesting personalities for whom Florida places are named is Dr. Joseph Braden, who came in the middle of the nineteenth century to Manatee County with his brother and several other families from Tallahassee after the crash of the Union Bank there. These adventurers became the pioneer sugar planters of the area, and Dr. Braden eventually built a house so impressive that it was called "Braden Castle." The ruins of it still stand near BRADENTON, and BRADEN CASTLE DRIVE goes past them. The name of the town was "Braidentown" when the post office was established in 1878; it later was corrected to "Bradentown"; and by 1924 it was Bradenton.

But one of the greatest originals of them all is the unbelievable Zephaniah Kingsley, of a prominent Scottish-American family, whose niece became James McNeil Whistler's mother, and who has his name written on Florida's map and his story indelibly printed in her annals. KINGSLEY, in Clay County, as well as KINGS-LEY LAKE, on which it is situated, was named for this wealthy slave trader and plantation owner of the late eighteenth and early nineteenth centuries. In 1790 Spain granted Kingsley a tract of land in Clay County; he had a plantation where Orange Park now stands and was largely responsible for the early development of the area. But it was to Fort George Island, in Duval County, that Zephaniah Kingsley brought his African queen wife, Anna Madegigine Jai, in 1817. He and "Ma'am Anna," as the slaves called her, lived for many years on the KINGSLEY PLAN-

TATION, the ruins of which are now one of the tourist sights of
the Jacksonville area. Kingsley was received into the "best" homes,
but his regal black wife, whom he had married in a tribal ritual
in Africa, it is said, was never recognized socially. The story is
one of the most poignantly intriguing of all the romantic Florida
tales. The Kingsley Plantation has recently been added to the
National Register of Historical Sites.

The murdered Dr. Henry Perrine is commemorated in Dade
County in the name of a town called PERRINE. Dr. Perrine was
granted a township of land in Florida by the United States government in 1838 in the midst of the Second Seminole War. He conducted tropical plant experiments in Florida (though not on his
grant) until he was killed by Indians in 1840 in the notorious
Indian Key Massacre, one of the bloodiest incidents in Florida's
wild history. Several neighbors shared his gory fate, but Dr.
Perrine's wife and children made a harrowing escape by hiding
in a turtle crawl under their burning house, standing in water
up to their shoulders. Eventually they fled in a boat and were
picked up by a passing schooner.

Story upon story emerges from the names of Florida places
commemorating men. Hundreds of other places in Florida have
been named for men locally prominent, though sometimes we find
that the cause of their prominence is now forgotten and in some
cases even their full names are forgotten. The places themselves
are nearly forgotten, too, sometimes, but most of them exist as
"settlements" or railroad stops if not as full-fledged cities or post
offices. In Appendix A is a list of some three hundred more places
bearing men's names, with as much information about the men
as is available.

WOMEN ON FLORIDA'S MAP

The naming of places for individuals seems to have resulted
principally in a map full of names of men. There is, however, a
fairly strong tendency among men in new territory to name
natural features for women; and sometimes cities, post offices,
and other man-made features also receive feminine names. Occa-
sionally places are named, rather impersonally, for famous
women, as in the case of England's Queen Charlotte, already
discussed, or for notorious women, like the mythical Gasparilla's Joseffa, also already mentioned. More often we find that the

feminine personal names are those of wives, sweethearts, mothers, or daughters of the namers.

Ordinarily the names honoring women are first names rather than surnames. Exceptions to this rule in Florida occur in the names of WIRTLAND (Jefferson County), HOGAN (Duval County), and SEARS (Hendry County). Wirtland was the plantation of Captain Lewis W. Goldsborough. He named it for his wife, who was the daughter of William Wirt, attorney general of the United States from 1817 to 1829. Hogan was settled by a woman named Eleanor Hogan in 1813. And Sears was named for the wife of Richard W. Sears of Sears, Roebuck & Co., because she was principal stockholder in the Standard Lumber Company, which established the settlement.

ARCADIA, county seat of De Soto County, was named in about 1885 for the daughter of an early settler, Arcadia Albritton. ARCADIA JUNCTION was an offspring. The name of BELL (Gilchrist County) was chosen by means of a beauty contest in which the winner's name was to be given to the new railroad station and post office (1903). The winner was Bell Fletcher, daughter of Daniel E. Fletcher, native Floridian and successful county farmer. Another community belle is remembered in the name of Franklin County's CARRABELLE, named in 1897 for Miss Carrie Hall. The name conferred at the time was "Rio Carrabelle," romantically enough, but the "Rio" was later dropped for practical reasons. CHARLOTTE LAKE, in Highlands County, commemorates Charlotte Bassage, the only child of a man named Bert Bassage.

DORA LAKE (Lake County) was named for Mrs. Dora Ann Drawdy, who in the 1880s was hospitable to United States government surveyors resurveying the Orange County boundaries. In appreciation, the surveyors named the lake adjoining her land in her honor. Later the nearby town, called by the interesting name of "Royellou" when it was established in 1882, in honor of three pioneer residents, Royal, Ella, and Louis Tremain, was renamed MOUNT DORA for the lake, which it overlooks from the summit of a plateau 266 feet above sea level.

LAKE DOT (Lake County) is named for Dorothy Norton. A place called ELINOR (sometimes spelled *Eleanor*) in Holmes County commemorates the wife of Elton Williams, who operated a sawmill there which he called "Elinor's Mill." An old Negro woman employed by George F. Drew, who became Florida's governor in 1877, is said to be the honoree of the name of ELLAVILLE, in Madison County, where Governor Drew built the largest sawmill in Florida. Gadsden County's FLORENCE was named in 1880 to honor Florence Hardee, daughter of Florida senator G. S. Hardee, once host to President Cleveland during his Florida honeymoon. Another FLORENCE, this one in St. Johns County, was named for a daughter of a settler.

LA BELLE, in Hendry County, was named by Captain Francis Asbury Hendry, for whom the county was named, in honor of two of his daughters, Laura and Belle; and NORTH LA BELLE came later. Another man, W. P. Henry, named LAKE GERTRUDE, in Lake County, for his oldest daughter. LAKE GRACIE (Lake County) remembers a Grace Pendry. LAKE HELEN, the name of both a town and a lake in Volusia County, was conferred in honor of Helen DeLand, daughter of Henry DeLand, for whom the city of DeLand is named. The town and lake were named by Mr. DeLand himself. Two Abrams girls, Irma and Joanna, are commemorated in the names of LAKE IRMA and LAKE JOANNA, both in Lake County. LAKE JOSEPHINE, in Highlands County, was named for a little girl, Josephine Spivey, who lived on the lake. Columbia County's LULU commemorates the sweetheart of Walter Gillen, a pioneer. Two young girls are remembered in the name of MARIANNA, in Jackson County, a town established in 1823 and named for Mary and Anna, daughters of Robert Beveridge and wife, in whose name the land was recorded. One other story states that the town was named for the wives of the two founders.

A small village called LAKE MARY, in Seminole County, was named after the lake that was named for Mary Randolph, wife of Major William Randolph. MARY ESTHER, in Okaloosa County, was named for two women, it is generally believed, though there is a difference of opinion as to which two women they were; some say they were the wife and daughter of the Presbyterian minister, a Professor Newton, who established the place; some say they were his two daughters. LAKE MERIAL, in Bay County, was named by another fond father, T. D. Sale, for his daughter; and LAKE MINERVA, in Lake County, was named for a lady named Minerva Gottsche, wife or daughter of one Augustus Gottsche, while a Nettie Morin gave her name to LAKE NETTIE, also in Lake County. Orange County's NONA LAKE commemorates the daughter · of a pioneer homesteading family. In 1877 Abraham Cavanaugh established a town in Escambia County which a Mr. Boley named OLIVE for his wife; and we are told that the United States Post

Office Department named THELMA, in Taylor County, for some official's lady.

Names can sometimes have a delightful multiple meaning, as is evidenced in the name of Florida itself and in the name of Charlotte County. ST. THERESA, in Franklin County, has a name which honors a Tallahassee girl while at the same time taking advantage of history to give the name a wider meaning. Theresa Hopkins was the girl honored; the fact that the seventeenth-century Spanish mission of St. Theresa, or Teresa, stood nearby prompted the "St." part of the name (or was it the other way around?). At any rate, local lore puts Theresa Hopkins among the women commemorated by Florida place-names.

One of the most misleading of Florida place-names to the casual observer is the name of WIMAUMA, in Hillsborough County. The invariable assumption is that it is one of the many Indian names which dot the map. The truth is, however, that this name commemorates the three daughters of the first postmaster there. Their names were Wilma (or Willie), Maude, and Mary; and the name Wimauma was formed from parts of their names in 1903.

🏵 OTHER COMMEMORATIVE NAMES 🏵

Place-names may commemorate more than people. Sometimes places are named so that men may remember an event which happened there. The most famous of such place-names in Florida is MATANZAS, a Spanish word meaning "slaughters" (see chapter 6). It was written on Florida's map in 1565 by Pedro Menéndez de Avilés, to commemorate his slaughter of the French Huguenots under Jean Ribault at a place on the south end of Anastasia Island near what has since been called MATANZAS INLET in St. Johns County. Now Florida has a MATANZAS RIVER in St. Johns and Flagler counties as well as the FORT MATANZAS NATIONAL MONUMENT on Anastasia Island.

Other names commemorate less famous events—often mere local incidents. BUCK HORN in Taylor County called to the minds of those who named it the killing of a buck during a cattle roundup, and BURNT MILL CREEK commemorated the burning of a sawmill on the banks of a creek in Bay County. ISTOKPOGA LAKE, in Highlands County, apparently was named because of a drowning there, for the word means, in Seminole-Creek, that a person was killed (*isti*, "person," *poki*, "finished"). The town of ISTOKPOGA in the same county takes its name from the lake. DEERHUNT, in Liberty County, obviously commemorates a hunt, while the name of HURRICANE ISLAND, in Bay County, is said to be for a hurricane that cut the island off from the mainland. Bay County's COURT MARTIAL, one of the more intriguing names in this category, was named for a court martial that General Andrew Jackson held there to try two army deserters; and CANTONMENT, in Escambia County, recalls that Jackson's troops camped there for a while. THLA-PAC-HATCHEE CREEK, in Osceola County, is one of several Indian names of the area which seem to commemorate bloody events, the meaning of this one being "fallen enemy creek."

Place-names also commemorate the ideas and ideals of the men who established the places. The county names of Union, Liberty, and Dixie are of this category, commemorating the common American ideals of union and freedom, and the regional adherence to a romantic Southern idea. UNION CITY (Union County) and UNION (Walton County) further commemorate the union ideal, while other names honoring the American dream of liberty are LIBERTY POINT (Glades County), LIBERTY (Liberty County), FREDONIA (Polk County), and FREEPORT (Walton County). Southern tradition is remembered again in the name of a small place called DIXIE in Hernando County. Another abstraction is honored in the names of the PEACE RIVER (or *Peace Creek*) in Sumter, Polk, and Manatee counties, and PEACE VALLEY in Polk County. These names were derived from the Spanish name of the river, which is shown on the earliest printed map of Florida (about 1587) as *Rio de Pas*, meaning "River of Peace." Others include FELLOWSHIP in Marion County; HARMONY CENTER in Hillsborough County; PROSPERITY in Holmes County; PROGRESSO in Broward County; WELCOME and WELCOME JUNCTION in Hillsborough County; CONCORD in Gadsden County; and ENTERPRISE and ENTERPRISE JUNCTION in Volusia County.

Another important category of commemorative place-names includes those which commemorate places elsewhere. Often when men settle in new territory they name the new place for the place they left behind. Thus, a considerable number of Florida place-names attest to the origin of her settlers, particularly after Florida became the property of the United States. Other place-names are transferred because of their pleasant sound to the namers, as in the case of LA CROSSE, a village in Alachua County. Miss Marion Futch, daughter of the namer, the late Mrs. John Eli

Futch, relates that in 1876 or 1877 John Futch (her father) and his brother Henry decided to buy cotton from farmers living around the Futch plantation; they constructed a small wooden building in which to store the cotton, which eventually led to the construction of a larger general store for groceries and dry goods. Eventually the store became the community's first post office also. In 1881 John Eli Futch married Harriet Amanda Strickland, and built a home for them near his store. Shortly thereafter, others came and built homes around the place. "So my mother said," Miss Futch reports, "'This place has got to have a name.' So she said, '*La Crosse*! That is what we will call it. I've always loved the name of *La Crosse*, ever since I read about La Crosse, Wisconsin.'" Such engaging whimsy may be behind other transfer namings.

Sometimes a place is named for another because the new place is felt to be somehow like the older place. In such cases the names might justifiably be categorized as descriptive rather than commemorative; the several names of Italian cities found on Florida's map or the names of some Spanish places, conferred on Florida places both because of a feeling for history and because of Florida's climatic similarity to parts of Spain, could be discussed as descriptive names. For practical reasons, however, all Florida place-names transferred from other places will be considered as commemorative of those places.

Florida has place-names transferred from almost all, if not all, of the other forty-nine states, showing the great extent to which she has served as a haven and a new frontier to those from all parts of the country. Some of these are listed in Appendix A, with what information is available concerning the namers and their reasons.

An especially interesting name is another Wisconsin transfer— EAU GALLIE, in Brevard County. Reports have persisted for years that the name is French for "bitter (or salty) water"; the town is near the salt-water lagoon called Indian River. But although *eau* is French for "water," there is apparently no French word resembling "gallic" which means anything like "bitter" or "salty." Strangely, the first illuminating clue to Eau Gallie's origin came from a children's book, *Caddie Woodlawn*, by Carol Ryrie Brink, a Newbery Award winner which tells the story of a pioneer Wisconsin family. They lived near a town called *Eau Galle*, a name so like that of the Florida town that a connection seemed inevitable. Subsequent correspondence with miscellaneous officials, including postmasters in both Eau Galle, Wisconsin, and Eau Gallie, Florida, led eventually to Mr. W. Lansing Gleason of Eau Gallie, the grandson of William H. Gleason, who came to Florida from Eau Claire, Wisconsin, which he founded, and established and named the Florida town. Near Eau Claire was a stream called the *Eau Galle River*. Because Mr. Gleason liked the name, his descendant reports, he gave it to the Florida town he founded in 1882—*Eau Gallie*. We can only suppose that Mr. Gleason was mistaken about the spelling or that it subsequently has changed. According to the same source, the name is a combination of French (*eau*, "water") and Chippewa Indian (*gallie*, "rocky"), resulting in "Rocky Water," probably descriptive of the abundant coquina rock in the area. The postmaster in Eau Galle, Wisconsin, Mr. V. M. Taylor, says that the Wisconsin name is pronounced exactly as the Florida one ("Oh-galley"), but he gives a different meaning for the Wisconsin name—"low water." Mr. Taylor indicates that the name is all French. If it is, perhaps the French *galet* ("pebble") is the original of the *Galle* part of the name. Its pronunciation, of course, is very nearly the same—"gal-lay." In any case, Eau Gallie is clearly a transfer name, commemorating a place in another state because a man from that state cast his lot with that of Florida a century ago. There are many other such place-names in Florida (see Appendix A), but no other yielded such an interesting detective story.

Two Florida place-names commemorate Canadian places, and it is probable that the gold rush of the 1890s was their inspiration. They are KLONDYKE, in Escambia County, and YUKON, in Duval County.

Local transfers, or places in Florida named for other places in Florida, have generally been discussed with the original name (as Micanopy Junction, discussed with Micanopy). It should be mentioned here, however, that this is another category of place-names commemorating places. GLEN ST. MARY (Baker County), for example, was named in the 1880s for the St. Marys River, which had been named *Rio de Santa Maria* by the Spanish and translated to *St. Mary's River* by the English. Also, a number of places in Florida have been named for the state itself: FLORIDA BAY (Monroe County), FLORIDA CITY (Dade County), FLORIDA TOWN (Santa Rosa County), CAPE FLORIDA (Dade County), the FLORIDA RIVER (Liberty County), and the FLORIDA KEYS, the general name for the chain of islands extending from Biscayne Bay to Key West and beyond. A town named for another town nearby is NEW PORT RICHEY (Pasco County), named for "old" PORT RICHEY about a mile away, which was named for its postmaster. Another local transfer is STETSON, in Volusia County, named for STETSON UNIVERSITY in nearby DeLand.

The number and variety of Florida place-names commemorating places in other countries is indicative both of the cosmopolitan nature of her population and settlement history and of the exotic appeal of her climate, topography, and romantic history. Some of her names from Mediterranean and tropical lands were given for romantic reasons, and other foreign names were given because her settlers wanted to commemorate their homelands. Appendix A contains a list of Florida place-names given to commemorate older places in other lands, with whatever information is available concerning reasons for the transfers. More than thirty countries are represented in this sample of ninety-seven names, with most of the transfer names, predictably, coming from Britain (chiefly England and Scotland), and from Spain and Italy. The names have been brought from every continent of the world, however, as the list in Appendix A will show. Its astonishing variety is typically Floridian—and typically American, of course—though the weighting of the particular imported names differs from state to state. In Florida's commemorative names, whether they honor people, events, ideas and ideals, or other places, we read a story distinctively her own.

4

"Many Pleasant Groves"

AN OUTSTANDING PHENOMENON of Florida place-names is the extent to which they describe Florida. An unusually large number of place-names—beginning with the name Florida itself ("because it appear'd very delightful, having many pleasant groves . . .")—tell what kind of place the state is, what trees and flowers grow there, and what natural resources and conditions have molded its destiny. Though descriptive names are common in every state, it would perhaps not be an exaggeration to say that Florida, a state whose prosperity has depended to an unusual extent upon certain of its natural conditions, has described these conditions in its place-names rather more than most states have done. The place-naming in this category has often been a form of advertising, so that few of the names recently bestowed are descriptive of the state's worst features, and some of the names which hinted of undesirable conditions have been changed during the American period. An example is the change of Mosquito County in 1824 to Orange County, the first feature being one of which Florida did not care to boast, while the second is one in which Floridians take great pride. Taking all the existing names together, however, we can form a fairly accurate picture of Florida's climate, situation, and topography. The names also describe to some extent the activities and occupations of the people.

The descriptive place-names fall into three major categories: those which describe the flora of Florida; those which describe

82

the fauna; and those which describe general climatic, situational, and topographical conditions and the occupations and activities growing out of such natural features and conditions. In the discussion which follows, examples of place-names in each category and subcategory are given. Additional descriptive names are listed in Appendix B.

🌼 FLORA 🌼

CITRUS TREES

It is no surprise to find that citrus trees have given rise to more Florida place-names than has any other single kind of plant. Since early Spanish times the orange tree has flourished in Florida, with wild orange trees abounding along the east coast before the disastrous freeze at the turn of the century. Today the state is the nation's leading producer of citrus and citrus products. The conspicuousness of the orange tree and other citrus trees on the peninsula of Florida is evidenced in the names of two of its counties, Orange and Citrus, as has been noted. Additional names proclaim it variously in English and in several other languages.

The dead language of the ancient Romans gives us AURANTIA, the name of a place in Brevard County. *Aurantia* is the plural of the botanical designation for a fruit of the orange species, *Citrus aurantium* (the Seville, or sour, orange). Aurantia was established for citrus cultivation in 1882 by the Bliss Company of New York. YALAHA, in Lake County, received its name from the Seminole-Creek word for "orange," while the name of ILLAHAW, in Osceola County, is another form of the same word. And it would be strange if the Spanish word for "orange" had not been used; so we find NARANJA in Dade County. These names, both Indian and Spanish, were given by later Americans who honored Florida's past.

CITRA, in Marion County, was so named by a committee in 1881 because citrus production was the principal industry there. The Mandarin orange, brought to Duval County from China, gave its name in 1841 to the village of MANDARIN in that county, while settlements called SATSUMA, in Jackson and Putnam counties, were named for a variety of orange also. Volusia County's SEVILLE got its name from the small wild Seville orange which flourished in that section. The Seville orange was imported to Florida by early Spaniards. Another variety of orange is honored in the name of TEMPLE TERRACE, in Hillsborough County, where groves of Temple oranges were planted by the founders in 1921.

Places in Orange and Putnam counties are called TANGERINE, for the small, sweet, and easily peeled citrus fruit by that name; and the lemon is the namesake for LEMON CITY, in Dade County, where a large lemon grove flourished when the place was named in the late nineteenth century. And LIMONA, established between 1835 and 1842 in Hillsborough County, got its name from the Spanish *limón* ("lemon").

Among the somewhat disguised citrus place-names is MONT-VERDE, in Lake County, so named for the hills of citrus groves which surrounded the town site at the time of naming. The town was established in 1885; its name means "green mountain." Other not-so-obvious citrus names include the many "fruit" names: FRUIT COVE, in St. Johns County, named in 1871; FRUIT CREST, in Palm Beach County; FRUITA, in Marion County; FRUITLAND, established in Putnam County in 1856; FRUITLAND PARK, in Lake County; and so on. "Grove" is still another synonym for "citrus" in Florida place-names, as in the name of Lake County's GROVE-LAND, named in 1911 for the citrus groves there, and in the names of other Florida places, though some of the "grove" names were inspired by the oak tree.

And there are many places whose names frankly include the words "citrus" and "orange," such as Alachua County's ORANGE HEIGHTS, named for an orange grove on a hill, and Clay County's ORANGE PARK.

THE PINE

Some have said that Florida's continuing prosperity has been due largely to two trees, the orange and the pine. Her place-names confirm the assertion, for the pine tree is very close to the orange tree in the number of place-names it has inspired in the state. That the pine tree has been a noticeable feature of the Florida landscape since discovery days is evidenced in the name of Pinellas County, evolved from the early Spanish *Punta Pinal* ("pine grove point"), which designated the peninsula now forming the greater part of the county. The pine names have doubled and redoubled through the years, until a sizeable list of them can now be compiled.

It includes BAY PINES, in Pinellas County; BIG PINE, in Monroe

County; PINE POINT, in Dixie County; and countless other names for stations, creeks, and settlements with the word "pine" in them. The name of SAPLINGS, in Flagler County, presents a variation, as does that of WOODVILLE, in Leon County, given for the pine woods there. PINEOLA (Citrus County) and PINETTA (Madison County) represent attempts to use the pine tree's name creatively.

THE PALM

The prominence of the citrus and pine trees and their importance to Florida's economy cannot be denied, but there are many who would guess that the palm—symbol of tropical leisure and lazy vacation living—has been more significant still. It is the palm which appears on the Great Seal of the State of Florida, and by an act of the 1953 legislature the Sabal palm (the native "cabbage palm" or "swamp cabbage") was made the state tree.

It is safe to say that of all her trees the palm is most symbolic of Florida in the American mind, for it is the palm which makes Florida scenery distinctly Floridian. Even with her green trees that "wave us globes of gold," her landscape might seem merely southern without the distinctive palm tree, which tells of her character as a vacation land and refuge from winter as no other growing thing could.

It is natural, then, that her place-names have honored the palm tree extensively. One of her counties has "palm" in its name— Palm Beach County—and many other places (towns, cities, streams, swamps, and "wide places in the road") have names which are tributes to this decorative plant so characteristic of the state.

CABBAGE CREEK, in Putnam County, and CABBAGE ISLAND, in Pinellas County, are two which honor the swamp cabbage, or Sabal palm. COCOA and COCOA BEACH, in Brevard County, are named for the cocoa, or coconut, palm, as is COCONUT GROVE, in Dade County. Manatee County's PALMA SOLA ("lonesome palm") is romantically named for a lone palm on an outlying key. Martin County has a PALM CITY, and Manatee a PALMETTO. And these are only a sample of Florida's many existing palm names.

THE OAK

The testimony of the palm names, describing Florida as a tropical paradise, is summarily contradicted by the oak names, which rise up in almost equal numbers to proclaim her a temperate one. Actually, of course, Florida is in the temperate zone, but her situation there is such that her climate has been frequently characterized as subtropical, and her vegetation is a mixture which announces her transitional position. Thus the appearance of the palm and the oak in such balanced proportion among her place-names constitutes a true description and is more logical than it seems.

LIVE OAK, the name of the county seat of Suwannee County, was given in 1885 for a majestic live oak under which section hands who were laying the railroad were accustomed to eat their lunch. RED OAK, in Madison County, was named in about 1869 for the magnificent red oak which shaded the country store in which the post office was established. Two other varieties of oaks growing in Florida are the namesakes for WHITEOAK, in Liberty County, and WATER OAK CREEK, in Bradford County, while numerous other place-names of Florida include the word "oak" in combination with "hill," "land," "grove," and the like. In Collier County a slightly elevated ridge grown with scattered oaks is called by the Seminoles SEHA-LEGGE, which we are told is derived from the Creek *seca* ("black jack" or "scrub oak") and *laiki* ("site").

Spanish Moss.—Wherever the oak tree is found, there abounds the Spanish moss, that gray mist that drapes the wooded Florida landscape in mystery and has given rise to legendary tales among both Indians and later settlers. Spanish moss, an air plant, is not peculiar to Florida, for it grows throughout much of the South, but it is particularly evident in this state; and though it attaches itself to other trees, it is especially luxuriant among the limbs of the oak tree. Place-names of Florida have honored the drooping moss. There is, for example, MOSS BLUFF, in Marion County, a place established before 1888 and named to describe the moss-draped trees nearby. And there is MOSSDALE, in Volusia County, established about 1858 and named for the same reason. MOSSY-HEAD, in Walton County, also got its name from the hundreds of moss-laden oaks in the vicinity.

THE CEDAR TREE

The cedar tree, as anyone could tell from place-names alone, is a part of the Florida landscape too. CEDAR KEYS, in Levy County, is on one of the CEDAR KEYS, or islands, and was named for them.

Index

B

Boca Grande, 104
Boca Quarasote, 39–40. *See also*
  Sarasota County
Boca Raton, 104
Boca Sarasota, 39–40. *See also*
  Sarasota County
Bocilia Island, 104, 195
Bocilla Pass, 195
Boggy, 195
Boggy Bayou, 114. *See also* Nice-
  ville
Boggy Branch, 195
Boggy Creek, 143, 195
Boggy Hollow Creek, 196
Boggy Point, 6, 196
Bogie Channel, 187
Bohemia, 5, 175
Boiling Creek, 189
Bokeelia, 104
Bon Ami, 113
Bonaventure, 130–31
Bond, 71
Bonifay, 152
Bonita Beach, 113
Bonita Springs, 193
Bothamley, 152
Botheration Creek, 117
Botts, 152
Boulogne, 171
Bovine, 184
Bowden, 152
Bowlegs Creek, 49
Bowles, 53
Bowling Green, 166
Boyd, 152
Boyette, 152
Boynton, 152. *See also* Boynton
  Beach
Boynton Beach, 152
Braden Castle, 152
Braden Castle Drive, 73
Braden River, 152
Bradenton, 73
Bradenton Beach, 152
Bradenton Junction, 152
Bradentown, 73. *See also*
  Bradenton

Bradford County, 27–28, 66
Braidentown, 73. *See also*
  Bradenton
Branchton, 152
Brandon, 71
Brandy Branch, 121
Brandy Creek, 196
Branford, 147, 165
Brent, 153
Brentwood, 153
Brevard County, 27, 37–38, 61
Brickton, 6, 102
Bridgend, 189
Bridgeport, 189
Briggsville, 70. *See also* Samsula
Brighton, 171
Bristol, 169
Broadbranch, 6, 189
Broad Creek, 196
Bronson, 153
Brooker, 153
Brooklyn, 168. *See also* Keystone
  Heights
Brooksville, 60
Brothers River, 105
Broward County, 31–32, 61
Browards Station (Broward's
  Neck), 153
Brown, 153
Brownsville, 153
Buck, 185
Buckeye, 181
Buckeye Creek, 181
Buck Horn, 77, 181
Buckhorn Creek, 185
Buckingham, 69
Buck Key, 185
Buena Vista, 6, 193
Buffalo, 167
Bull Creek, 94
Bullfrog Creek, 5, 94
Bulow, 153
Bunker Hill, 166
Bunnell, 153
Burbank, 69
Burnett's Lake, 153
Burnt Grocery Creek, 117

Burnt Mill Creek, 77, 142
Bushnell, 71
Butler, 153

C. de Cañareal, 144
Cabbage Creek, 85
Cabbage Island, 85
Cabo de Cañaveral, 144
Cacema Town, 90–91. *See also*
 Kissimmee
Cadica, 145–46
Cairo, 170
Calhoun, 153
Calhoun County, 25–26, 59
Callahan, 71–72
Callaway, 153
Caloosahatchee River, 51, 141
Caloosa Lake, 51
Calos, 8, 15–16, 141. *See also*
 Charlotte County
Calvary, 132–133
Campbell, 71
Campbellton, 153
Camp Johnston, 66
Camp Roosevelt, 61
Canal Basin, 189
Canal Cross, 189
Canal Point, 189
Canaveral, 89–90
Canaveral Harbor, 89–90
Candler, 153
Cantonment, 78
Cape Blanco, 196
Cape Canaveral, 61, 89–90
Cape Canaveral City, 89–90
Cape Florida, 80
Cape Kennedy, 61, 89–90
Cape Malabar, 170
Cape Sable, 6, 105
Cape San Blas, 130
Capitola, 103
Captiva Island, 56–57, 122–23
Carabay, 141. *See also* Sarabey

Carlos Bay, 56. *See also* Gasparilla
Carrabelle, 75
Caryville, 72–73
Caseeme, 90–91. *See also* Kissimmee
Cassadaga, 167
Casselberry, 153
Cassia, 181
Catawba, 181
Catfish Creek, 97
Cat Island, 184
Cattockowee Hatchee, 143
Causeway Community, 189
Cautio, 143
Cayo Agua Key, 189
Cayo Costa, 196
Cayo Hueso, 8, 24. *See also* Key
 West
Cedar, 87
Cedar Bluff, 87
Cedar Creek, 87
Cedar Key, 86–87. *See also* Cedar
 Keys
Cedar Key Junction, 87
Cedar Keys, 5, 86–87, 92
Cedar Landing, 87
Celery, 88
Center Hill, 103
Center Park, 194
Central, 194
Central City, 194
Century, 114
Cerro Gordo, 144
Chacala, 47
Champaign, 171
Charlie Apopka Creek, 187–88
Charlotte Bay, 15–16. *See also*
 Charlotte County
Charlotte County, 8, 15–16, 51
Charlotte Harbor, 8, 15–16, 51,
 53, 56
Charlotte Haven, 15–16. *See also*
 Charlotte County
Charlotte Lake, 75
Charm, 6, 193
Chassahowitzka, 91, 181
Chattahoochee, 9, 105
Chattahoochee River, 105

Cowhead Creek, 184
Cowhide Creek, 184
Cow House Creek, 95–96
Cow House Island, 95–96
Cow House Slough, 95–96
Cow House Swamp, 95–96
Cow Log Branch, 184
Cow Pen Branch, 184
Cowpen Lake, 6, 95–96
Cow Pen Slough, 184
Crackertown, 8, 121
Crandall, 154
Crawford, 154
Crawfordville, 64
Creighton, 154
Crescent Beach, 196
Crescent City, 196
Crestview, 196
Criglar, 154
Crooked Creek, 190, 196
Crooked Island, 196
Crooked Lake, 68. See also Babson
  Park
Crooked River, 196
Cross City, 196
Crown Point, 196
Crystal Bay, 190
Crystal Beach, 190
Crystal Lake, 190
Crystal River, 190
Crystal Springs, 190
Cubee Swamp, 185
Cuchiyage, 127. See also Mate-
  cumbe
Cuckoo Point, 6, 186
Cudjoe, 116–17
Cudjoe Key, 116–17
Cuke, 7, 116
Culbreath, 154
Cumberland Sound, 170
Cumpresco, 115. See also Volco
Curlew, 6, 186
Curry, 154
Cuscawilla, 48. See also Tuscawilla
Cutler, 154
Cynthiana, 166
Cypress, 5, 178

Cypress Creek, 87, 178
Cypress Gate, 178
Cypress Lake, 87. See also Lake
  Hatchineha
Cypress Pond Branch, 87
Cypress Slough, 87

Dade City, 64
Dade County, 21, 64
Dallas, 169
Damietta Mosquito, 55. See also
  Ormond
Dancy's Place, 154
Dania, 5, 175
Danzig, 175
Davenport, 64
Davie, 154
Davis Islands, 68
Daytona, 154. See also Daytona
  Beach
Daytona Beach, 154
Daytona Crest, 154
Daytona Shores, 154
Deadmans Bay, 123
Deadmans Key, 123
Decatur, 170
Deep Bottom Creek, 190
Deep Branch, 190
Deep Creek, 190
Deep Head Branch, 190
Deep Lake, 190
Deer Creek, 185
Deerfield Beach, 185
Deerhunt, 78
Deer Island, 5, 185
Deer Lake, 185
Deerland, 185
Deer Park, 95, 185
Deer Prairie Slough, 185
Deers Island, 185
Deers Run, 185
DeFuniak Springs, 72
Deland, 67–68, 76

E

Frog Creek, 94
Frontenac, 46
Frostproof, 6, 193
Fruita, 84
Fruit Cove, 84
Fruit Crest, 84
Fruitland, 84
Fruitland Park, 84
Fruitville, 177
Fruitville Junction, 177
Fukechatte Leyge, 140–41
Fulford, 156
Fullers, 156
Fullerton, 156

Gadsden County, 23, 59, 64
Gainer, 156
Gainesville, 64, 118–19
Gainsboro, 156
Galt City, 73
Galvez Springs, 144
Gandy Bridge, 73
Ganymede, 134
Garcon Point, 142
Gardena, 88
Garden City, 5, 88
Garden Springs, 42. See also Ponce
    de Leon Springs
Gardenville, 88
Garfield, 60–61
Gasparilla, 56–57
Gasparilla Island, 56–57
Gasparilla Key, 56–57
Gasparilla Sound, 56–57
Gatlin, 64
Geneva, 174, 175
Genoa, 172
Geronimo, 51–52
Gibsonton, 156
Gifford, 73
Gilchrist, 64
Gilchrist County, 32, 61, 64

Gin Branch, 121
Gladecrest, 196–97
Glades, 196–97
Glades County, 36–37, 196–97
Gladeview, 196–97
Glass, 156
Glencoe, 156
Glendale, 197
Glennel, 112
Glenoak, 178
Glen St. Mary, 80
Glenwood, 181
Glenwood Terrace, 181
Glory, 133
Goethe, 156
Golden Beach, 112
Golden Egg, 9, 135
Golden Rod, 87
Goldsboro, 170
Gomez, 44
Gonzalez, 43
Gonzalia, 43. See also Gonzalez
Goodno, 156
Goolsby County, 32. See also
    Hardee County
Gopher Ridge, 5, 186
Gorrie Bridge, 69
Gorrie Square, 69
Gotha, 5, 172
Goulding, 156
Graceville, 66
Grand Island, 197
Grand Rapids, 166
Grand Ridge, 166
Grand View, 193
Grant, 156
Grassy, 156
Grassy Island, 68. See also Davis
    Islands
Greenacres City, 181
Green Cove Springs, 181
Green Creek, 181
Greenfield, 181
Greenhead, 182
Green Pond, 182
Green's, 156. See also Greensboro

Hibernia, 5, 155–56, 172
Hickoria (Hicoria), 182
Hicks' Island, 49
Hicpochee Lake, 197
Higgins, 157
Highland, 197
Highland City, 197
Highland Park, 197
Highlands County, 36
High Springs, 106
Higley, 157
Hildreth, 157
Hillcrest Heights, 197
Hilliard, 157
Hillsboro Bay, 16–17, 54
Hillsboro Beach, 54
Hillsboro Inlet, 54
Hillsboro Lighthouse, 54
Hillsboro River, 16–17, 54
Hillsborough, 54
Hillsborough Bay, 16–17
Hillsborough Canal, 54
Hillsborough County, 16–17, 54
Hillsborough River, 54
Hillside, 197
Hilolo, 187
Hinson, 157
Hinterland, 197
Hiwassee, 170
Hobay, 125. *See also* Hobe Sound
Hobe Sound, 125, 134
Hodgson, 157
Hoe Bay, 8, 125. *See also* Hobe Sound
Hogan, 75
Hog Island, 96
Hog Master's Lake, 142.
Hogtown, 119, 142
Hogtown Creek, 142
Holder, 157
Hollandale, 127–28. *See also* Hallandale
Holley, 157
Holly Hill, 88
Hollywood, 165
Hollywood-by-the-Sea, 165. *See also* Hollywood

Holmes Beach, 157
Holmes County, 29, 47
Holmes Creek, 29, 47, 143
Holmes Valley, 29. *See also* Holmes County
Holopaw, 102
Homeland, 197
Homestead, 197
Homosassa, 182
Homosassa River, 182
Homosassa Springs, 182
Honey Heights, 7, 112
Honeymoon, 128
Hopkins, 157
Hornsby Spring, 157
Horseshoe Beach, 113–14
Horseshoe Cove, 113–14
Horseshoe Point, 113–14
Houston, 157
Howey-in-the-Hills, 157
Hurricane Creek, 197
Hurricane Island, 78
Hypoluxo, 197

I

Iddo, 122
Idlewood, 102
Illahaw, 83
Immokalee, 99
Imperial River, 112
Indialantic, 7, 115
Indian Ford, 197
Indianola, 112
Indian Pass, 198
Indian River, 35
Indian River County, 35, 97–98
Indian Rocks Beach, 198
Indian Springs, 198
Indrio, 7, 115
Indrio Beach, 115
Industria, 128
Inglis, 66
Inlet Beach, 189
Interbay, 189

L

Two Egg, 7, 120

The U.S. Geographic Board says firmly, "Not Cedar Key," though locally the town is often called that. The islands were named for the cedar trees on them, and pencil factories operated in Cedar Keys until the cedar was depleted. The town makes claim to settlement by the Spanish in 1525, but 1850 is generally given as the founding date of the present town.

Also in Levy County is LEBANON, named for the biblical Lebanon, famous for its cedars, because the cedar tree grows here, too. And in the same county we find ROSEWOOD, named for the red cedar trees in the vicinity.

CEDAR in Citrus County, CEDAR BLUFF in Calhoun, CEDAR CREEK in Baker, CEDAR LANDING in Marion, and CEDAR KEY JUNCTION in Alachua are other cedar names, while TORREYA STATE PARK, in Gadsden County, is named for the Torreya tree, a rare variety of cedar growing on the east bank of the Apalachicola River.

THE CYPRESS TREE

The cypress, a big-kneed swamp tree that often grows in water, has given its name to a number of places and natural features in Florida, where it grows from one end of the peninsula to the other. There are, for instance, seven streams called CYPRESS CREEK in Florida: one each in Washington, Pasco, Calhoun, Gulf, and Hamilton counties and two in Hillsborough County. We find, also, CYPRESS POND BRANCH in Okaloosa County, CYPRESS SLOUGH in Okeechobee County, BIG CYPRESS BRANCH in Liberty and Walton counties, and LITTLE CYPRESS CREEK in Walton County.

Besides these and other names which contain the familiar word "cypress," we find in Florida such place-names as LAKE HATCHI-NEHA (Polk County), which is from the Seminole-Creek *achinaho* ("cypress tree"). The body of water so designated was called "Cypress Lake" on maps as early as 1839; so the present name is either a return to an older Indian name or a recent application for romantic reasons.

FLOWERS

In addition to the numerous names associated with trees, various flowers of Florida have inspired names for her places. A bouquet of such names includes GOLDEN ROD in Orange County, IRIS in Dade County, JESSAMINE in Pasco County, LANTANA in Palm Beach County, LOTUS in Brevard County, OLEANDER in Dade County,

OLEANDER POINT in Brevard County, MAGNOLIA SPRINGS in Clay County, MAGNOLIA GROVE in St. Johns County, and MYRTLE GROVE in Escambia County.

More general flower names, honoring in one stroke every variety of blossom, are Lake County's BLOOMFIELD, Citrus County's FLORAL CITY and FLORAL ISLAND, Okaloosa's GARDEN CITY, Orange County's WINTER GARDEN, Hillsborough's GARDENVILLE, Seminole's GARDENA, and Hillsborough's FLORA—the last one summing it all up by commemorating the Roman goddess of flowers.

MISCELLANEOUS PLANTS AND TREES

Attempts at classifying large numbers of items frequently end up helplessly with a tremendous class called "miscellaneous." So it is with the "flora" place-names of Florida. Literally dozens of her names describe her by pointing to her plant life in a specific or general way; so great is their variety that classification after a certain point is impossible.

APPLE CREEK, in Columbia County, is for the crabapple tree. ATTAPULGUS CREEK, in Gadsden County, is from Creek *atapha* ("dogwood"), and *algi* ("grove") making "dogwood grove." The tropical facet of Florida's character is reflected in the names of BAMBOO, in Sumter County; the BANANA RIVER, in Brevard County; and BANYAN, in Brevard County. Palm Beach County's BEAN CITY, Santa Rosa's BERRYDALE, and Volusia's CELERY suggest some of the agricultural interests of Floridians. HOLLY HILL in Volusia County, MULBERRY in Polk County, and JUNIPER in Gadsden County mention three more trees that abound in Florida; Volusia County's SPRUCE CREEK, Putnam's PECAN, and Escambia's WALNUT HILL name three others.

Monroe County's TORCH KEYS, made up of BIG TORCH, MIDDLE TORCH, and LITTLE TORCH, were named for the torchwood tree, a small tropical native tree which burns slowly and can be used for torches. LAUREL (Sarasota County), LINDEN (Sumter County), MANGO (Hillsborough County), MANGROVE POINT (Hillsborough County), MAPLE (Citrus County), and LIGNUM VITAE KEY (Monroe County) make a list which testifies to the diversity of Florida's physical conditions. WAHOO, in Sumter County, receives its name from the Creek *uhawhu*, for the winged elm or white basswood. VINELAND, in Orange County, was named for the grape industry in the region. Manatee County has a WILLOW, and Sumter has a

WILDWOOD, named in 1878 when the telegraph operator at the station in the forest at the end of the line headed his dispatches "Wildwood."

One of the most interesting of the "flora" names of Florida is CANAVERAL. This name, which (when written in correct Spanish as *Cañaveral*) means "canebrake," or "place of reeds," was left on Florida by the Spaniards more than four hundred years ago. In 1565 Menéndez, who founded St. Augustine, built a fort called *Santa Lucia de Cañaveral* on the promontory we have called CAPE CANAVERAL for so long; and "Prom. Cañaveral" is the name of an east coast point of land on the Le Moyne map, which records the Ribault expedition of the 1560s. But on Thanksgiving Day, November 28, 1963, in an access of grief and out of an intense desire to honor the slain President John Fitzgerald Kennedy, the new President Lyndon Baines Johnson announced that Cape Canaveral would henceforth be CAPE KENNEDY. It had been six days since the assassination which had made Mr. Johnson president; the United States Geographic Board had approved the renaming, at his request, the day before. A note in the "American Name Society Bulletin" says, "It took only three hours to change a name that had been in effect for four centuries."

That the change was too impulsive is attested to by the fact that before the sixties were over, Florida's senators (Spessard Holland and Edward J. Gurney) had introduced into Congress a bill to restore the name of Canaveral to the Cape. The bill died in the Senate Interior Committee, but Senator Gurney tried again. On July 21, 1972, the Senate passed unanimously his resolution to restore the Spanish name to the Cape, but the measure was referred to the House Science and Astronautics Committee, where, Senator Gurney tells us, "according to press accounts, the influence of certain Massachusetts politicians effectively killed this measure." In 1973 he re-introduced the matter, but Senate leadership decided that in view of the action taken by the House in 1972 the Senate should defer action on the proposal until it secured passage in the House. In the summer of 1973 the measure was introduced into the House.

Meanwhile Florida citizens were expressing themselves in numerous letters "to the editor" and to the United States Geographic Board, as well as in petitions to Congress. Their sentiment seemed overwhelmingly to be that the late president's memory and leadership are rightly honored in the name of the

John F. Kennedy Space Center on the Cape—a new name announced by President Johnson on that same grief-laden November day—but that for the land area, a name of such long standing as Cape Canaveral should not be cast aside. Then the 1973 Florida legislature, weary of waiting, adopted a bill which restored the name Cape Canaveral to all official state maps and documents regardless of what name the federal government chose to call the place. Throughout the ten years since the change, local citizens had been clinging tightly to such names as PORT CANAVERAL, CANAVERAL HARBOR, and CAPE CANAVERAL CITY, which had been attached to places on the Cape long before 1963.

The will of the people was clear, then, and with dramatic suddenness the United States Board of Geographic Names scheduled an October 8, 1973, hearing on the Florida legislature's request for restoring Cape Canaveral's ancient name. And on October 10 Florida papers carried the headline "Cape Is Canaveral Again." Presumably the matter is settled, and Florida now has back its Cape Canaveral, one of the very few remaining descriptive names bestowed by the Spaniards.

That our Indian predecessors in Florida were prone to describe her vegetation in the names they gave is shown by Indian place-names that we have retained—sometimes without knowledge of their meanings and nearly always in a state of corruption which makes it difficult to discover their meanings. Among such names is KANAPAHA, attached to a small community and a lake in Alachua County. The name has been conjectured to mean "bead grass," a variety which grows in the area (Seminole-Creek *kunawa*, "bead," plus *pahi*, "grass"). Other speculations declare the name to be related to "skunk grass" (from *kunu* or *konip*, "skunk," plus *pahi*); "earth grass" (from *ikana*, "earth" or "ground," plus *pahi*); or to be a misapprehension of *pakanaho*, the Creek term for the wild plum. One authority, however, believes that the name is a relic of the ancient Timucua Indians, long gone from the Florida scene, since the village of Kanapaha is within the old Timucuan province of Potano. This authority points to the Timucuan *cani* ("palmetto leaves") and *paha* ("house") as the possible origin, since the Timucua thatched their pole houses with palmetto leaves. In any event, all guesses point to vegetation of some sort native to Florida.

Another Indian name which may or may not be properly placed among the "flora" names is KISSIMMEE, the name of the county seat of Osceola County and of several other places and natural features in the area. One conjecture is that it begins with the Seminole-Creek *ki* ("mulberry" or "mulberries"), and that Seminole-Creek *asima* ("yonder") may be the second element. The name is of considerable antiquity and wide application. "Cacema Town" is written on a 1720 military map and "Casseeme" on one of 1837, both of them in the general area where the name *Kissimmee* is now used. It is probably derived from one of the lost dialects and is thus beyond translation. Of course folk legend makes its interesting contribution: A brave tells his Indian lover how beautiful she is. To this she replies, "Well, kiss-i-me."

CHASSAHOWITZKA is the name of a swamp in Hernando County. According to one authority, it signifies "hanging pumpkins," from Seminole *chasi* ("pumpkins") and *wiski* ("hanging loose"). Another interprets it as a compound of Creek *chasi* ("pumpkin") and *houwitchka* ("to open"), thus "pumpkin opening place."

Sometimes the white man has taken the Indian names whose meanings he is familiar with and has translated them into English. A few examples are found in the names of BIG CYPRESS SWAMP in Collier County, for which *Atseenahoofa*, from Creek *achenaho* ("cypress") and *taphe* ("broad"), appears on a mid-eighteenth-century map; WIDE CYPRESS SWAMP in Orange County, once designated *Atseenatopho*, from the same roots; and PINEY POINT in Taylor County, shown formerly as *Ocitlota Funka*, from the Creek *chula* ("pine"), *ote* ("island"), and *funka* ("projection" or "point"). The name of ROYAL PALM HAMMOCK in Dade County was translated from *Tallasoculsa*, the Seminole word for "coconut palm grove."

In a few cases it is probable that the translation was the other way around—that is, that the red man translated into *his* language the name given to a place by the white man. A confusing example of such an occurrence is the Seminole *Tolopchopco*, or *Talahk Chopko Hatchee* ("River of Long Peas"), now called the PEACE RIVER (Polk and Charlotte counties). The casual observer might assume—and has often done so—that the present name arose from a misunderstanding of the white man's original translation from the Seminole, for the river has been shown as *Peas Creek* and *Pease Creek* on nineteenth-century maps. However, the name *Rio de Pas* (Spanish "River of Peace") appeared in this vicinity on the first printed map of Florida (ca. 1587), and *R. de la Paz* is at the head of an unnamed bay on the West Coast on the map drafted by Ferdinand Columbus, illegitimate son of Christopher Columbus, in 1527. Le Moyne's map of 1591 shows *F. Pacis* (Latin for "River of Peace"). It is unlikely that these early designations arose from misunderstanding, for there is no basis for homonymous confusion of the terms for *peas* and *peace* in Spanish or French (that is, the two words in those languages do not sound in the least alike). Not until after English-speaking people had settled in Florida did the name *Tolopchopko* appear on the map—and in any case the sixteenth-century Spanish and French explorers preceded the Seminoles in Florida by two hundred years. It is evident, therefore, that when speakers of English translated *R. de la Paz* and *F. Pacis* to *Peace River*, the later Indians who had learned that English *pease* or *peas* designated a certain vegetable used *their* name for that vegetable to designate the river they heard the white man call *Peace*. Perhaps, even, white men themselves had become confused before that time and were themselves responsible for the Indians' mistranslation. The names have, at any rate, been confused since that time, as nineteenth-century maps and twentieth-century histories clearly show. The United States Geographic Board has settled the matter by fixing the name as the Peace River, a name honorably come by and legitimized by the record, such as it is.

Atsena Otie, a name derived from the Creek ("Cedar Island"), was once the name of the main island of the Cedar Keys group— now called DEPOT KEY—and apparently it was taken over in translation as the white man's name for the entire group.

Other Indian names have simply been replaced by the white man's names without attempts at translation. Though a discussion of those which described the flora of Florida might be interesting here, it would be of little avail, for the description given in the current names covers the same ground. The fact that Florida is "very delightful, having many pleasant groves," as the first Spaniards saw it, is amply borne out in the names given to its places by both Indians and white men through the years.

❀ FAUNA ❀

Florida's wildlife—animals that have roamed her swamps and woods since prehistoric times and some that have migrated or been brought here in later times—have furnished names for her places, too. And these names, as surely as those taken from her plant life, describe the kind of land she is.

REPTILES, INSECTS, AND ANIMALS

The alligator is about as synonymous with Florida in many minds as is the palm tree. This weird anachronism left over from a vanished age has inhabited her swamps and streams farther back than the memory of man goes. Though fascinating to tourists from what they consider a safe vantage point, the alligator is, after all, a reptile and shares with other reptiles a certain unpopularity, so that place-namers of fairly recent times have not tended to attach its name to places which they hoped would attract settlers or tourists. However, before Florida became self-conscious, a good many alligator names were bestowed, and some of them still exist. They designate, for the most part, natural features rather than man-made communities, and some of them are in the Indian tongue, or a corruption thereof. ALLAPATTAH, corrupted from Seminole-Creek *halpata* ("alligator"), is the name of a community center in Miami (Dade County) and of a post office station there. A large marshy area between the St. Lucie River and Lake Okeechobee is also called the ALAPATA or ALAPATTAH FLATS, from the same derivation. The ALAPAHA RIVER in Hamilton County is thought to be another corruption of the same word, and the LITTLE ALAPAHA RIVER in the same county is an offspring. There are at least three bays called ALLIGATOR BAY—one off the coast of Franklin County, one off Monroe County, and one off Dade County. The map shows ALLIGATOR REEF off Monroe County. ALLIGATOR CREEK is ubiquitous; Gulf, Sarasota, Pinellas, Escambia, Okaloosa, Santa Rosa, Franklin, Wakulla, Liberty, Madison, Washington, Jackson, Holmes, Dade, Charlotte, Nassau, Bradford, and Hamilton counties, if not others, boast one. Old Indian names for the Dade and Charlotte creeks are *Halbatahatchee* and *Halpatah Hatchee.* Osceola, Liberty, and Columbia counties each have an ALLIGATOR LAKE. HALPATIOKEE MARSH, in St. Lucie County, and the HALPATIOKEE RIVER in neighboring Martin County are named from *halpata,* plus *oki* ("water"), and the name means "alligator water." Two early names of Columbia County's Lake City (renamed in 1859) were HALPATA and ALLIGATOR, after an Indian village formerly there whose head man was *Halpatter Tustenugee,* or "Alligator

Warrior," and this name change is indicative of the trend toward more inviting names by the American place-namers.

Another reptile, the snake, inhabits Florida, too. Here again there has been no wish to advertise the fact, so that no towns or counties are named for snakes. However, some topographic features have been named for them, both in English and in the Seminole-Creek language. Off Dade County there is SNAKE BIGHT (the topographical term might well be a pun in this case); in Monroe County there is SNAKE CREEK; off Levy County there is SNAKE KEY; in Dade County there is the SNAKE RIVER CANAL; in Baker County there is MOCCASIN CREEK, for the deadly water moccasin; in St. Johns County there is MOCCASIN BRANCH; and Leon County has a community called MOCCASIN GAP. The Seminole-Creek *Chittohatchee* ("snake river") was formerly applied to two streams, one in Osceola County and one in Monroe County, but the names have been changed to TEN MILE CREEK and RODGERS RIVER, respectively. One railroad station—CHETOLAH, in St. Lucie County— may have been named from *chitola* ("rattlesnake"), the designation of a Zuni clan, but there is no absolute certainty as to this origin.

Floridians have worked to rid the state of the pesky mosquito and have likewise put some effort into taking the unromantic word *mosquito* off the map. As has been mentioned earlier, in 1845 they changed the name of *Mosquito County* to Orange County. Once, too, before the arrival of the English, the HALIFAX RIVER (Volusia County) had been called the *Mosquito River*. But some mosquito names live on regardless of the unfortunate association. MOSQUITO CREEK and SOUTH MOSQUITO CREEK are in Gadsden County, MOSQUITO CREEK in Okeechobee County, and MOSQUITO INLET off the coast of Volusia County. In the main, though, the mosquito-control program has been fully as effective on the map as it has been on the land.

Six streams named BEE BRANCH, a BEETREE CREEK (Alachua County), and a BEE RIDGE (Sarasota County) are among the places named to honor another native insect, while Hillsborough County's BULLFROG CREEK, Clay's BULL CREEK, and Hillsborough's FROG CREEK tell of the swamp creature whose voice enlivens the night air of Florida in so many locations.

The bear is abundantly represented in Florida place-names, mostly in names attached to streams and natural features, there being six streams called BEAR BRANCH in the state and nine called

BEAR CREEK, as well as sundry other features—e.g., BEAR GAP, in Lake County—named in honor of this animal, which still roams wild in parts of Florida.

More than a dozen names—including Osceola County's DEER PARK, Monroe's FAT DEER KEY, and Flagler's NEOGA—are reminders that Florida is a happy hunting ground for big game. *Neoga* is a corruption of *naoge* ("deer"), the name of a Seneca clan of the Iroquois Confederation, and is an imported name.

The beaver, the fox, the rabbit, the raccoon, the panther, the wildcat, and the wolf appear in place-names of Florida. So does the turtle, both land and sea varieties. The most famous of the "turtle" names is DRY TORTUGAS, the name of a group of islands in Monroe County sixty-nine miles west of Key West. *Tortugas* is Spanish for "turtles." The islands were so named by Ponce de León because it was there during his 1513 voyage of discovery that he and his men replenished their failing food supply by capturing 170 turtles in a very short time. Fort Jefferson, a Civil War base and now a national monument, is situated on the Tortugas. (In it was once imprisoned Dr. Samuel A. Mudd, charged with giving aid to John Wilkes Booth, the assassin of President Lincoln.)

Florida's special sea animal, the manatee, already mentioned as the namesake of Manatee County, is honored in several other place-names as well; and the playful otter, which romps in Florida's wilderness waters, is mentioned in the name of Levy County's OTTER CREEK, both a town and a stream, as well as in the names of other streams and natural features located throughout the state. Trapping otters was once an important industry in Levy County.

Two domestic animals, not native to the state but brought over by the early Spaniards, have left their names upon the Florida map. They are the cow and the hog. In 1521, on his second voyage to Florida, Ponce de León brought cattle with him, and cattle-raising is one of the oldest and most important of Florida's industries. The Indians had no native word for "cow," as has been previously pointed out, and so they adopted the Spanish word *vaca*, which in their speech became *waca*—also recorded as *wacca* and *wakka*. The cow names on Florida's map, besides the ubiquitous COW CREEK and similar names, include the VACA KEYS (Monroe County), COW HOUSE CREEK (Hillsborough County), and WACAHOOTA (Alachua County). The second of these names—COW HOUSE or COWHOUSE—also designates an island, a slough, and a swamp in Hillsborough County, and is an interesting relic of history, for it is a translation of the Seminole term *Wacca Hute,* signifying "cow pen." Alachua County's WACAHOOTA, then, is another rendition of the same term, and is said to be derived from the fact that Billy Bowlegs, one of the Seminole War chiefs, built his cow pen there. It may be worth mentioning that despite its new spelling, the name is pronounced locally "wocca-hooty," as if it were still in its earlier form. COWPEN LAKE, in the same area, would seem to be another English translation of this Indian name.

In connection with the cattle names, it may be remembered that Jacksonville was once *Waca Pilatka,* or "Cow Crossing," and that the antiquity of some of the cow names indicates how important cattle have been to Florida for several hundred years.

The hog is represented in the names of a few rural features and places such as HOG ISLAND, at the entrance of the Suwannee River in Levy County, HOG ISLAND off the coast of Pinellas County, HOG ISLAND in Lake George in Putnam County, and DUROC—the name of a breed of hog—in Clay County. STOCK ISLAND, the name of one of the keys in Monroe County and the community thereon, was given because in early days Key Westers used to keep their cattle and other livestock there before butchering them.

BIRDS

The trees, the waters, and the skies of Florida are inhabited by various birds, of course, and her place-names tell us so: BIRD KEY designates a key—also called BIRD ISLAND—off the coast of Pinellas County; a key off the coast of Hernando County; a key off the coast of Monroe County; and a key in Terra Ceia Bay, off Manatee County.

The cuckoo, the curlew, the duck, the dove, the eagle, the flamingo, the gull, the crow, the osprey, the owl, the parrot, the pelican, and the wild turkey are some of the specific birds mentioned in Florida place-names. And the name of the Hardee County seat, WAUCHULA, though it is one of considerable mystery, may have been formed from a careless pronunciation of Creek *watula* ("sand hill crane").

There is also much doubt concerning the origin of ORTEGA, a name attached to a residential section of Jacksonville and to a creek in the same county (Duval), but it means in Spanish "hazel grouse" or "quail," and many of these are said to have been in the area in early days. The name dates from the time of the second Spanish occupation.

FISHES

Some of the bird names—for example, the osprey and pelican names—as well as the water names tell by association of fishes. But many place-names go further than this and describe Florida directly as an angler's heaven.

At DEVIL FISH KEY, off Hillsborough County, President Theodore Roosevelt is said to have landed a large devil fish. Monroe County has an ANGEL FISH KEY, a JEWELFISH KEY, and a JEWFISH KEY, as well as a group of islands called OYSTER KEYS and a group called TARPON BELLY KEYS. The large silver gamefish called the tarpon, which is caught in the area, is mainly inedible, but early settlers found that a thin filet taken off the belly was good to eat. There is also a PORPOISE KEY in Monroe County, named for the playful mammal that romps in Florida waters.

Broward County's POMPANO BEACH is named for another prominent Florida fish. And a favorite freshwater fish of Florida natives is named in CATFISH CREEK (Polk County), while the trout is mentioned a number of times in the names of Florida streams. Even the dreaded shark is memorialized—as in Monroe County's SHARK POINT and SHARK RIVER.

The meaning of APOPKA is uncertain; some guesses make it a "flora" and others a "fauna" name. It is the name of a lake in Orange County, adjacent to Lake County, and of a town near that lake in Orange County. Evidence is strong that the name is from two Creek words—*aha* meaning "potato" and *papka* meaning "eating place"—for on at least two nineteenth-century maps the name is spelled *Ahapopka*—with hyphens in one of the spellings—*A-ha-pop-ka*. Since the whole *apopka* name cluster is connected with lakes and streams, however, there are grounds for agreement with the often-made assertion that the name is a shortened form of Seminole-Creek *Tsala Apopka*, and thus actually means "trout eating place" rather than "potato eating place." At any rate, it is one of the descriptive place-names of Florida, and trout from Lake Apopka might well have been its inspiration.

❁ OTHER DESCRIPTIVE PLACE-NAMES ❁

Among the variety of things that other descriptive place-names of Florida tell us is that Florida is a land of many waters, with its thousand miles of seacoast and its numerous lakes and rivers. Seven of the county names mention the waters: Bay, Gulf, Okaloosa ("black water"), Lake, Indian River, Okeechobee ("big water"), and Palm Beach. Scores of her minor names corroborate the description.

SALTWATER NAMES

Names proclaiming the state's saltwater atmosphere include ATLANTIC BEACH, in Duval County, and BAHIA HONDA KEY (Monroe County). *Bahia Honda* is Spanish for "deep bay"; the water in the channel here runs from 22 to 28 feet deep. COQUINA (Duval County) is named for the coquina rock, made up of marine shells and coral. The name of Lee County's ESTERO is the Spanish word for "estuary," or "swell of the sea." Citrus County, which borders on the Gulf of Mexico, has a GULF HAMMOCK. In Pinellas County there is a GULFPORT, so named because it also borders on the Gulf.

MARINELAND, in Flagler County, proclaims Florida's coastal location, as does TIDEWATER, in Levy County—and as does the name of the SPANISH HARBOR KEYS in Monroe County, where, they say, the Spanish pirates used to hide. The name of SEABREEZE, in Volusia County, is another which describes this situational feature of Florida. The community of Seabreeze is now a part of Daytona Beach, but the name is still current. SALT SPRINGS, in Marion County, is an inland spring, but its name tells of the salt seepage which can and does occur from the sea in some inland areas. The water of Salt Springs is distinctly brackish.

FRESHWATER NAMES

That there are many lakes and streams in Florida is evident in scores of her place-names—those of towns, cities, and stations as well as the specific names of bodies of water. The cluster of ANCLOTE names is among these. *Anclote* is Spanish for "stream anchor, grapnel, kedge." There is an ANCLOTE in Pinellas County, named for the ANCLOTE RIVER, which received its name because it was a place of refuge for sea-going boats during rough weather; and there are the ANCLOTE KEYS, in Pasco County, named for the basin or bay inside the keys.

Pinellas County's county seat, CLEARWATER, is another prominent place with a "water" name; and a town called DELTA, in Escambia County, is—as one would expect—at the mouth of the Escambia River.

FENHOLLOWAY is the name of a town and a river in Taylor County. It is corrupted from Creek *feno* ("bridge") plus *halwi* ("high")—thus "High Bridge." This name, which Sidney Lanier, in his 1876 guide to Florida, called *Finalawa*, also tells of inland water. Collier County's IMMOKALEE is of Cherokee Indian derivation—*ama* ("water"), plus *kalola* ("tumbling"). The name INTERLACHEN, in Putnam County, describes the little town's situation between two lakes. Osceola County's LAGOVISTA has a name made up of the Spanish words *lago* ("lake") and *vista* ("view"); this is not a true Spanish name in form and has been manufactured according to an English word-formation pattern—"Lake View"—rather than the Spanish pattern, which would call for *Vista del Lago*—"View of the Lake." LAKE CITY (Columbia County) and LAKELAND (Polk County) are other "lake" names, while MIDRIVER (Broward County) tells of flowing inland water, as does RIVER JUNCTION (Gadsden County), where the Flint and the Chattahoochee rivers join to form the Apalachicola. RIO MAR, in Indian River County, is Spanish for "River Sea" (though it is not an authentic Spanish name but an American formation), because the town is between the Indian River and the Atlantic Ocean. Pinellas County has a RIO VISTA, whose name, like that of LAGOVISTA, is an American-formed Spanish name intended to mean "River View." Authentic Spanish would be *Vista del Rio*.

The name of Lake County's OKAHUMPKA may be translated "Single Lake" or "Lonely Water." It is on the site of an Indian village known as early as 1813 and called "Okeehumptee." The name is a combination of Hitchiti *oki* ("water") and Seminole-Creek *hamki* ("one").

PALATKA, in Putnam County, is named for an Indian town, *Pilatko*, formerly at or near the place. The name was probably shortened and corrupted from Seminole-Creek *pilotaikita*, meaning "crossing." The city of Palatka is on the St. Johns River, where a bridge now makes the crossing; and EAST PALATKA is across the river from it.

Among other Indian "water" names is SOPCHOPPY, the name of a town and of a creek in Wakulla County. It is derived from Creek *sokhe* ("convulsive" or "twisted") and *chapke* ("long"), meaning "Long Twisted Stream."

An interesting cluster of related Indian names which speak of Florida's waters includes Withlacoochee, Withla, Lacoochee, the Little Withlacoochee River, Willacoochee, and Welaka. The first—WITHLACOOCHEE—is the name of two rivers, one in North Florida bordering Madison County and the other in West Central Florida rising in Polk County, and of a bay into which the latter river flows. It is compounded of Creek *we* ("water"), *thlako* ("big"), and *chee* ("little")—hence, seemingly, "Little Big Water," though *big water* usually means "river" and may specifically designate a river of lakes. The name of Polk County's WITHLA is an abbreviation of Withlacoochee, and the name of Pasco County's LACOOCHEE is the same name abbreviated from the front. In view of Withlacoochee's meaning, the name of the LITTLE WITHLACOOCHEE RIVER (Hernando County) works out to "Little Little Big Water River" or "Little Little River River." WILLACOOCHEE, the name of a creek in Gadsden County and of a landing on the Florida East Coast Canal in St. Johns County, has the same derivation as Withlacoochee; and the name of WELAKA, in Putnam County, is made up of the first two words of the name—*we* and *thlako*—designating a "big water," or river of lakes. It is fair to assert that Gadsden County's present LITTLE RIVER is a part of this cluster also, the present name being a translation of the former *Weeklakatchee*, formed from the same words from which Withlacoochee, Willacoochee, and the shortened forms were derived. Little River was shown on an eighteenth-century map (the Purcell-Stuart map, 1778) as *Weeklakatchee, or Little Big River.*

NAMES DEPICTING NATURAL BEAUTIES AND CLIMATIC ADVANTAGES

Florida has depended to an unusual extent upon natural beauties and climatic advantages for prosperity. Consequently many Florida place-names reflect the desire of the residents and developers to advertise these natural advantages.

BELLEAIR, in Pinellas County, BELLE GLADE, in Palm Beach County, and BELLE MEADE, in Collier County, are three such names. The first was given by Henry Plant in 1896, when he built his Belleview Hotel, and is a French word combination meaning "beautiful air," though properly the adjective should be *bel*, since French *air* is masculine in gender. The second, Belle Glade, is a French-English combination dating from the 1920s and meaning "Beautiful Glade"—the "glade" referring to the Everglades. Belle

Meade, the last of the three, is a French-English combination, with misspelling, meant for "Beautiful Meadow."

PLAYA LINDA, Spanish for "Pretty Beach," is the name of a place in Brevard County, written on recent maps as PLAYALINDA BEACH, resulting in the tautological "Pretty-Beach Beach." The place now called SAFETY HARBOR, in Pinellas County, is said to have been described by the Spanish pirate Gomez as "God's resting place." SUMMERLAND KEY, in Monroe County, has a pleasant Florida name. And ZEPHYRHILLS, in Pasco County, which had been settled in the post–Civil War era as *Abbott*, was renamed in the early twentieth century to tell of the breezes over the hills in that area.

Important among the names of approbation are the "sunshine" names. Florida's official nickname is "The Sunshine State"—a sobriquet that appears on her automobile license plates—and sunshine is one of her chief commodities. Such names as the following advertise that commodity: SUN CITY (Hillsborough County); SUNNILAND (Collier County); SUNNYMEDE (Osceola County); SUNSET (Hillsborough County); SUNSET ROAD (Dade County); SUNSHINE BEACH (Pinellas County); and SUNNYSIDE (Lake County).

The "winter" names are also particularly significant as advertising names, for Florida has proved to be a haven from the harsh winters of the North. Her place-names have not neglected to point out this fact, as evidenced in such names as WINTER BEACH (Indian River County); WINTER HAVEN and WEST WINTER HAVEN (Polk County); WINTER HOME (Orange County); WINTER PARK (Orange County); and WINTERLEA (Polk County).

ENVIRONMENTAL OCCUPATION NAMES

Some place-names are descriptive of what happens at the places, what men do there, or what purposes the places serve, rather than describing their natural features. The pine and citrus names and other names already mentioned hint at such things, but some names are more direct.

ALLIANCE (Jackson County) was named for the Farmers' Alliance Organization and thus tells of the agricultural pursuits which were the mainstay of the community. AZUCAR (Palm Beach County) means "sugar" in Spanish; and the place is owned outright by the United States Sugar Corporation for the production of cane sugar.

The name of BALLAST POINT (Hillsborough County) tells that in earlier days vessels discharged their ballast (rock) at this point, or sometimes, if in need of ballast, took rock here.

In Escambia County the name of BRICKTON tells of the brick kilns in the vicinity, for West Florida is a land of red clay much used in the production of bricks. The name of CORONET (Hillsborough County) was derived from that of the Coronet Phosphate Company and speaks of the phosphate-mining industry, which is important in Florida. FAIRGROUNDS, a suburb of Marianna in Jackson County, tells in its name that county fairs were once held on the spot. Another name telling of agriculture is that of FARM-DALE, in Bay County. FREIGHT LINE JUNCTION (Escambia County) tells of shipping interests, while the name of HOLOPAW (Osceola County) says much the same thing in another language. The name is guessed to be connected with the Seminole-Creek *halatipuichita* ("to haul or draw as with a horse"), and signifies, then, the place where something is hauled. The place is the site of an important lumber mill. IDLEWOOD, in Gulf County, is the site of a hunting and fishing lodge and tells in its name of pleasure and vacation pursuits. LOGGING RIVER (Hardee County) tells of the lumber industry in Florida, as does LUMBERTON (Pasco County).

As a matter of fact, most of the "mill" names of Florida speak of the lumber industry by their reference to sawmills either now in operation or in operation at the time of naming. Some of them are MILL BAYOU (Bay County); six streams named MILL BRANCH scattered through the state; MILL CITY (Calhoun County); MILL CREEK (one each in Calhoun, Lafayette, Manatee, and St. Johns counties, as well as thirteen other MILL CREEKS throughout the state); MILLCREEK (St. Johns County); MILL GROVE (Wakulla County); MILLVILLE (one each in Bay and Wakulla counties); MILL-VIEW (Escambia County); MILLWOOD (Marion County); and MOLINO (Escambia County). *Molino* is the Spanish word for "mill." Even the name of NOMA (Holmes County) is derived from the lumber industry, for it is from the Noma Mill Company, which operated a sawmill there. ADAMS MILL CREEK (Walton County) is one of the mill names not connected with the lumber industry. Once upon a time a grist mill was operated on its bank by an Adams family.

POSTAL COLONY (Lake County) speaks of Florida as a place of retirement; it is a colony for retired postal clerks. QUAY (Indian River County) tells of shipping by water. RELAY (Flagler County) derives its name from the fact that it was built on the site of a relay station for a stagecoach line in earlier days. On SHINGLE CREEK (Orange County), as the name implies, early settlers made shingles for houses in Orlando. SILO (Lafayette County) apparently derives its name from the fact that here green fodder was converted into silage for cattle.

SOUTHERN MINE (Citrus County) recalls the phosphate mining industry of Florida. SUGARTON (Hendry County) echoes the message of Azucar in saying that sugar is produced in this section of Florida. TEXTILE CITY (Volusia County) is obviously named for a textile operation. TRUCK CENTER (Seminole County) and TRUCK-LAND (Lee County) speak of the trucking in connection with Florida agriculture. Orange County's WEWAHOTEE tells us that trains once took on water here, for in the Creek language it means "water house" or "water tank" (*wewa*, "water," plus *huti*, "house"), and it is true that the Florida East Coast Railroad had a water tank here at the time the place was established.

Charlotte County's WHARF is another place-name that tells of shipping by boat. And names like FERREL STILL (St. Johns County) do not proclaim Florida as a state of moonshiners, but speak of the turpentine and naval stores industry, which has been an important adjunct of the hospitality of her soil to the pine tree. The stills referred to are turpentine stills.

LOCATION NAMES

Names which describe places merely by showing their location in terms of direction from or proximity to other places are the least significant of the descriptive names. In themselves they tell us little about the state or its people that we cannot learn from other names. But Florida, like other states, has her share of places with such names.

Some of these are CAPITOLA (Leon County), so named because it is near Tallahassee, where the state capitol is located; CENTER HILL (Sumter County), so named because the post office was on a hill which was then the exact center of the county before Lake County was created from a part of Sumter County; and KEY WEST (Monroe County), so named in an interesting instance of folk etymology because it is the westernmost of the main group of Florida Keys.

MIDWAY (Gadsden County) was midway between Quincy and Tallahassee by routes existing at the time of its naming. Brevard County's SOUTH MERE is supposed to be so named because it is near the boundary line between Seminole and Brevard counties—*mere* means "boundary"—but the *south* is not accounted for in this explanation, for the place is on the east-west boundary line. WEST GATE is at the western entrance to West Palm Beach, in Palm Beach County. And countless other "west," "east," "north," "south," and "middle" names exist. About all that such names tell us is that the places designated by them are located in a particular direction from some other place, though often their references to the other places and the generic affixes attached to them—"river," "bay," "cape," "bluff," etc.—do repeat the message conveyed by the names of the other places or give us a little message of their own. Thus they augment the total description of Florida given by its place-names.

MISCELLANEOUS DESCRIPTIVE NAMES

ALTAMONTE SPRINGS (Seminole County) has an American-made, half-Spanish name meaning "High Hill Springs." ARTESIA (Brevard County) got that name because the water supply there was wholly from artesian wells. Highland County's BASKET LAKE is shaped like a basket.

A number of *Boca* ("mouth") names are a part of Florida's Spanish heritage, and help describe her irregular coastline. BOCA CHICA, on BOCA CHICA KEY in Monroe County, has a name that is Spanish for "Little Mouth," originally referring to a narrow channel here. Pinellas County's BOCA CIEGA BAY is Spanish for "blind mouth," probably referring to obstruction by dense vegetation. BOCA GRANDE (Lee County) is Spanish for "Big Mouth" and refers to a passage from the Gulf. More interesting is Palm Beach County's BOCA RATON, Spanish for "Rats' Mouth"—shortened from the authentic Spanish *boca de ratones*, a term used to designate a reef of hidden rocks which chewed ships' cables as rats might. And Lee County's BOCILLA ISLAND is apparently an English corruption of the Spanish diminutive for *boca—boquilla*, meaning "little mouth." The supposition seems to be confirmed by the presence of a settlement on the island called BOKEELIA, which preserves the Spanish pronunciation of *boquilla* in an English phonetic spelling.

Sand, both on her beaches and inland, is one of the Florida hallmarks. The folk-saying that if a traveler ever gets Florida sand in his shoes, he will surely come back—or perhaps never get away—is a well-known one; and the word *sand* often figures in Florida book and periodical titles as being significant of the state—for example, *Sand in My Shoes, Footprints in the Sand, Florida's Golden Sands,* etc.

Her place-names, too, mention the sand, in at least three languages. *Sable* means "sand" in French and is an obsolete word for "sand" in Spanish, and it is from the latter source that the name CAPE SABLE (Monroe County) probably came. OCTAHATCHEE, the name of a lake and a settlement in Hamilton County, is from a Creek word combination of *oktaha* ("sand"), and *hatke* ("white"). The earlier spelling—*Oktahatko*—rules out the supposition that the last element is the familiar *hatcha* (or *hatchee*) for "creek" or "river"; so "White Sand" it seems to be—and truly descriptive it certainly is, for the white sands of Florida are a marvel to newcomers year after year. SAND CUT ("cut" is synonymous with "inlet" in Florida place-name usage) is a Palm Beach County "sand" name, while in Franklin County there are SAND ISLAND and SAND ISLAND PASS; in Pinellas County we find SAND KEY; in Walton and Holmes counties we have SANDY CREEK; and in Monroe County there is SANDY KEY.

The intriguing name of the BROTHERS RIVER (Gulf County) rather unexpectedly turns out to be descriptive also. The river is made up of several branches from the same source, known as *Little Brother, Big Brother,* etc., because of their common origin. The CHATTAHOOCHEE RIVER, which rises in Georgia and joins with the Flint River to become the Apalachicola River at Florida's northern border, has a Florida town named for it—CHATTA-HOOCHEE, near the place where the rivers come together. The name—from the Indian *chat-to* ("stone"), plus *ho-cha* ("marked" or "flowered")—was originally given because of colored or marked stones found in the river. The name of the CONCH KEYS (Monroe County) came, of course, from the name of the conch, a tropical shellfish common in the area—and natives of the Key West vicinity are also colloquially called *conchs* because of the local abundance of these shellfish.

The beautiful name of CORAL GABLES (Dade County) came from the name of the first house built there, its gables decorated with coral rock. Equally attractive is ISLAMORADA, the name of a place on Upper Matecumbe Key, in Monroe County. It is made up of Spanish words meaning "purple island" and was given because the island appears purple when viewed from the sea.

DELRAY BEACH (Palm Beach County) has an American-concocted name of Spanish flavor, said to be either from the Spanish *del rey*, meaning "of the king," or from the Spanish *del rayo*, "of the ray," referring to the sun. The specific part of the name dates from 1895, though the generic part—"beach"—was not added to it until sometime in the 1930s.

PAHOKEE is a Florida place-name with an ancient and honorable native history. It is from the Seminole-Hitchiti *pahi* ("grass"), and *oki* ("water"), adding up to "Grass Water"—or more poetically, "Grassy Waters"—a term long ago applied by the Indians to the Everglades. It appeared on the Bruff map of 1846 as "Pay-hay-okee" and was also rendered sometimes as "Pay-hai-o-kee." The present contracted form, Pahokee, is the name of a town in Palm Beach County, on the shore of Lake Okeechobee amid the rich mucklands of the Everglades. It was founded in 1922 after a committee of men, which included the father of Alton C. Morris, had "stepped off," or selected, the site for a spillway later to be the center of a truck-farming shipping area. At that time the only access to the outside world for the settlers was by boat across Lake Okeechobee, and surviving pioneers remember nostalgically the *Lily*, a paddle-wheeled steamer, and the *Harry L.*, which once or twice a week brought news from Okeechobee City and West Palm Beach—including news of the Armistice of World War I, two days after the war was declared ended in 1918.

HIGH SPRINGS, a town in Alachua County, was so named because of a spring formerly located on the top of a hill there. The name was given in 1898, though the town is older. It was first known as "Sanaffee," a corruption of the name of the nearby Santa Fe River, and then for a while (beginning in 1886) as "Orion," presumably for the constellation so named, or for the hunter in Greek mythology who became the constellation, though no one is sure of this.

Florida's swamps are often alluded to in her place-names. One of these is OPALOCKA, the name of a town in Dade County. It is from Seminole *opilwa* ("swamp"), and *lako* or *thlako* ("big"). The name is of somewhat recent application and is said to apply to a hammock situated near the town. Somewhat similar in meaning is the name of OTAHITE, a small place in Okaloosa County. This one is perhaps from the Creek *otahita* ("damp place"), referring to the seepage streams common in the area. The guess that it might have been named for the Otaheite orange is discounted by citrus experts, who believe that the species is too obscure to have been known there.

The mournful name of the PERDIDO RIVER, forming the western boundary of Florida, is Spanish for "lost." It was given, it may be conjectured, because of the "lostness," or loneliness, of the area—or perhaps because someone or something was lost there.

The provocative PICOLATA, designating a place in St. Johns County, is a name of doubtful origin, but one guess is that it is from the Spanish *pico*, plus *lato*, or "broad bluff," describing the ground on which the Spanish fort at this site was built. Another guess is that the name is of Indian origin; one writer connects it with *Holahta*, which in the Apalachee, Creek, and Timucuan languages meant "blue" and often formed part of the title of Seminole chiefs. In various spellings, the name has appeared on Florida maps and charts since the early eighteenth century at least.

The name of PUNTA RASA is just as frequently spelled "Punta Rassa," if not more frequently, but the United States Geographic Board has fixed it as *Punta Rasa* and firmly stipulates, "Not Punta Rassa, Puntarasa, nor Puntarassa." The name is obviously Spanish, but there are conflicting translations, some saying "raveling point" and others "flat point." It has been observed that the coastline of Sanibel Island, opposite Punta Rasa, presents a ragged or raveled appearance. However, *Punta Rasa* is good Spanish for "flat point" (or "unobstructed point"), and it is probable that *rassa* is simply a misspelling of *rasa*; there does not seem to be a similar Spanish word meaning "raveling." This Lee County place, which was once a busy beef-shipping center and, as the terminus of the cable to Cuba, was the first place in the United States to learn of the sinking of the *Maine*, is now virtually a ghost town, roads and bridges having passed it by in this century. It dates at least from the second Spanish period.

Whether or not *Punta Rasa* describes a ragged coastline, there seems no doubt that the RAGGED KEYS of Dade County got their name from such a circumstance. And most of the "shell" names of Florida—SHELL CITY (Charlotte County); SHELL CREEK MANOR (Charlotte County); SHELL KEY (Monroe County); and SHELL POINT (Wakulla County)—tell us in another way of her proximity to the sea. However, Flagler County's SHELL BLUFF was named for a hill of snail shells left by Indians.

The name of TERRA CEIA, a town on TERRA CEIA ISLAND in Manatee County, is another interesting example of changes wrought in names when they are shifted from one language to another. It is apparently a corruption of the Spanish *Terrasilla,* the pronunciation of which is similar to the current pronunciation of the present form—"terra-sée-ya." *Terrasilla,* from *tierra* or "earth," means "little land." The late interpretation "heavenly land," based upon the assumption that *Ceia* is a corruption of the Spanish word *cielo* for "sky" or "heaven," seems to have no basis in fact or likelihood. There is also a TERRA CEIA BAY and a TERRA CEIA JUNCTION in Manatee County, both of them also being namesakes of TERRA CEIA ISLAND, the original "little land."

There is a hilly area in Orange County—south and southeast of Lake Apopka—called THLAUHATKE HILLS. The name is believed to be a shortened form of Creek *thlane* ("mountain"), combined with Creek *hatke* ("white"), meaning "white mountain." The hills here are mantled with white sand. In a Seminole War journal this area is mentioned as "The Thlauhatke or white mountain, an elevated range of hills," and the writer says that "the ascent in many places was so difficult as to render drag ropes and heavy details of men necessary to take the baggage wagons over the heights."

One of Florida's most famous place-names is that of the city of MIAMI, in Dade County, and of the river which flows through the city. Miami is the largest and perhaps the most widely known city in the state. It received its name from the river, which, before the drainage canals lowered the waters of Lake Okeechobee, afforded a canoe trail to the lake. *Miami* is a part of a Seminole name-cluster which includes the *Myakka* variants as well. It is of ancient usage in Florida, being the earliest known name for Lake Okeechobee—recorded in the form *Mayaimi*—and its meaning is not now traceable. However, authorities tentatively agree on "it is so wide" or "big water," a reasonable assumption backed by the report of Fontaneda—an early Spaniard who lived captive among the Calusa Indians for a time—that *Lake Mayaimi* was so called because it was so large. (Here again an amusing folk legend is often told: An Indian brave told his sweetheart that she was beautiful, whereupon she replied, "My! *Am* I?") *Myakka* and its variants are thought to be corruptions of the same early word. And the famous Tanner map of 1823 shows Lake Okeechobee as "Lake Macaco," doubtless a variant of *Myakka.*

Though the meaning of TAMPA is not now known, we can be reasonably sure that somehow it described the place to which it was attached four hundred years ago. One guess is that it means "a nearby place," from the Creek *itimpi* ("near it")—presumably from the closeness of the original Indian village to the bay which is now called TAMPA BAY. Another is that it means "split wood for quick fire"—referring to the driftwood along the shore. The name has been current in Florida at least since the sixteenth century, however, having been mentioned by Fontaneda, in his relation of 1575, as the name of a Calusa town. (In Spanish times the name of the Indian village took such forms as "Tanpa" and "Timpe.") In this light it is difficult to accept interpretations based on similarity to Creek words, for the renegade Creeks came to Florida more than a century later. At least as early as 1705 a bay on the Gulf Coast was designated "B. Tampa," and by the late eighteenth century the name Tampa Bay was firmly attached to the bay where it now rests. The present city of Tampa, located on and ultimately named for the bay, is at least in the vicinity of the Calusa town which Fontaneda mentioned. It is one of Florida's largest and most picturesque cities, with many an exciting story in its past. It began as the Seminole War "Fort Brooke" (1823), became Tampa Bay (though the "Bay" was soon dropped) when later settlers preferred that name for their first post office in 1831, and boomed as a training camp for soldiers and as a take-off point for Cuba during the Spanish-American War. In 1876 poet Sidney Lanier went to Tampa in search of health, took up residence at the Orange Hotel, and soon was entertaining the cream of the city's society with flute solos. Inspired by the city's natural characteristics, he put the name of Tampa into poetry in "Tampa Robins"—"The robin laughed in the orange tree,/Ho! Windy North, a fig for thee!"

And of course the name of Florida's capital city, also a descriptive one, is of major importance. TALLAHASSEE has a name of ancient application in its vicinity, the present Leon County. A map of 1767 shows an Indian village named *Tallahassa Talofa*. Creek *Talwa* means "town," and *ahassee* means "old," so that TALLAHASSEE is correctly translated "Old Town." Since *talofa* also means "town," the name of the Indian village would seem tautological, but it apparently indicates that the town occupied a site formerly occupied by another town; and it is thought that *Tallahassa Talofa* was the site of the former mission town of San Luis de Talimali, the Spanish capital of the province of Apalachee, which was near the present Tallahassee. When Florida's capital site was selected in 1824, there was no occupation of the settlement, but the so-called Tallahassee Indians were still nearby. Mindful of history and conscious of the romantic sound of the name, Octavia Walton, daughter of George Walton, secretary of the territory of Florida (1822–26), chose Tallahassee for the name of the new capital city. In various forms—including *Tallassee* and *Tulsa*—the name has been of widespread use wherever Creek Indians wandered. It is said that the site for Florida's Tallahassee was selected because it was midway between Pensacola and St. Augustine, the capital cities of the Spanish Floridas, East and West. The story is told that two horsemen set out, one from each of these cities, and that by agreement the place where they met was designated as American Florida's capital—and the daughter of American Florida's secretary was allowed to choose the city's name.

Of course, there are many more descriptive names which were not discussed. There seems to be no end to the names and the stories behind them. And one more thing is clear about Florida's place-names: that they describe her in great detail, her perfections and her flaws, her glory and her homeliness, but most of all her compelling beauty and romance.

5

"Some Record of What We Were"

ALL NAMES TELL SOMETHING about the people who gave them. But some, especially, go beyond commemorating people, places, and things, or describing the land, and reveal humor and whimsy, religious and literary backgrounds, and folk activities and lore. They give us the "personality" of the people, arise from or give rise to folk tales, and show how silly, religious, ambitious, imaginative, or playful the people were as they named the land.

Florida, as much as any land, has aroused a sense of poetry in the people who settled here. So a fair number of her place-names were given as much for their music as for their meaning. Some, indeed, have no discernible meaning. Dade County's BAL HARBOUR is one of these, with its pleasant and apparently meaningless "Bal," and the exotic air lent by the British spelling of *Harbor*. The "Bal," however, turns out to have an unexpected meaning. A newsletter on file in the village manager's office there reveals that it is the first syllable of the word *balanced*—used because the town is "balanced" between Biscayne Bay and the Atlantic Ocean. Originally the place was called "Bay Harbour," but the residents were dissatisfied with that name because it gave the impression that the village was not on the ocean. Bal Harbour was their solution. EMERALDA, in Lake County, may have been so named because of its verdure—or perhaps the name was suggested by the name of the heroine of Victor Hugo's *Notre Dame de Paris*, Esmeralda, or another Esmeralda. Broward County's FLORANADA connotes flowers, as do FLORINDE (sometimes FLORINDA) in Polk County,

111

FLOWEREE in Hendry County, and FLOROSA in Okaloosa County, while Putnam County's FLORAHOME suggests both flowers and security.

GLENNELL, in Hillsborough County, had its name assigned by the railroad because of the attractive sound of it and because it fitted the remoteness of the place. GOLDEN BEACH, in Dade County, has a name given by subdivision developers in the 1920s for its advertising value. HONEY HEIGHTS (Lake County) capitalizes upon alliteration and sweetness of imagery, while Lee County's IM-PERIAL RIVER apparently was so named because of the impressive-ness of the name. The name of INDIANOLA (Brevard County) was a coinage suggested by the Post Office Department because of the Indian mounds in the vicinity. LAKE GEM (Orange County) is one of the metaphorical descriptive names that praise as they describe. LECANTO (Citrus County) is thought to have some refer-ence to the music of the area's songbirds (from Italian *canto*, mean-ing "song," with the French definite article *le*), but is a coinage more useful for sound than for description. FLORAL BLUFF (Duval County) was obviously named entirely imaginatively, for it is said that neither flowers nor bluffs are there.

WOODLAWN, a settlement and cemetery in St. Johns County, has a pleasant name popular for cemeteries and subdivisions, and the name of LYRATA (Brevard County) connotes music and grace (cf. *lyre*). The name of PARAGON (Broward County) reflects the pride and hope of its founders. The names of MONARCH (Sumter County) and WINDSOR (Alachua County) seem to have been chosen for their regal sound. The latter was settled and named by Eng-lish planters in 1846. Other names apparently selected for their euphony and pleasant connotations are VANDOLAH (Hardee County), BELVEDERE (Palm Beach County), BLOSSOM (Manatee County), and OWANITA (Lee County)—though this last place may be named for a girl (the name being, possibly, a spelling of *Juanita* or a possible feminine formation from Owen).

When we hear of SOLANA (Charlotte County), we feel certain that its namers wanted to honor the sun, Florida being a land of sun-worshippers, as well as to make a name with a pretty sound. And in Dade County the inhabitants of a place called "Snake Creek" longed for beauty and romance and renamed their town ULETA, a name borrowed from the scenario of a South Sea moving picture filmed in the area. TARU, in Manatee County, could hardly have been named for the desert in British East Africa, but its un-English sound is romantically suggestive of faraway places.

Other names selected for the desirable images they evoke are FLORIDALE (Santa Rosa County); BONITA BEACH (Taylor County); BELLE HAVEN (Santa Rosa County); DEL RIO (Levy County), the name of this place meaning simply "of the river" in Spanish, but sounding pleasantly exotic to American ears; FAIRVIEW (Putnam County); BELLEVIEW (Escambia County), using a popular American combination of French and English to mean "beautiful view"; SUNBEAM (Duval County); BELLE GLADE (Palm Beach County), another combination of French and English; BELLE ISLE (Orange County), utilizing the French "beautiful" and the poetic English word, directly from Old French, for "island"; and two more BELLEVIEWS, one in Marion County and one in Pinellas County. Such names as these, like EL PORTAL (Dade County), often were taken from predecessor real estate developments in the 1920s. *El Portal* means, in Spanish, "the gate" and was, at the time it was named, the highway entrance to Miami from the north.

MAYPORT (Duval County) is a nineteenth-century naming (1830) which looks back to the sixteenth century and the brief Florida adventure of the French Huguenots, who had called the St. Johns the "Rivière de Mai" because they discovered it on the first day of May. Mayport, on the St. Johns, was so named in memory of that lost name.

LAPARITA, in Lee County, is a station with a cleverly chosen Spanish name; it means "the little stop; the short stay," and at the same time has a pleasantly exotic sound to American ears. EL DESTINO (Jefferson County) was chosen by John Nuttall of Virginia in 1828 as the name of a tract of land near Tallahassee, which he obtained from the United States government and hoped to develop. The name is Spanish for "The Destination" or "Destiny." The French BON AMI, or "Good Friend" (Liberty County), is another foreign-language name bestowed by Americans for exotic appeal as well as for meaning. ESPANOLA (Flagler County) was so named because of the pleasant sound of the name and its recognition of Florida's Spanish heritage, as was SIESTA (Sarasota County), connoting rest and idleness in a way impossible to achieve with an English word. The naming of FAVORITA or FAVORETTA (Flagler County), established as a turpentine still in 1910, sprang from the same sort of interest in Florida's Spanish heritage.

SHAMROCK, in Dixie County, was named for good luck, possibly by an American of Irish origin. Maybe HORSESHOE COVE, HORSESHOE POINT, and HORSESHOE BEACH, also in Dixie County, were named for good luck too— or maybe the namers thought the cove was shaped like a horseshoe. In Okaloosa County the town of NICEVILLE, originally called "Boggy Bayou," was given that name at the suggestion of the postmaster, apparently because it seemed to him to be a nice ville. A place called "Teaspoon" in Escambia County was renamed CENTURY because the construction of a lumber mill was begun there in the first month of the twentieth century.

Orange County's PINECASTLE got its name from the tree house of a Florida poet, Will Wallace Harney, who was also editor of Osceola County's first newspaper. When Harney left Kissimmee, he went to Orange County and built a house in a large pine tree, calling it his castle. The town of Pinecastle thus got its name.

LADY LAKE (Lake County) was romantically named for a nearby lake which the Indians called "Lake Lady" because, it is said, they found a drowned white woman floating on its surface. The settlers, who had moved here in 1884 from nearby Slighville in order to take advantage of the railroad that had just come through, won out in their fight for this picturesque name over the railway authorities, who wanted to call the place "Cooper."

The search for originality in place-names is as evident as the search for beauty and romance. In both searches, meaning was important too, but meaning in the final result is not always apparent to the casual eye. For instance, a stranger might long wonder about the name of EKAL (Sumter County) before he realized that it is simply *lake* spelled backwards. Other reverse spellings used for place-names include Hillsborough County's REMLAP, so named because the Potter-Palmer interests had holdings there; NOLEM, in Sumter County; and SENYAH, in Volusia County. The name of WABASSO, a village in Indian River County, is said by one Indian-name authority to be a reversal of *Ossabaw*, the name of an island and a sound off the coast of Georgia. NEDRA (Alachua County) appears to be a reverse spelling of *Arden*.

A type of word formation used extensively in the creation of meaningful new place-names is that of the compounding of syllables from two separate words to form an entirely new word. Such a name is FLOMICH (Volusia County), formed from the first syllable of *Florida* and the first syllable of *Michigan*, the latter state being the native state of the founder. Other similar concoctions are LAKE TALQUIN (Gadsden County), a combination from *Tallahassee* and *Quincy*, because it is near both of these cities; MARICAMP

(Marion County), formed from *Marion* and *Camp*; MODELLA (Dade County), from *Model Land Company*, the name of an organization which developed the area; OKEELANTA (Palm Beach County), a blend of *Okeechobee* and *Atlantic* because it is near both the lake and the ocean; PENNSUCO (Dade County), from the *Pennsylvania Sugar Company*, which colonized the place for sugarcane planting; PHOSLIME (Marion County), from the phosphate and limerock there; PHOSMICO (Polk County), from *Phosphate Mining Company*; SANLANDO (Seminole County), from *Sanford* and *Orlando* because it is between the two cities; TAMIAMI, a village in Lee County and a canal following the TAMIAMI TRAIL, a highway which connects Tampa with Miami (hence the name, a blend of *Tampa* and *Miami*); KANFLA (Santa Rosa County), from the first syllable of *Kansas* and the abbreviation for *Florida*; WAYLAND (Lake County), a compound of syllables from *Waycross* and *Lakeland*, once the name of the railroad on which it is located—now the Seaboard Coast Line; and VOLCO (Volusia County), from *Volusia County*. This name was given by the Volusia County Cypress Company in 1922, following a precedent set by the *Cummer Cypress Company*, which had called the place *Cumpresco*. MANASOTA (Sarasota County) is obviously a blend of *Manatee* and *Sarasota*, Sarasota County having been a part of Manatee County until 1921.

In some instances compounds and blends have been from other languages or have been a mixture of English and other languages. BELMAR (Hillsborough County) is probably a combination of syllables from Spanish words for "beautiful sea." INDRIO and INDRIO BEACH (St. Lucie County) take their names from the nearby Indian River, but with the Spanish *rio* substituted for the English *river*. Another name formed partly from *Indian River* is INDI-ATLANTIC (Brevard County), located between the Indian River and the Atlantic Ocean. MANAVISTA (Manatee County) has a name made up of the first part of *Manatee* plus the Spanish word for "view." The names of VALROY and VALRICO, both in Hillsborough County, use Romance language elements suggesting "royal valley" and "rich valley." And Orange County's ORLO VISTA, the first part of which is a shortening of *Orlando* and the second the well-known Spanish "view," apparently means "view of Orlando," for Orlando is not far away.

Sometimes place-names are shortened forms of other place-names— as OKALOO, in Okaloosa County, is shortened from the county name. This type of naming has already been observed in Withla and Lacoochee, made from parts of Withlacoochee, and is also seen in the transfer name WISCON, from *Wisconsin.*

PHOSPHORIA (Polk County) is a name made up as a euphonious reminder of the phosphate mining activity in that county.

An interesting form of name-making, which is a little like folk etymology and has a touch of humor in it, is found in the name of JANE JAY (Polk County), which surely is a humorous spelling of "J. 'n' J." for some railroad or business now forgotten. Analogous to it is TEEN JAY (Alachua County), for "T. 'n' J.," the old Tampa and Jacksonville Railroad that used to run by the station there. JAY-JAY, on the Indian River, is another name of this nature, being for the J. J. Parrish Packing House located there.

The true acronym—composed of the initial letters of a phrase— occurs in SUMICA (Polk County), which came from the first letters of the important words in *Societé Universalle, Mining, Industrie, Commerce et Agriculture,* the name of a French company which owned land at the site of this village. KICCO, in Polk County, is another example. It was named from the initials of the *Kissimmee Island Cattle Company.* The town of NALCREST, in Polk County, begins its name with the initials of the postmen's union, the National Association of Letter Carriers (NALC); it is a village which the union built especially for retired postal employees.

When down-to-earth, rural folk are naming places, they some- times name them "what comes naturally," and we find several delightful examples of such naming for towns in Florida. CUKE, in Levy County, was named for the common term for the cucumbers raised there; and in St. Johns County is a town named SPUDS, the colloquial name for potatoes, which are grown extensively in the area. Calhoun County has its ROAST EAR and Flagler County its POTATOVILLE, while Monroe County has its CUDJOE KEY and a settlement thereon called CUDJOE. According to some sources, *Cudjoe* is a contraction of "Cousin Joe's," but it might be pointed out that it is also the colloquial pronunciation of *kudzu,* the name of an Oriental vine which grows tenaciously and with jungle-like luxuriance in Florida's wet places. It seems reasonable, there- fore, that "Cousin Joe's" is a folk etymology for the colloquial name of this vine, and that actually Cudjoe Key and Cudjoe got their names from the vine. Others aver that Cudjoe was named for one of the last Seminole chiefs. And it is true that in the Seminole treaty of 1832 an interpreter is identified as "Cudjo" and that the name of a Chief "Coi-had-jo" appears in the preamble to that treaty as well as in the 1833 treaty signed at Fort Gibson.

Other casual, "folksy" names in Florida include the names of PICNIC (Hillsborough County), a crossroads town near a place where church picnics once were held; PIN HOOK (Marion County); HEN SCRATCH (Highlands County); RAMROD KEY (Monroe County); SONNY BOY (Seminole County); SUNDAY BLUFF (Marion County); and TEA TABLE KEY (Monroe County). All such names have the character of casually bestowed nicknames which grew into a habit and finally found a permanent place on the map. PICTURE CITY (Martin County) suggests some local incident or attraction, and Gadsden County's SAWDUST speaks of sawmilling, as does SAWPIT CREEK, in Duval County. YELLOW FEVER CREEK (Lee County) calls to mind a danger and a sadness very real in nineteenth-century Florida, long since eradicated by the work of Dr. Walter Reed and the heroes who helped him.

Long forgotten griefs and gaieties are suggested in the names of BURNT GROCERY CREEK (Santa Rosa County); FIDDLESTRING BAY CREEK (Liberty County); BOTHERATION CREEK (Washington County); SUNDAY ROLLAWAY CREEK (Franklin County); FODDER-STACK SLOUGH (Osceola County); and STARVATION BRANCH (Liberty County).

KNOCK 'EM DOWN KEY, in Monroe County, is said to have been so named because two sponge fishermen had a bloody fist fight there years ago. "They must have had two battles—one more violent than the other," remarked the *Key West Citizen* in an article about the names of keys printed November 15, 1964, "since we have both BIG KNOCK 'EM DOWN and LITTLE KNOCK 'EM DOWN Keys."

In the same article the *Citizen* reported the story that BIG COPPITT KEY (also in Monroe County) was really named "Big Carpet Key" (because of its carpet of greenery perhaps?), but southerners spoke the name as it "came natural" to them to speak it, and northerners mistakenly changed the "Carpet" into "Coppitt" on the charts.

FORT LONESOME is the name of a settlement in Hillsborough County. Who named it nobody knows for sure, but why it was so named is clear, though Mrs. Hazel Doyle, who has operated a store there since 1934, says it is not so lonesome any more. "Every little pig trail's got a slew of people around it," she says of the prosperous citrus-growing area (as reported in a news story published in the *Gainesville Sun*, January 27, 1970). Mrs. Doyle believes the place was named by WPA workers before she arrived.

LEISURE CITY, in Dade County, has a very Floridian name, suggesting vacations in the sun, but it is not actually a resort town. A migrant workers' camp is located there, and it is also the residence of many of the nearby Homestead Air Force Base's personnel.

The intriguing name of PEGHORN, in Osceola County, has the following story behind it: At that place, in 1883, there was a country store operated by a man known today only as Mr. Franklin, obviously a man of imagination and some education. Mr. Franklin had a wagon which he used for hauling supplies to the store, and he called it the "Cornucopia Express." When the country people thereabouts had the name explained to them, one of them exclaimed, "Well, if that's a horn of plenty, it must be a peg horn!" To explain this rather puzzling story, we have had two suggestions: we are told that the alto horn, among bandsmen, is called a "peck horn" and that the villager may have been misunderstood. The alto horn is smaller than a baritone horn or an upright bass horn, and the point of the remark might have been a disparagement of the wagon: "Your wagon's not very big to be a horn of plenty, it must be just a peck horn." The other suggestion comes from a friend who interprets the remark as praise rather than disparagement of the wagon, and points out that *peg* may have been an idiolectal pronunciation of *big*. Because the remark tickled the villagers, they began to call the place Peghorn, and so it has been ever since. In just such ways are names sometimes given, and behind even the homeliest of names unsuspected sophistication may lurk.

Even names which sound rather dull often have lively stories surrounding their selection. An interesting one concerns the naming of GAINESVILLE, in Alachua County. It has been seriously reported by a few old-timers that Gainesville was so named because it "gained the vote" when an election was held to determine a new county seat for Alachua County in 1853. In a sense this report is true, though it grew out of a pun, obviously unrecognized as such by some hearers, and does not negate the fact that the city is named for General Edmund Pendleton Gaines, an Indian fighter. Before 1853 the county seat of Alachua County was at Newnansville, but the boundaries of the county had changed so that Newnansville was no longer a central or convenient location for the seat of government. So an election was scheduled to determine whether it should be moved to a more central location. The settlers in the centrally located area of an early settlement called "Hogtown" were eager to have the county seat near them, and to that end one of them offered land for the courthouse, and streets and lots were laid out around a courthouse square. When the question of a name for the new town came up, County Commissioner William I. Turner, an influential man, proposed *Gainesville* in honor of the aforesaid general. Mr. Turner had, however, an opponent in the person of another prosperous and influential citizen, Mr. William H. Lewis, who wanted the place named *Lewisville* in his own honor. A barbecue to which all citizens were invited was held at nearby Boulware Springs, and the matter was hotly argued. Mr. Turner finally made the punning proposition, accepted by the opposition, that "if we *gain* the courthouse we will call it *Gain*esville, and if we *lose* the courthouse we will call it *Lewis*ville." The courthouse was gained, and that is how Gainesville was named for Edmund Pendleton Gaines. (The oft-repeated tale that Gainesville was once known as "Hogtown" is refuted by careful historians, who point out that no one inhabited Gainesville's corporate limits when it was platted and that maps drawn after its settlement still showed Hogtown two miles to the west of it.)

DUMBFOUNDLING BAY (Dade County) is a name with humor in it, and so is EARLY BIRD (Marion County). The former could be a folk etymology of *Dumfermline* (after the Scottish town). Lake County's FIDDLE LAKE got its name, according to early settlers, from an incident in which a merchant lost some violins in the lake. In Polk County, in the city of Lakeland, there is a lake which was renamed LAKE WIRE when a telegraph line was stretched along its shore. Alachua County has a sinkhole so deep and weird (legend has it that it is bottomless) that the folk named it the DEVIL'S MILLHOPPER, and there are a number of folk legends explaining why the sinkhole is there.

When a group of Dunkards from Virginia founded a town in Palm Beach County, they named it CHOSEN because it was their chosen home. And in 1868 a man named J. Z. Dixon called a little place on the Indian River (Brevard County) CITY POINT, an example of wishful thinking which never got beyond the wishing stage, for City Point is still a rural point. COSME, in Hillsborough County, may have been named from *cosmos*, for "order" or "harmony," but it could be a back-formation from the flower-name *cosmos* (misinterpreted as a plural), though "cosma" would be the expected result of such a back-formation.

Legend has it that a place called O'LENO, in Alachua County, got its name from a gambling game, Keno. Through folk corruption, *Keno* is said to have become *Leno*, then *Old Leno*, and finally O'Leno, although to many people this seems highly unlikely. In Escambia County there is a station called QUINTETTE, and they say it was probably the fifth station to be placed along the railroad (1903).

A confusing example of cultural naming is seen in the name of Gadsden County's GRETNA. Here a settlement was begun in 1897 by a naval stores company, though at first it was not a town and apparently did not have a name officially bestowed upon it. But places must be called something, and the story goes that the Negroes called it "Gritney" and said it was because there was so much sand there. When a turpentine still, homes for officials, and a commissary were built, a post office was established and the postmaster—a Mr. J. W. Mahaffey—is said to have modified the Negroes' name for the place to Gretna, as a more dignified name for the post office. It must be said, however, that there is considerable doubt surrounding this story. It is far more likely that the Negroes' "Gritney" (still a current pronunciation) may have been a corruption of the name as it is now spelled. *Gretna Green* in Scotland may have been the original inspiration.

STARR, in Jackson County, is reported to have received its name from the fact that it was on a "star route"—that is, that mail was delivered to the area by contract from the government to an individual.

Jackson County's TWO EGG arouses more curiosity than many Florida names, and there are several stories current as to its origin, all centering around a country store where two eggs were involved in a purchase. An article in the *Florida Times-Union* for September 20, 1953, reports that two brothers started a country store there but had not decided upon a name until their first customer asked for two eggs. Others say that a child came in, placed two eggs on the counter, and said, "Mamma says send her one egg's worth of bladder snuff and one egg's worth of ball potash." Whether the two eggs were the payment or the purchase, they furnished Florida with an intriguing folk name.

A place called RATTLESNAKE, halfway between St. Petersburg and Tampa, was established by a canner of rattlesnake meat. Mr. George K. End began his business in Arcadia in the early 1930s, but moved nearer to a large population center, petitioned for a post office named Rattlesnake, and got it! Besides canning the reptile meat for food, Mr. End packaged rattlesnake oil for the treatment of rheumatism, and rattlesnake venom for hospital and laboratory use. The story is that he died of a rattlesnake bite; and there is no longer a post office at Rattlesnake, which is hardly even a village any more.

A pioneer resident of ECHO, in Levy County, says that the place was named for a brand of whiskey. The drinking habits of an early settler also account for the name of NORUM, in Washington County. This place was once called *Wilder*, but the man who eventually established a post office there (a Mr. Bostick) was very fond of homemade rum. One day he and a friend drove to Wilder to get some, and while the friend went to get the liquor, Mr. Bostick, waiting in the buggy, thought about the prospect of establishing a post office at Wilder and was meditating upon what he would call it when his friend came back and announced, "No rum." Or so the story goes. WHISKEY GEORGE CREEK (Franklin County) may have a "drunk" story or a "moonshine" story embedded in its name, as also may BRANDY BRANCH (Okaloosa County) and GIN BRANCH (Liberty County), though the latter two names may simply have been given to describe the appearance of the water in the streams.

A name of good-natured derision reflecting the historical and cultural background of Floridians is that of YANKEETOWN, partly in Levy County and partly in Citrus County. This town was founded in the 1920s by the Knotts family of Gary, Indiana, who had a fishing camp and a few houses there. They planned to call their town *Knotts*, but the southerners thereabouts called the place, in fun, Yankeetown. The Yankees accepted the challenge and called it that officially when the town was incorporated in 1925. A subdivision laid out nearby accents the humor of the situation with its answering name of CRACKERTOWN.

ELKTON (St. Johns County) is said to have acquired its name because a Mr. B. Genovar had just joined the Elk's Club when he purchased the site. In a glow of fraternal pride he named the place *Elk Town*, and it afterward became Elkton. It should be mentioned, however, that *Elkton* is a "stock" name, occurring in Maryland, Kentucky, Michigan, Oregon, South Dakota, Tennessee, and Virginia. The name of Suwannee County's PADLOCK goes back to the days when the state "farmed out" its prisoners to individuals (paying $800 a month for the care of a gang). Charles K. Dutton kept a gang and padlocked them at this place at the end of each day's work; so when a railroad station was established here, Padlock was felt to be an appropriate name. Ironically, the forests surrounding Padlock had for years after the Civil War been called FREEDMAN'S HOUSE because a few freed slaves bought farms there.

ERIDU and IDDO, in Taylor County, were named by J. E. Willoughby, a former railroad engineer, according to an article in the *Florida Times-Union* for September 20, 1953, "for reasons known only to him." Another writer says, without revealing a source for the information, that Eridu is a derivative of *Eridanus*, the Latin name for the River Po; and no one has suggested a derivation for Iddo. However, it should be pointed out that Eridu was an ancient city of Mesopotamia, thought to have been the prehistoric capital of the Sumerian federation, and that archaeological excavations of it were in progress in 1918, at which time the name was undoubtedly in the news. As for Iddo, a man by that name is referred to as "Iddo the seer" and "the prophet Iddo" in 2 Chron. 9:29, 12:15, and 13:22. It would be an amazing coincidence indeed if Mr. Willoughby had actually manufactured both of these names and stumbled upon two proper names already in existence. It is much easier to believe that the bestowal of the names Eridu and Iddo was a quiet joke by a man who had an eye for the unusual and obscure.

LOSTMANS RIVER (Monroe County) hints of wilderness and a local incident. Lake County's MASCOTTE was named by a Boston settler for the ship that brought him to Florida; it sailed from Boston to St. Petersburg in the 1880s. In Manatee County the place called NEON got its name from a neon sign; and Monroe County's NO NAME KEY seems the result of a fruitless effort to think of a name. The *Key West Citizen* (November 15, 1964) says, "Everybody ran out of names before they ran out of islands." NONSENSE CREEK, in Manatee County, and PERKY, in Monroe County, suggest folk whimsy; and PIRATES COVE (Monroe County) bespeaks imaginative consciousness of a colorful past. So does SANTOS, in Marion County, an American-bestowed name (ca. 1883) following the Spanish tradition set in Florida, *santos* meaning, of course, "saints."

The name of CAPTIVA ISLAND, in Charlotte Harbor, suggests

some intriguing incident or custom in Florida's wild past, but nobody knows the real story. It is said that the pirate Gasparilla kept his wives (those captive Spanish and Mexican maidens) there, but the story is spoiled by the knowledge that the island, with its present name, was on maps printed before the legendary Gasparilla is supposed to have come to Florida—and that the pirate probably never existed anyway.

TELEGRAPH CREEK (Lee County) commemorates the stringing of the telegraph wires through Florida in the pioneer days. Hardee County's TEXACO perhaps was named for a gas station.

WHITE CITY (St. Lucie County) was so named because its founders, a group of Danish immigrants from Chicago, 1893, did not allow Negroes to live there. The name of Marion County's BED-ROCK may be literal, but it is also a fortunately figurative name choice to suggest solidity and permanence. NEWPORT (Wakulla County) may seem to be only an American stock name, but this one has a local meaning. When Port Leon was destroyed by a tidal wave in 1843, refugees from there founded a "new port," away from the shore of the Gulf.

DEADMANS BAY (Dixie County) has a name suggesting a story, but information on it is so confused that one can make little of it. STEINHATCHEE, the name of the river that flows into Deadman's Bay, appears to be derived from Creek words signifying "dead man's river," and it is probable that the bay was named for the river. A town and a spring in Lafayette County, where the river rises, have the name *Steinhatchee*, too, and there is also a DEADMANS KEY, in neighboring Levy County. HANDSOME CREEK (Duval County) and PIONEER (Escambia County) belong among the cultural names by reason of their connotative quality. STATE LINE (Gadsden County) might well be a descriptive name, but its bluntness and homeliness prompted its being placed here; it is one of those names which simply "happened" and is thus a true folk name. LOST CREEK (Wakulla County) and MUTTER CREEK (Walton County) have this natural quality too, with a touch of imagination added.

Every year a little post office in Orange County becomes a bee-hive of activity during the Christmas season, for the name of it is CHRISTMAS. Thousands of pieces of holiday mail from all over the United States are sent there to be postmarked "Christmas." The place acquired its name because a United States Army fort was established there on one Christmas Day during the Second

Seminole War. The settlers called it *Fort Christmas* in honor of the day, and the town that later grew there retained the specific part of the name. Like the Spanish saints' names among the place-names of Florida, this name tells us not only on what day the place was named but what kind of people named it. There is also a CHRISTMAS CREEK nearby; and off the coast of Dade County is a key called CHRISTMAS POINT, the story of whose naming is unknown.

Some of the oddities that occur when place-names are transmitted from one language to another might logically be pointed out in the discussion of cultural names. An interesting one is embodied in the name of BLACK CREEK (St. Johns County), which came from Spanish to English with a meaning exactly the opposite of that of its original name. The Spaniards called the stream *Rio Blanco* ("White River"); and by a sort of folk etymology (note the similarity in sound of *blanco* and *black*) it became Black Creek for the Americans. By a similar process KEY WEST evolved from *Cayo Hueso*, it being a fortuitous circumstance that it is one of the westernmost of the Florida keys, though the Spanish name meant "Bone Key." To speakers of English the Spanish *Hueso* (pronounced "wáy-so") sounded enough like the English *West* to encourage a logical supposition that it meant just that. The word *Cayo* they knew, and correctly translated it as "Key."

The name of WAUKEENAH, in Jefferson County, has been "translated" as an Indian name. One authority gives Seminole-Creek *wacca* ("cow"), and *ina* ("body")—thus "cow's body"—as the probable origin, but here again we have an unexpected source in the Spanish name of *Joachina*. *Joachina* was the name of John G. Gamble's plantation a few miles west of the present Waukeenah. He had named it for a lady of Spanish descent who lived in Pensacola, and the American (as well as Spanish) pronunciation is perfectly represented by the present spelling. When the post office which had been established at the plantation was moved to the crossing of the St. Augustine Road (ca. 1827), the settlement there—first called *Marion Cross Roads*—was afterward known as *Joachina*, but the spelling was "Indianized" to its current form.

SAMPALA LAKE (Madison County) offers another example of either folk etymology or corruption or both. One authority connects it doubtfully with the Seminole *sampa* ("basket"), but another is more convincing when he points out that it is an Indian corruption of *San Pablo*; for the Franciscan mission of San Pedro y San Pablo de Porturiba was located near this lake. *Sampala*, of course, could just as well be an English—i.e., American—corruption of *San Pablo*. The existence of SAM PEYLOR LAKE in the same area illustrates another step in folk etymology on the part of the Americans.

BENOTIS (Taylor County) is an oddity said to have been derived by the Post Office Department from the Latin *nota bene*. Perhaps some official, faced with assigning a name to the new post office, was inspired by an "N.B." on the papers pertaining thereto.

A resort on Long Key, an island in the Gulf near St. Petersburg (Pinellas County), has a name—PASS-A-GRILLE—which has puzzled many people, but one writer tells us that the original form, shown on an 1841 map, was *Passe-aux-Grilleurs* ("Pass for the Grillers") and that this was the point where fishermen stopped to cook, or grill, their meals. We are not told why the name was in French, but it is understandable that Americans smoothed the difficult phrase into something they could more easily say.

The possible corruption of Spanish *San Juan* to *Suwannee* has already been noted. And the latter is a name that has been of such widespread use in Florida that it has been subject to further modification. An interesting example is Madison County's SUWANOCHEE SPRINGS, which adds the Creek *chee* ("little") to the possibly pseudo-Indian *Suwannee* to make "little Suwannee." Another is the aphetic WANNEE (Gilchrist County), which was originally shown on the map (1870) as *Suwannee*.

The name of HOBE SOUND (Martin County) has an unusually interesting history. It is assumed to be an English phonetic rendering of the Spanish *Jobe* or *Jove*, and was a name applied to the inlet here and to the Indians who lived in the vicinity at least as early as the seventeenth century. English maps and chronicles of that century show the names of *Hobay* and *Hoe Bay*. Assuming the name to have been derived from the Spanish, some mapmakers spelled the name *Jobe* or *Jove*—and assuming further that the name referred to the king of the gods in Roman mythology, they sometimes changed it to *Jupiter*. The latter name stuck to the area and was applied by Americans to a fort built during the Seminole War at the site of old *Hoe Bay* or *Hobay* Indian village, later to a lighthouse which replaced it, and inevitably to the town which grew up around it. Meanwhile the inlet, or sound, retained the older name, finally rendered *Hobe*, and by that name it is known today. Thus are Hobe Sound and JUPITER (Palm Beach County) related. The actual derivation and meaning of the original name is not known. The likelihood that the Spanish rendering was simply a phonetic spelling of an Indian name already existing is strong, so that *Jupiter* is one of those "mistakes" in naming which enliven the study of place-names.

A significant part of Florida's heritage, as mentioned earlier, is the Indian place-names left on her map. Conscious of this heritage, the white man has given many Indian names himself. One of the white man's Indian namings is APOXSEE (Osceola County). J. E. Ingraham, vice-president of the Florida East Coast Railway and president of the Model Land Company, gave this name, a respelling of the usual transliteration of Seminole-Creek *apaksi*, meaning "tomorrow"; and whether he meant it to connote the happy, lazy "tomorrow" philosophy which Mexico's *mañana* brings to mind or whether he spoke in it of a shining future, it is truly a Florida cultural name in its origin and meaning.

KOLOKEE. in Seminole County, is a settlement homesteaded by Negroes; its name is from the Seminole-Creek *kulki* ("lamp"), and it is pleasant to think that the name was chosen to suggest light and comfort. In De Soto County there is a place called NOCATEE. It comes from the Seminole-Creek *nakiti*, meaning "What is it?" Humor and whimsy seem to underlie this name, but if there is a story we do not know it. NITTAW, in Osceola County, was named when the Florida East Coast Railway went through in 1910; it is Creek *nitta*, or "day." SALOFKA (Osceola County) got its name from the Creek word for "knife," *eslafka*. Many of the Indian namings by the white man seem somewhat aimless and are more a recognition of a romantic heritage than a careful application of meaning. Particularly in the counties with Indian names there seems to have been an effort to bestow Indian names upon the towns and stations.

Like Wakulla and Escambia, the name OCALA (Marion County) is so ancient that its meaning is now unknown. It is of Timucuan derivation, *Ocali* being the name of the Timucuan province through which de Soto passed in 1539—somewhere, it is thought, on the shores of the Silver River, near the present Ocala. The present city, formerly called *Fort King*, was named Ocala in the 1840s in recognition of that older time. Translations of the name are guesses only. But like Wakulla its last two syllables suggest the *kala* or *kali* which in several Indian dialects means "a spring of water." And like Wakulla, the name Ocala occurs where there is an especially large and beautiful spring. The OCALA NATIONAL

FOREST, spreading across several counties in the Middle Florida area, also honors this ancient past with its name.

SARASOTA, already discussed as a county name, is another cultural inheritance whose source is lost in antiquity. It is the name of the county seat of Sarasota County, of SARASOTA HEIGHTS, EAST SARASOTA, and SARASOTA KEY (Sarasota County), and of SARASOTA BAY (Sarasota and Manatee counties).

Other names whose antiquity defies attempts at translation include those of the village of AUCILLA and of the AUCILLA RIVER in Jefferson County and of WACISSA and the WACISSA RIVER in the same county. According to one Indian-name authority, the Aucilla River—encountered in many variations on old maps, including *Assilly, Oscillee, Scilly,* and *Asile*—formed the ancient boundary between the territory of the Timucua and that of the Apalachee Indians, and the name is Timucuan. The name of Wacissa is probably of Apalachian origin, an early form of it (dating from the first Spanish period) being *Bacica*.

The CHIPOLA RIVER, flowing through Jackson, Calhoun, and Gulf counties, also has a mystery name, derived possibly from the long-dead Chatot tongue. TOCOI and TOCOI JUNCTION (St. Johns County) hark back to the aboriginal Timucua, who had a village of that name in the vicinity of St. Augustine, while MATECUMBE, on UPPER MATECUMBE KEY, has a name whose meaning has been the subject of much interesting guesswork but may never be definitely known. It has been conjectured by more than one person, for example, that the name is corrupted from that of the Indian village which Fontaneda called *Guaragunve* and translated "Pueblo de Llanto," or "town of weeping," while the Federal Writers' Project says that Matecumbe is from an Indian corruption of the Spanish *Mata Hombre,* "kill man," which was a translation of *Cuchiyage,* the Indian name of the island. Nobody really knows, and Matecumbe must join the other names which hint at an impenetrable past. There is also a LOWER MATECUMBE KEY in this name cluster.

A few names which, like those transferred intact from foreign places, reflect the cultural heterogeneity of Florida are VALKARIA, in Brevard County; KORONA, in Flagler County; and HALLANDALE, in Broward County. Valkaria, modified from the name of the *Valkyries* of Scandinavian mythology, was named by Mr. Ernest Svedelius, a Swede, who settled there in 1895. The name was formerly spelled *Valkary.* Korona is a Polish settlement; the name, ultimately Latin, means "crown." Hallandale's early settlers were largely Hollanders, and its name is a variant of "Hollandale." This Broward County town, one of the oldest on the lower east coast, was established in 1898. LABUENA (Baker County) is another American-bestowed name which takes note of the Spanish past; it means "the good." INDUSTRIA (Taylor County) appears to be a Latin name, for the word, in Latin, means "diligence," and thus it is a cultural name, not only reflecting the ideals of its founders but the educational background of one or more of them as well.

Other miscellaneous cultural names are UTILITY (Polk County); STANDARD (Marion County); SANS SOUCI (Pinellas County) and SANS SOUCI (Pasco County), French for "without care"; PLACIDA (Charlotte County), a feminine Latinized version of "placid"; MUTUAL (Citrus County); PANACEA (Wakulla County), which means "cure-all" and has reference to a group of springs nearby which are supposed to be health-giving; LIKELY (Martin County), whose founders must have thought it a likely place to build; and HONEY-MOON (Duval County).

A rather large group of more easily classifiable cultural names are those which reflect religious beliefs and affiliations. A sizeable number of Florida places bear names which recall the sixteenth-century Spanish commitment to the Roman Catholic Church, for it was the Spanish explorers' custom to give to a place the name of the saint on whose day the place was discovered or established. Some of the saints' names, like *Rio de San Juan*, now known as the ST. JOHNS RIVER (from which St. Johns County received its name), have been Anglicized, but they still remind us of the stately, cere-monious Spaniards who claimed this land for His Catholic Majesty the king of Spain. Some of these Catholic names have shifted locations, but all are a heritage from those days. Other names of the "St. Johns" cluster are ST. JOHNS BAY (Duval County); ST. JOHNS BLUFF (Duval County), where the French Fort Caroline was built in 1564 and renamed *San Mateo* by the Spanish Menéndez when he captured it on St. Matthew's Day in 1565; and ST. JOHNS PARK (St. Johns County).

ST. AUGUSTINE, called sonorously *San Augustin de las Floridas* ("St. Augustine of the Floridas"), *el siempre fiel Ciudad de San Augustin* ("the ever faithful City of St. Augustine"), and the like in old Spanish documents, was established in 1565 by Pedro Menéndez de Avilés and named by him for St. Augustine, Bishop of Hippo, on whose feast day, August 28, he discovered St. Augustine's harbor after having first sighted the coast of Florida on August 25. It has been continuously settled ever since and is the nation's oldest city. Other names of the cluster are ST. AUGUSTINE BEACH, ST. AUGUSTINE HARBOR, and NEW AUGUSTINE, all in St. Johns County.

The ST. MARYS RIVER, now forming the northeast boundary of Florida, was called by the Spanish *Rio de Santa Maria* and translated by the English. LITTLE ST. MARYS RIVER and ST. MARYS (Nassau County) are of the same family. SANTA MARIA, a place in Santa Rosa County, takes its name from the early Spanish saint's name for Pensacola Bay—*Santa Maria de Galvez.* SANTA ROSA COUNTY, SANTA ROSA ISLAND, SANTA ROSA SOUND, and the village of SANTA ROSA, discussed among the county names, also reflect the Roman Catholic faith of Spain.

The name *Baïja de S. Ioseph* appears on the earliest printed map of Florida, about 1587. The *Baïja de S. Ioseph* shown is in the approximate vicinity of the present ST. JOSEPH'S BAY (off the coast of Gulf County), and so the latter name seems to be a direct inheritance from the Spanish explorers. POINT ST. JOSEPH is an offspring, as is PORT ST. JOE, which has gone far to secularize the original religious connotations of the name. Port St. Joe is a city on St. Joseph's Bay, built to replace the old town of St. Joseph, a "lost city" destroyed in 1841 by a yellow fever epidemic and a tidal wave.

The name of the SANTA FE RIVER, which forms the northern boundary of Alachua County, came from the early Spanish mission *Santa Fe de Toloca*, meaning "Holy Faith of Toloca," and from its name followed also SANTA FE LAKE and the village of SANTA FE, also in Alachua County. Ironically, this river with the holy name appears to have been the same one that de Soto called "River of Discords" because of an argument among his band on its banks. Many of Florida's natural features had several names during the first century or two of Spanish rule. Corrupted spellings of the Spanish *Santa Fe* appearing on the nineteenth-century maps are *Santaffey* and *Santaffe* (among others), but in the end the original Spanish spelling was recognized and fixed.

The procession of saints' names continues with ST. ANDREWS BAY (Bay County), from which were named ST. ANDREW—now a part of Panama City—and ST. ANDREWS SOUND. Off the coast of Franklin County is ST. VINCENT ISLAND, where the Spanish Franciscan mission of Cape San Vicente once stood; and an arm of

Apalachicola Bay off Franklin County is called ST. VINCENT SOUND from the same source. CAPE SAN BLAS (Gulf County) was named by the Spaniards for the martyred bishop of Sebaste in Armenia; and the town of SAN BLAS (Bay County) got its name from the same ultimate source. Wakulla County's ST. MARKS was established in the early eighteenth century by Don José Primo de Rivera, probably on the feast day of St. Mark; it was first a fort— *San Marco de Apalache*—for the protection of the Apalachee Indians, and is now a fishing village. The ST. MARKS RIVER, rising in Leon County and flowing through Wakulla County, got its name from the fort, and ST. MARKS JUNCTION (Leon County) has been a later product of the naming.

The name of ANASTASIA ISLAND, off the coast of St. Johns County, is reported to be a corruption of the Spanish name *Santa Estacia*, given to the island by Pedro Menéndez when he landed there on this saint's day in 1565; there is a town on the island which was called ANASTASIA after it, as well as ANASTASIA STATE PARK. *Anastasia* is also a feminine proper name derived from the Greek for "resurrection"; it was the name of a fourth-century martyr who in medieval legend was associated with the Virgin's midwife. ST. LUCIE, which has already been noted as a county name, was a Spanish naming for a Roman Catholic saint; and from that sixteenth-century naming has sprung not only the county name but likewise the name of ST. LUCIE, a city within the county; the names of the ST. LUCIE CANAL (Martin County); ST. LUCIE INLET (Martin County); and ST. LUCIE RIVER (St. Lucie County). In Bay County the name of SANTA CRUZ, Spanish for "Holy Cross," remembers a number of missions established by the Spanish in northwest Florida under that name. Duval County's ST. NICHOLAS, or FORT ST. NICHOLAS, was devoutly named by the Spaniard Don Manuel de Monteano in 1739. In the same county SAN PABLO got its name from the Spanish mission of San Pablo, which once stood in the vicinity. The former PABLO BEACH, now incorporated into Jacksonville Beach, also had this background.

Not all of the Roman Catholic place-names in Florida were bestowed by the Spanish; some have been given by later Catholics; and some have been given by non-Catholics following the precedent of the Spanish explorers. LORETTA, in Duval County, dates from the establishment of a Catholic mission honoring a shrine in Loreto, Italy, during the time of the British occupation, around 1775; the town was named by a Father Veil. BONAVENTURE

(Brevard County) is thought to have been named for St. Bonaventura, Italian scholastic theologian canonized in 1482. But the word *bonaventure* is also the name of a type of sailing vessel and was formed from the Italian words for "good luck." SAN JOSE, in Duval County, was started during the boom of the 1920s and seems to have been given its saint's name as a bow to the Spanish past and for the sake of atmosphere rather than for religious reasons. In Putnam County the town of SAN MATEO, Spanish for "St. Matthew," was established in 1867; apparently its name was inspired by tradition and by knowledge of the older San Mateo, a fort established by Menéndez on the site of the French Fort Caroline near St. Augustine. ST. LEO, in Pasco County, was established as a Benedictine abbey in 1889 and named for the canonized Pope Leo I. Lee County's SAN CARLOS is Spanish for "St. Charles"; and SEBASTIAN, in Indian River County, was named for the Roman St. Sebastian, martyred in the third century.

Other saints' names on the Florida map are ST. CATHERINE (Sumter County); ST. FRANCIS (Lake County); ST. JAMES CITY (Lee County); ST. JOSEPH (Pasco County); ST. JOSEPHS BAY and ST. JOSEPHS SOUND (Pinellas County); ST. MARTINS KEY (Citrus County); ST. THOMAS (Pasco County); SAN [*sic*] HELENA (Leon County); and SAN ANTONIO (Pasco County). The last name is said to have been given in the 1880s by its founder, Judge Edmund F. Dunne of Arizona, in fulfillment of a promise made by Judge Dunne to the saint to whom he prayed for rescue while lost in the Arizona desert. Doubtless in recognition of Florida's Spanish tradition, Judge Dunne transposed *St. Anthony* to its Spanish form.

Though the Spanish left us many religious place-names and inspired many others, the Indians have left little evidence of their religion on the map. Only one town—Gulf County's IOLA—seems to have a Seminole religious name. Here stood an ancient Seminole town whose name appeared in many forms—including *Iolee* and *Yanollee*—before it became fixed as Iola. It is believed to be a variant of "Yahola," the name of a male deity to whom appeals were made in cases of sickness or emergency. It became the cry uttered by the attendants while the chiefs were taking the "black drink" and is a part of the source of Osceola's name.

Another name with non-Christian religious connotations, though it is not truly a religious name in the spirit of its naming, is that of MECCA and MECCA JUNCTION, in Seminole County. The name recalls, of course, the spiritual center of Islam, but it is an American naming (1912) and was thought of, doubtless, in the sense of a haven or goal reached after a pilgrimage.

ST. GEORGE'S ISLAND and ST. GEORGE SOUND, off the coast of Franklin County, are thought to have been named by the British for the patron saint of England, and are not a part of the Roman Catholic parade of saints' names. JOHNS PASS (Pinellas County) is reported to have been named by the British also and was recorded on early maps as *St. Johns Pass.* Johns Pass is a settlement, but the name is also applied to a pass between two keys off the Pinellas County coast.

The less colorful Protestant names are more characteristic of the later settlement history of Florida. SHAKER VILLAGE (Osceola County) is one of the few Protestant religious place-names which do not come directly from the Bible. (This is a primary distinction between the Catholic and Protestant names—that Catholic names come from church literature, while Protestant ones tend to be chosen directly from the Scriptures.) Shaker Village was established in 1905 by a colony of Shakers from New York State; the venture was unsuccessful, and the name is only a memory now; the village site is occupied by a small tourist camp.

A biblical name in Putnam County is that of PENIEL, taken from Gen. 32:30, "And Jacob called the name of the place Peniel: for I have seen God face to face, and my life is preserved." SALEM, in Taylor County, was established in 1842; its name is the ancient name of Jerusalem, "city of peace." PROVIDENCE (Union County) was established about 1830 and was named, like many other American places, for the divine protection hoped for there. There it also a PROVIDENCE in Polk County. Possibly MAGDALENE (Hillsborough County) is a biblical name (for Mary Magdalene); and certainly MOUNT ARARAT (Volusia County) is—so named, it is suggested, because the hill there has two peaks, as does Mount Ararat in Armenia, where Noah's ark is said to have rested. NEEDLES EYE (Marion County) obviously came from the Scriptures (see Matt. 19:24), as did SHILOH (Brevard County), named for the place where the ark of the covenant rested for three centuries and where the boy Samuel had his vision (1 Sam. 3:21). ACHAN (Polk County) is a biblical name (see Josh. 7), though one wonders at the naming, for Achan was no hero. ANTIOCH (Hillsborough County) was named for the biblical Antioch, where Paul started his first missionary journey: "And the disciples were called Christians first in Antioch" (Acts 11:26). A place in

Marion County has the connotative biblical name of CALVARY; and in St. Lucie County there is an EDEN.

Other biblical names include INTERCESSION CITY (Osceola County), which was settled in 1934 by members of the House of Faith, a non-denominational Christian sect holding to the original teachings of John Wesley. The site, donated to the House of Faith by J. W. Wile, an Indianapolis philanthropist, was then a ghost town left over from Florida boom days; and it is interesting to note that the religious name given it in 1934 is similar in sound to the name it bore when it was originally platted—*Interocean City*, describing its position between the Atlantic Ocean and the Gulf of Mexico. Also in Osceola County is a place called WESLEY CHAPEL. Two little neighboring places in Alachua County are called ADAM and EVE, though perhaps as an expression of whimsy more than for religious reasons. SAMPSON CITY and the SAMPSON RIVER in Bradford County might well be named for the biblical strong man Samson (Judg. 13–16), but information on the name is lacking. There is a SAMPSON, as well as a SAMPSON CREEK, in St. Johns County too. Gadsden County's GLORY is a rousing Protestant name with a gospel-meeting sound; and SHARON, in the same county, takes its name from the Song of Sol. 2:1—"I am the rose of Sharon, and the lily of the valleys." There is also a SHARON in Clay County. Leon County's LUKE may be for the biblical St. Luke, and Okaloosa County's DORCAS for the woman who "was full of good works and almsdeeds which she did" (Acts 9:36).

Near Jerusalem, centuries ago, was a holy place (perhaps more than one) called *Bethel*, Hebrew for "House of God," where Abraham pitched his tent and built an altar (Gen. 12:8), where Jacob had his dream (Gen. 28:10–19), where at one time the ark of the covenant was kept (Judg. 20:27), and where Samuel stopped yearly when he went out to judge Israel (1 Sam. 7:16). Churches and settlements have been named throughout America for Bethel, and Florida is no exception, as Wakulla County's BETHEL will testify. Two other biblical names are JOSHUA CREEK (De Soto County) and MIZPAH (Duval County). The latter name—now used as a parting salutation—means literally "watchtower" and is from Gen. 31:48–49. LOVEDALE (Jackson County), summing up the entire Christian philosophy in its first syllable, was named for a church and a school of that name more than half a century ago.

When people are naming places, they tell also what they have read and what stories and myths have kindled their imaginations. In Florida there is a sizeable group of "literary" place-names— names taken from the secular reading of those who named them. Classical mythology accounts for more than half of them. In Volusia County there is a GANYMEDE, named for the Trojan youth who was carried off to be cupbearer to Zeus. HESPERIDES, in Polk County, was named for the Greek garden where the golden apples grew that Hercules sought as one of his twelve labors; the namer of the Florida Hesperides chose the name aptly to identify a place where citrus fruits ("golden apples") grow in astonishing abundance.

The name of JUPITER (Palm Beach County) has been mentioned in reference to the naming of Hobe Sound. This place, as well as JUPITER INLET, was named for the Roman deity in an accidental way, but when JUNO, in the same county, was named, it was no accident. The place was named for the wife of Jupiter, queen of the Roman gods, and the name was given to match that of Jupiter. In 1888 a railroad connected the two places, which were eight miles apart, and the two stops between them were named MARS and VENUS for the god of war and the goddess of love. Settlers in the area nicknamed the line the "Celestial Railroad," and the literary joke is now a part of Florida's lively past.

There is also a NEPTUNE in Palm Beach County for the Roman god of the sea, and there is a NEPTUNE BEACH in Duval County. Charlotte County has its MARS; St. Lucie its JUPITER RIVER; and Highlands County its VENUS. In Putnam County there is POMONA, established sometime before 1884 and aptly named for the Roman goddess of the fruit of trees. The names of JOVITA and LAKE JOVITA (Pasco County) pose a problem, but they seem to mean with their Spanish diminutive ending (which is erroneously feminine) "Little Jove," or "Little Jupiter." JUPITER in Gadsden County, ATHENA in Taylor County, and the RIVER STYX in Alachua County are other classical names.

The settlement of MARATHON, on Key Vacas in Monroe County, recalls the famous fifth-century (B.C.) battle of the Greco-Persian War at Marathon, from whence a Greek soldier ran all the way to Athens to tell of the Greek victory. NEREUS, in Liberty County, is apparently named for the Greek sea god Nereus, father of the Nereids, though Liberty is an inland county. In Brevard County, on the Canaveral peninsula between the Banana River and the Atlantic Ocean, there is a place called OCEANUS, named for the god and the personification of the stream Oceanus in Greek mythology. And Florida has its EUREKA (Marion County), a word from the Greek which signifies triumphant discovery, said to have been exclaimed by Archimedes when he discovered a method of determining the purity of the gold in King Hiero's crown. There is also EUREKA MINE, in Citrus County. ELECTRA, in Marion County, was named either for the lost star of the Pleiades (perhaps because of the obscure location of the place) or for Electra, the daughter of Agamemnon in Greek legend and drama. The name of ARCADIA, county seat of De Soto County, is the same as that of the region of Greece used by the bucolic poets as the setting for a life of ideal contentment and simplicity—but in view of the "Arcadia Albritton" story (see chapter 3), it cannot be regarded with certainty as a classical name.

Literary names from sources other than classical include one name from a fairy tale—GOLDEN EGG, in Seminole County, from the well-known story of the goose that laid golden eggs. And FAIRYLAND itself is a town in Brevard County. It is uncertain where the name of BELLEISLE (Bay County) came from, but it is reported that it was named by Mrs. W. H. Covington, whose husband operated a turpentine still here, because the name in a book appealed to her. When Escambia County's TARZAN was established as a spur of the Louisville and Nashville Railroad in 1921, its tangled, jungle-like location suggested its name, taken from that of the jungle hero of Edgar Rice Burroughs' series of Tarzan books so popular with young Americans.

The name of Taylor County's MANDALAY was inspired by Rudyard Kipling's popular poem "The Road to Mandalay"; and TRILBY (Pasco County) got its name in the 1890s when George Du Maurier's novel *Trilby* (1894) was popular. The town was called "Macon" before, but the citizens renamed it for the heroine of the novel; so that there could be no mistake about the name's source, they named a SVENGALI SQUARE and a LITTLE BILLEE STREET too, for other characters in the novel.

Two of Florida's place-names—MINNEHAHA LAKE, in Lake County, and the village of NOKOMIS, in Sarasota County—were inspired by one of America's favorite poets, Henry Wadsworth Longfellow, from his poem *Hiawatha*.

It would be strange not to find names from Shakespeare in the literary place-names of an English-speaking land, and Florida has her share. In Brevard County we find ORSINO, lifted from the pages of *Twelfth Night; or, What you Will*, in which play appears Orsino, sentimental Duke of Illyria. And Shakespeare's star-cross'd lovers, Romeo and Juliet, are on the map of Florida, though Juliet's name is misspelled. The towns, ROMEO and JULI-ETTE (Marion County), were obviously named as a pair. Local legend has it that in one of these places lived a boy and in the other a girl whose families were enemies and that their story ended as tragically as that of Shakespeare's lovers, but perhaps this is legend only, for the story cannot be confirmed.

Lake County's ELDORADO was named either for the legendary treasure city of South America, or for the place of gold and jewels which figures in Voltaire's *Candide*. In Spanish it means "the golden." Floridians like to say that the name is truly descriptive as applied to the Lake County village, for in this area the golden fruit of the citrus trees abound.

A place called SORRENTO, in Lake County, is said to have been named in 1875 for a book entitled *Agnes of Sorrento*, which was popular at that time. UTOPIA (Okeechobee County) and UTOPIA (Sarasota County) take their names from the title of Thomas More's *Utopia*, the story of an ideal land. Dade County's ALADDIN CITY obviously got its name from the pages of the *Arabian Nights*; and it was so named because it grew like magic when it was begun in the Florida boom days. From the medieval Arthurian cycle some-one drew the name of AVALON, in Santa Rosa County, or perhaps it came from the song of that name, popular in the second decade of the present century. Another romantically chosen name is that of SHALIMAR, in Okaloosa County. Shalimar was named by one of the daughters of the founder, from the sentimental song "Pale hands I loved beside the Shalimar." Her father, James E. Plew, started a winery here just after the repeal of the prohibition amendment and called his product "Shalimar Wine."

In a discussion of the cultural aspect of place-naming, the phe-nomenon of legend must be reckoned with. Legends surrounding the origins of place-names usually grow up *after* the naming, when the folk attempt to "explain" a name whose origin or meaning is lost to them. Sometimes, perhaps, a place-name story is true but cannot be confirmed, and it thus takes on the quality of uncertainty which is the essence of legend. "They say" is the beginning of all such stories. They say, for example, that the lake called ORCHARD POND in Leon County was once an orchard which sank and filled with water. Since many of Florida's sinkholes have appeared overnight, we cannot dismiss this story as a mere fabrication. In fact, it is highly probable. They say that Levy County's CHIEFLAND was settled by a Creek Indian chief in 1842, after the wars with the whites were over, that he operated a large farm on these acres, and that members of his tribe lived about on smaller farms and worked for him. They say that Nassau County's TIGER ISLAND was so named because two men hunting for deer there before the Civil War (perhaps in the British period) killed two large panthers, locally called tigers.

They say of BAGDAD, in Santa Rosa County, that one Joseph Forsythe killed a man in New Orleans sometime during Florida's early territorial days, that he fled in a crude boat to Pensacola Bay, and eventually bought a tract of land near the present site of Bagdad, took in a partner, and went into the sawmill business. Difficulties in getting the lumber to the point on the Blackwater River where it could be shipped to New Orleans were enormous, but were overcome, and a settlement grew around the place where the lumber was stacked. And finally, they say, the name of Bagdad, originally the *Bagdad Land and Lumber Company*, was chosen from the *Arabian Nights* because of the fantastic difficulties overcome by the mill owners. There is a BAGDAD JUNCTION in Santa Rosa County, an offspring of the first Bagdad.

Tradition has it that FALMOUTH, in Suwannee County, was named for a pointer dog—the favorite dog of a resident named Colonel Duval. Falmouth was killed while hunting, they say, and the colonel changed the name of the town, originally called *Peacock*, as a memorial to his pet. OLD WOMANS BLUFF, in Franklin County, was so named because during the Civil War, every time a riverboat passed this bluff on the Apalachicola River a woman stood there, and the deckhands became accustomed to looking for her. Her identity was never known, but the deckhands began to call the place Old Womans Bluff, and so it has been ever since. On WEDDING ROCK in the Suwannee River a young couple was married in order to circumvent the threat of the girl's father that if she married anywhere on land or water he would kill her. A minister to whom the desperate lovers told their story took them to a rock in the river and performed the ceremony—and Wedding Rock it became. Or so they say.

All such stories—and others of like nature which have appeared in this book—may or may not be true. There are other place-name stories, however, which are patently untrue, though often amusing. Many of them grow up around names in foreign tongues and are a sort of folk etymology, based on the sound of the names. There is, for example, the well-known "explanation" of the origin of the place-name MIAMI. With variations it goes like this: A young man loved an Indian maid in those parts. One day he told her how beautiful she was, whereupon she replied, "My! *Am* I?"—thus, mysteriously enough, furnishing a name for the locality. One feels that the remark is hardly of the significance necessary to occasion the naming of a place, even assuming that the Indian maid spoke English, but still such folk legends flourish.

There are the various stories involving MICANOPY's naming—one attributing the name to the fact that an Irish merchant there was slow in paying his creditors, and someone, perhaps the Indians, said of him, "Micky no pay"; or the one that says the name arose from the Indians' repeated statement when they bought supplies at the place, "Me can no pay"; or the one that tells of an Indian who offered to open a particularly difficult crate of merchandise with the words "Me can opey." These are only three of several stories "explaining" the name of Micanopy.

Such a story is also told of the name of ESTIFFANULGA, in Liberty County. Here, they say, a traveler came upon the dead body of an Indian and remarked, "He's stiff and ugly." Of UMATILLA they tell the tale that it was once an Indian village where the squaws had been given orders not to speak to a white man. One day a party of whites came through, and one of them asked a squaw the name of the place. Mindful of her orders, she looked inquiringly at a nearby brave, who graciously said, "You may tellum." As for TARPON SPRINGS, they say that its name arose from the exclamation of a visiting lady, "Oh, see the tarpon spring!" when she saw the dolphins leaping offshore. Folk legends such as these are lively and colorful, and they illustrate the point that a name must have a meaning, and the folk will invent one if necessary.

In many ways, then, the names people place on the land and what they say about the names reveal the culture of a people— what they have been, what they have done, what they have laughed at, and what they have believed in. So it has been in Florida; and though the land is now crowded with names, still they shift and still new ones will come, to record what we are becoming. SATELLITE BEACH (Brevard County), for instance, is a new place-name which announces Florida's entrance into the space age, via the Kennedy Space Center, while such names as CHITTY CHATTY

CREEK (Sumter County), MURDER CREEK (Okaloosa County), FLOPBUCK CREEK (Charlotte County), and GUNSTOCK BRANCH (Santa Rosa County) still survive from her pioneer past to suggest what she used to be.

What the future holds for Floridians we cannot know, but we can be certain that as time goes by, the names on Florida's map will continue to record what we become and preserve some record of what we were.

6

Ghosts on the Land

THOUGH NAMES, even when we have forgotten their meaning, have tremendous staying power—witness the ancient Ocala, Sarasota, Matecumbe, Wakulla—many are lost as the years go by. Some are lost by chance and some are lost "on purpose," discarded in favor of newer and shinier ones. Florida has its gallery of ghost names, some of them still haunting the land though they are gone from the new charts and the new maps.

❀ INDIAN NAMES ❀

Students of history can hear the strange syllables of names given by long-gone Indian tribes whispering over the land. "A-LI-MA-CA-NI!" the breeze sobs softly over Fort George Island (Duval County). And over the Blackwater River in Okaloosa County the tree branches tap out the harsh, staccato syllables of FUKECHATTE LEYGE. At the mouth of the St. Marys River (Nassau County), where Jean Ribault and his men stayed a day and a night in May of 1562, the winds and the waters weep for the land of CHICORA, because its name and its people are gone. And near Cape Canaveral (Brevard County) ghostly voices cry "A-BA-IO-A," the name of a vanished village near which Ponce de León anchored in that 1513 Maytime after he first found Florida.

They say that *Alimacani*, as nearly as can be determined (by comparing its sounds with those of Timucuan words which were translated), means "sweet land by the sea." It was the Timucuan name for Fort George Island and for a Timucuan village on the island when Ribault landed there on the last day of April in 1562 and was given hospitality by the tall Indians whose land it was. The devout Huguenot Ribault is reported to have knelt and given thanks to God for safe passage and prayed for the welfare of his new friends. Then, it is said, he tried to explain to the chief, by signs, his worship of one God in heaven. The chief quickly understood, and replied by raising two fingers to show that his people worshipped two gods—the sun and the moon. The sun and the moon still light the land, but their worshippers are gone, like the name, from that "sweet land by the sea." *Fukechatte Leyge* is the forgotten name for the upper reaches of the Blackwater River and is derived from Creek words meaning "Red Clay Place." The meaning of *Chicora* is not known, but it was the name of a land "where people lived long"; the meaning of *Abaioa* has also been lost.

The clicking consonants of TACATACOUROU are also gone from the land, but when Dominique de Gourgues, a young Frenchman of Catholic family, came to Florida at the beginning of 1568 to avenge the insult done to the French king and to all France when the Spaniards slaughtered Jean Ribault and his compatriots at the place later called *Matanzas*, he first anchored at the mouth of a river which the Indians called Tacatacourou, he said. This was, apparently, the same river called by the Spanish the *Rio de Santa Maria* and by the French the *Seine*, though some report that it was the *Somme* that the French called it. Today it is the St. Marys River, so translated from the Spanish by the English and Americans. But the French and Indian and Spanish ghosts remain, to remind us of Florida's varied history.

GUALE, CALOS, YS, and APALACHIE were names of Florida "provinces" when the white man came. They are gone now, though extant names (e.g., "Apalachicola," "Caloosahatchee") call to mind some of them. MACARISI, ALOMATO, TAPOQUI, and SELOY, which were Indian villages in the St. Augustine area, are gone too, taking the meaning of their names with them. SARABAY (sometimes written on the old maps as *Carabay, Sarandy,* or *Sarauay*) is what the Indians called the river which is now Fort George Inlet, according to the account of the crusade of "le capitaine Gourgues." In 1539 the Spaniard Narváez and his men left AUTE, an Indian village near Wakulla Springs, a heap of smoking ruins, after first finding and taking a large store of corn. A town called AYUBALE once stood near the present Monticello, and Spanish priests and soldiers fell there when the English raided Florida in 1702 in the service of Governor James Moore of the colony of Carolina.

Many more lost aboriginal names haunt the land. The story of their passing is the story of a people's passing too, and of cruelty and treachery we do not like to acknowledge.

Some lost names directly honored the red men of Florida, the later arrivals as well as the aborigines. SUMULGA HATCHEE, which once designated a stream that is now "Burnt Mill Creek," in Jefferson County, is a name which could well have been another designation for the Seminole people. The last element of "Sumulga" is thought to be the Creek *Ulga* or *Algi*, meaning "people," or "clan," while the first part may have been derived from Creek *sumka* ("deserter"), making "people who deserted." TEQUESTA, the obsolete aboriginal name for Biscayne Bay, referred to the Tequesta, or Tekesta, Indians, who formerly inhabited the shores of the bay. There was once, also, a TEKESTA near Miami on the site of a Spanish Jesuit mission wiped out by Indians in 1571. YAMASEE POINT was a one-time designation of what is now GARCON POINT, in Santa Rosa County. *Yamasee* was the name of a tribe related to the early Creeks; they were one of the earliest Indian groups to repopulate Florida in the eighteenth century and were the precursors of the Seminoles.

Members of another Creek community—the Okchai of Alabama—who eventually became incorporated into the Seminole nation, were once commemorated in OKCHOYCE, the name of a creek between Washington and Bay counties. In Alachua County the present Lake Levy was once called HOG MASTER'S LAKE, for some forgotten Seminole chief called "the Hogmaster." An Indian village of the 1820s near the present Gainesville was called HOG-TOWN, apparently from this same source, and the name HOGTOWN CREEK for a small stream in the vicinity is still extant to commemorate the Indians who inhabited the area. The obsolete CHI'S CUT for a river in Dade County is thought to have been a corruption of the name of an Indian guide to the American troops during the Seminole War; and a creek and other natural features in Sumter and Marion counties were once called OTEE EMATHLA after the leader of the Oklawaha band of Seminoles and principal counselor to Chief Micanopy. TOCOBAGO was Menéndez's name for Tampa Bay (1567), named for a contemporary Timucuan chief.

WEEKAYWEE HATCHEE is what the Indians used to call Holmes Creek (Holmes, Jackson, and Washington counties). Like most of the authentic Indian place-names, it is descriptive, meaning "Spring Creek" ("spring" used here in the sense of "spring of water"). This same creek also bore the Creek name ACHATTO, meaning "Stones There." Lost names like the Creek CATTOCKOWEE HATCHEE, meaning "Bloody Stream," seem to memorialize the violence characteristic of so much of Florida's early history. This creek in Osceola County is now called, tamely enough, "Boggy Creek." PUNTA TANCHA is an early name for the southern extremity of the Florida mainland; it may be a Spanish-Calusa combination meaning "Corn Point." SANTAFFY—a corruption of "Santa Fe"—is what the Indians once called the Santa Fe River.

Among the Indian ghosts on the land is the lost name for Florida itself. Antonio de Herrera, royal Spanish historiographer, relates that the aborigines told Juan Ponce de León that the land was called CAUTÍO, a name given to it by the Lucayans, who lived in the Bahamas. When Juan Ponce asked the Indians why that name was given to it, they said it was because those who lived there wore plaited palm leaves. How credible this report may be is uncertain, but apparently the name Cautío was applied at least to some portion of Florida. It is interesting to note the report of a twentieth-century student of the Seminole language that the Seminoles, in their own language, still call Florida KANYUKSA, a combination of Creek *Ekan* ("land"), and *Yuksa* ("end of it"), which adds up to "land's end"—and which, like most of the Indian names, is a descriptive tag, perfectly applicable to a peninsula.

🏵 EARLY SPANISH NAMES 🏵

A host of long-lost Spanish names also haunt Florida. RIO DE JOVENAZO was an early designation for the Escambia River, which was once called that in honor of the Duke of Jovenazo, a member of the war committee in Madrid in the late seventeenth century. The early Spaniards called the St. Johns River the RIO DE SAN JUAN and sometimes the RIO DE SAN MATEO; and RIO DE SANTA MARIA was their name for the St. Marys River. NOMBRE DE DIOS ("Name of God") is another Spanish name gone from the map, but once upon a time, in 1606, Bishop Altamirano of Cuba visited a Father Romero

there, and confirmed Doña Maria Menéndez, an Indian chief-
tainess who had married a member of the great Menéndez family
of St. Augustine. "Nombre de Dios" is still used to designate an old
Catholic mission in St. Augustine.

Besides such typically religious Spanish names as these, other
names have disappeared. LA REVUELTA ("The Revolt") was once a
name for Nassau Sound—in memory of some unknown rough
sixteenth-century happening. LAGO DEL CONEJO ("Lake of the
Rabbit") was a name given in 1539 by men in the de Soto expedition to what is now Lake Thonotosassa in Hillsborough County,
seemingly because a rabbit frightened their horses there and
caused considerable delay.

On the earliest printed map of Florida for which there is record
(about 1587), there are at the lower end of the Florida peninsula
RIO DE CANOAS ("River of Canoes"), RIO DE PAS ("River of Peace"),
AGUADA ("Watering Place"), and C. DE CAÑAREAL (obviously meant
to designate CABO DE CAÑAVERAL, meaning "Reed Field Cape").
Northward along the peninsula on this early map are many other
lost descriptive Spanish names—RIO DE CORIENTO ("River of Current"?), IUAN DE PONTE (a garbled rendition of Juan Ponce's name?),
BAÿA DE SPŌ SANTO ("Bay of the Holy Spirit," named by de Soto in
1539), BAÿA DE BAYOS ("Bay of Bay Horses," named by Narváez in
1539), BAÿA DE S. IOSEPH ("Bay of St. Joseph"), RIO DE FLORES
("River of Flowers"), RIO DE LAS PALMAS ("River of the Palms"), RIO
DE PESCADORES ("River of Fishermen"), and others. It appears that
early Spanish explorers principally gave names to streams and
bodies of water, since they did not establish settlements to any
extent. Some of the Spanish names on this early map are still
extant, but they are usually translated into English. Lovers of
picturesque names will mourn the loss of those such as Rio de
Flores and Rio de las Palmas.

Homelier Spanish names rustle among the ghosts also—names
like CERRO GORDO ("Fat Hill"), which was once the name of a town
that served as the second county seat of Holmes County. Places
with the unmistakably Spanish names of MANUELS and GALVEZ
SPRINGS are mentioned in the account of Andrew Jackson's wait
outside of Pensacola for Spain's formal transfer of Florida, but are
not now discoverable on the Florida map (though they may still
exist in the oral tradition as the names of "settlements" or "communities" in the Pensacola area). A Spanish-named place once
written about was DIEGO, in Duval County.

🏵 FORGOTTEN FRENCH NAMES 🏵

And of course French names are among the lost. As a matter of fact, all the names given by those ill-fated men who attempted to claim Florida for France in the 1560s were wiped from the map by the Spaniards who slaughtered the men; and the Spanish word "Matanzas" ("butcheries" or "slaughters") is their only living memorial from that time. For a little while, the beautiful name RIVIÈRE DE MAI ("River of May") was on the land, given to the St. Johns River by Jean Ribault on May Day in 1562. René de Laudonnière's French "River of Dolphins," where he saw the dolphins leaping in the sun, is regrettably gone also. So brief was the French chapter in Florida's history that maps showing the French-given names are few, and we have only a suggestion of what they were like. We know that their Fort Caroline (LA CAROLINE) was the earliest white settlement in the Florida territory. René de Laudonnière built it and named it in 1564, in honor of Charles IX of France, near St. Johns Bluff in the present Duval County; and Pedro Menéndez de Avilés reported in a 1565 letter to Philip II of Spain that eight or ten children had been born there, and that the population numbered fifty persons in all. It was because of the colony of La Caroline and its threat to Spanish supremacy in Florida that Philip had reversed his own 1561 order that no further attempts be made to colonize Florida, and had sent Menéndez there to expel the French and establish a permanent Spanish colony. His soldiers captured Fort Caroline and killed all but a few of the Frenchmen. Among those who escaped and finally reached France was Jacques Le Moyne, a young artist who later wrote a narrative of the French colony and illustrated it with pictures that have become famous. He published, also, a map which shows Florida as the sixteenth-century French explorers conceived of it.

Some of the names on the Le Moyne map are in Latin—e.g., PROMONTORIUM GALLICUM ("French Cape") and LACUS AQUAE DULCIS ("Lake of Fresh Water"). This latter name applied, apparently, to what we now know as Lake Okeechobee. Such names as F. PACIS (*Fluvium Pacis*, or "River of Peace"), F. CANOTIS ("Canoe River"?), and SINUS JOANNIS PONCE ("Bay of Juan Ponce"?) were apparently translated into Latin from the Spanish names. Also on the Le Moyne map are quaint recordings of Indian names mixed with Latin topographical terms. SARSOPE appears as the name of a *lacus* ("lake") and of an *insula* ("island") and MARRACOU, MAYARCA, and CADICA appear as names of villages. Perhaps *Sarsope* is an earlier form of the present Sarasota, and Mayarca a version of Myakka.

Ghosts they are, in any case—ghosts that mourn French Florida and call forth the shadowy forms of those who planted France's flag on this New World peninsula for a little while. The names make us see again the placard placed by Menéndez at the place (Matanzas) where he slaughtered the defenders of that short-lived French colony under Jean Ribault—"I do this not as to Frenchmen but as to Lutherans"—and the bitter answering one "le capitaine Gourgues" is said to have placed there three years later when he avenged the massacre by executing Spaniards on the same spot— "I do this not as to Spaniards . . . but as to traitors, robbers, and murderers."

✵ AMERICAN NAMES ✵

Some forthright American pioneer names, whose inventors were careless of euphony and pleasant connotations, have also been lost—many of them deliberately—since Florida became conscious of her destiny as a tourist haven. A few mosquito names have been eliminated, as noted earlier, for there is no longer a MOSQUITO COUNTY—it was changed to "Orange County" in 1824—and the erstwhile MOSQUITO RIVER is now the Halifax River. Some alligator names have also been eliminated, though a good many remain as the names of natural features.

So down-to-earth as to seem only a joke are two lost names reported to have been earlier designations of Milton, in Santa Rosa County: SCRATCH ANKLE and HARDSCRABBLE. The latter is somewhat of a "stock" American pioneer name, it seems, apparently signifying hard times in a hard land. The former has the same general connotation, suggesting particularly the presence of insects of one sort or another and of rough undergrowth catching the ankles. The earlier name of Alachua County's Melrose— SHAKERAG—is also interestingly inelegant, and that inelegance is the reason it is no longer extant. The name came about because the place it designated was the site of much pony-racing, and a white rag was waved as a signal for races to begin.

PEASE CREEK was the name first given to the town in Polk County which was later named "Bartow" in honor of a Confederate hero.

This homely name was a transfer from the Peace River, known at one time in its history as "Pease Creek" because of a misunderstanding (see chapter 4).

THOMPSON'S ISLAND was the first United States name for Key West—given in 1822 in honor of Secretary of the Navy Smith Thompson when a United States naval base was established there. JONESBORO was the name of Dunedin from the time of the town's founding in the 1850s until 1878, doubtless in honor of an early settler. ROWLAND'S BLUFF was the former name of Branford; it, too, must have been for a pioneer citizen.

A more noble name—SUTHERLAND, for the late-nineteenth-century duke of Sutherland—was replaced in the 1920s by the typical "boom" name "Palm Harbor." The place is in Pinellas County; the lost name was given in 1888 by the town's founders, a group of real-estate promoters, in anticipation of a substantial financial investment in the new development by the duke. He did not rise to the occasion, so abandonment of the name brought on no qualms of conscience. But it is a lost name which calls forth a romantic Florida story—the story of a nobleman who deserted his family in England, built a clapboard manor house on thirty pine-grown acres overlooking a lake near Tarpon Springs in 1889, and lived there for two years with the woman he loved, a commoner, Mrs. Mary Carolina Blair, of London. The little Episcopal church in nearby Dunedin was the scene of their wedding in 1888.

MINERAL CITY, former name of Ponte Vedra, and MILLVILLE, the name of a town that is now a part of Panama City, are lost names that show the plain, matter-of-fact naming style of busy American pioneers, while the new name for Mineral City—PONTE VEDRA, bestowed in 1932—reveals the urge toward the picturesque and the exotic which beset later Floridians. The same type of change took place in the replacement of WISCONSIN SETTLEMENT by "Orange City" (Volusia County), though this change was made in 1880, much earlier than the Ponte Vedra one.

MASSACRE is the grim lost name of St. Catherine, in Sumter County. The place is near the site of the Dade Massacre. (Perhaps the inhabitants grew squeamish about calling their home by a name with such cruel connotations.)

WANTON is a lost American name for Micanopy (Alachua County). It is easy—and interesting—to assume that the name referred to the lawlessness, or wantonness, of the area, but the truth is that the place was called that for a first settler, Edward

M. Wanton, one of the men who managed Don Fernando de la Maza Arredondo's Spanish land grant for him. (The grant, made in 1817, led to the first white settlement in what is now Alachua County. That first settlement was at the present Micanopy.)

We do not know why Trenton, in Gilchrist County, was once called JOPPA, or why Taylor County's Perry was once called ROSE-HEAD, or why the name GRUELLE was given and why it was later replaced by "Rochelle" in Alachua County. But these names wander among the ghosts over the land, as does LAUREL GROVE, which Zephaniah Kingsley, when he lived there, called what is now Orange Park (Clay County).

Some place-names were lost by natural destruction—because the places themselves were lost. In the 1830s there was a ST. JOSEPH in what is now Gulf County, a town that quickly became a rival port to nearby Apalachicola and a resort town for wealthy planters. A line of packets ran between St. Joseph and Liverpool; a railroad, wharves, and warehouses boosted its prosperity; but its barrooms, cheap hotels, and gambling houses gave it an unsavory reputation. In 1841, what many people regarded as retribution struck. A yellow fever epidemic was followed by a severe hurricane which destroyed the town, and its people abandoned the spot. When the city was later rebuilt, it was given the somewhat irreverent name of "Port St. Joe," which it bears today.

PORT LEON, in what became Wakulla County, was wiped out by a tidal wave in 1843. This town, which was for a few months the county seat of the new Wakulla County, had, besides a waterfront on the Gulf of Mexico, a railroad—with horse-drawn cars on it at first—and seemed destined for considerable prosperity; but like St. Joseph, it had the reputation of being a wicked city. There was no church, and Sunday was spent in "playing Billiards, Drinking, Swearing, Smoking, etc.," according to a contemporary account. It was said at the time that God destroyed it because "he was sorely displeased at what he saw." Settlers from there founded Newport, safely away from the coast, the same year.

Another pioneer American town in the same area—MAGNOLIA, founded by the Hamlins of Maine in 1827—was dead before 1840 because the railroad from St. Marks to Tallahassee bypassed it. It stopped growing after 1836, all the high hopes of its founders drooped, and its residents deserted it. Some citizens moved to the new—and doomed—city of Port Leon to the south, others to St. Marks. The warehouses were empty; the hotel which had advertised itself as the "best on the Gulf" had no guests. And now the ghost name Magnolia sighs in the pines above the spot, where only a graveyard remains.

The lost names mingle with the living ones to create the whole picture of Florida through the decades. Some of the names gone from the map linger on the lips of the people, so that they are not wholly lost; others can be discovered only by reading old records and examining history. Then we can hear them whispering in the wind and crying in the waters as we travel Florida—the Indian, the Spanish, the French, and the American ghosts on the land, reinforcing all that the living names tell us of the Florida history and romance.

Appendix A

Additional Commemorative Names

ALAMANA (Volusia): For the settler, J. A. Alaman (ca. 1902).

ALDRICH LAKE (Orange): For the first settlers who homesteaded here, of Scottish origin.

ALFORD (Jackson): For S. A. and Chauncey Alford, pioneer naval stores operators in that vicinity (ca. 1890).

ALLENDALE (Volusia): For two brothers, Thomas and William Allen, who, respectively, built the Congregational Church there, and owned fifty acres of orange groves. (Originally established as "Halifax City" by the East Florida Land Company in 1870; present town begun in 1913 by Cornelius Christiancy.)

ALLENHURST (Brevard): For Commodore J. H. Allen, who formed with his associates a hunting club there in 1907 or 1909. (Formerly known as "Haulover"; established by Captain D. Dummitt in 1852.)

ANTHONY (Marion): For Colonel B. C. Anthony, said to have come from Indiana. (First called "Anoty Place"; established 1878.)

ASHTON (Osceola): For family of first settlers. (Formerly "Ashton Station"; established 1884-85.)

AYCOCK (Jackson): For the Aycock brothers, lumber manufacturers there from 1900 to 1920.

BAILEY (Madison): For General William A. Bailey, who owned a large plantation and many slaves there in the 1830s. When the railroad came in about 1903, it passed through part of the old

Bailey property; and when a post office was eventually established it was given the name of Bailey in honor of the general.

BAKER MILL (Hamilton): For George Baker, who started a sawmill there in 1887.

BARBERVILLE (Volusia): For J. D. Barber, who settled there about 1882. (Area homesteaded and cleared before the Civil War.)

BARRINEAU PARK (Escambia): For W. C. Barrineau, a pioneer (1911).

BARTH (Escambia): For the Barth family (1910).

BASCOM (Jackson): For a member of the Bevis family, who established the place (1890).

BAYOU GEORGE (Bay): For a family who settled there in 1886.

BELLAMY (Alachua): Probably for John Bellamy, contractor for part of the old Bellamy or Federal Road from Pensacola to St. Augustine (ca. 1885).

BELLVILLE (Hamilton): For Colonel James E. Bell, first settler (before 1885).

BETTS (Bay): For J. S. Betts, of Ashburn, Georgia, sawmill man and one of the first settlers in the area.

BISHOPVILLE (Volusia): For Robert J. Bishop, a turpentine operator who purchased land there in 1900. (Formerly known as "Astor Junction" and later "Eldridge"; named Bishopville in 1911. Railroad station still called "Eldridge.")

BLANTON (Pasco): For a prominent South Florida family.

BOARDMAN (Marion): For L. Boardman, thought to have been an early settler (1863).

BONIFAY (Holmes): For a prominent family named Bonifay (1882).

BOTHAMLEY (Seminole): For the owner of a turpentine camp opened there in 1888.

BOTTS (Santa Rosa): For the Botts family (1890).

BOWDEN (Duval): Settled by Uriah Bowden in 1787. (Originally "St. Anthony's" or "San Antoni.")

BOYD (Taylor): For J. B. Boyd.

BOYETTE (Hillsborough): For Thomas Boyett.

BOYNTON BEACH (Palm Beach): For Major N. S. Boynton of Port Huron, Michigan, who built a hotel there. (Founded in 1896, first called "Boynton," name changed to Boynton Beach in 1925.)

BRADEN CASTLE (Manatee): See Bradenton discussion in chapter 3. Also in Manatee County are BRADEN RIVER, BRADENTON BEACH, and BRADENTON JUNCTION.

BRANCHTON (Hillsborough): For an early resident, James Branch.

BRENT (Escambia): For F. C. Brent, who built a summer home there because of the healthy location among pine woods. (Established about 1870; formerly called "Brentwood.")

BRONSON (Levy): For an early settler. The WPA Florida Guide indicates that the site of Bronson, county seat of Levy County, was originally called "Chunky Pond," and in 1844 was given its present name. The date varies in other accounts, but is always in the nineteenth century, in the American period.

BROOKER (Bradford): For a bridge across the Santa Fe River named after Ed Brooker, a farmer in that area. (Post office established and named in 1894 by Thomas R. Collins; a settlement began in the vicinity in 1838.)

BROWARDS STATION or BROWARD'S NECK (Duval): The site of the old Broward plantation, settled by John Broward in 1854.

BROWN (Holmes): Settled by Joe Brown, head of the Farmer's Alliance of Holmes County.

BROWNSVILLE (Escambia): For L. S. Brown, known as "Clean-Sweep Brown" because he and all his chosen candidates were elected to the city council when the municipal government was formed.

BULOW (Volusia): For Charles Bulow, who purchased the place and built a sugar mill there in 1830–31. (Established by James Russell in 1812.)

BUNNELL (Flagler): For Alva A. Bunnell, who founded it in 1880.

BURNETT'S LAKE (Alachua): For Samuel W. Burnett, builder of the first courthouse in Alachua County (in Newnansville, about 1823).

BUTLER (Jackson): For C. J. Butler, who owned the land (1892).

CALHOUN (Calhoun): For the Calhoun brothers, who operated a large farm and sawmill there immediately after the Civil War.

CALLAWAY (Bay): For the first sawmill operator in the section.

CAMPBELLTON (Jackson): For Judge R. L. Campbell, former resident of the county (1840 or earlier).

CANDLER (Marion): For the Candler family (1883).

CASSELBERRY (Seminole): By and for Hibbard Casselberry, local horticulturist. (Formerly "Fern Park"; renamed in 1940s.)

CLARKWILD (Hillsborough): For two pioneers, Mr. Clark and Mr. Wilder.

COACHMAN (Pinellas): For S. S. Coachman.

COATSVILLE (Holmes): For Marion Coats, who had a gristmill and a cotton gin there.

CODYVILLE (Flagler): For Cody Turpentine and Farm Land Company, who established it about 1901.

COLEE (St. Johns): For a pioneer Florida family.

COOK (Bay): For an early settler and long-time resident.

COURTNEY (Brevard): By and for a homesteader (ca. 1870).

CRANDALL (Nassau): For a prominent family living there in 1884. (Formerly "Township" and "Fort Henry.")

CRAWFORD (Nassau): Established by W. R. Crawford in 1883.

CREIGHTON (Volusia): For E. R. Creighton.

CRIGLAR (Jackson): For J. H. Criglar, who operated a mill there.

CULBREATH (Hamilton): For Tom Culbreath, who settled there in 1884.

CURRY (Monroe): For a family who came there from the Bahamas.

CUTLER (Dade): For an early settler, probably in 1890.

DANCY'S PLACE (Putnam): For Colonel Dancy, prominent Florida orange grower and planter, who had a plantation there.

DAVIE (Broward): For the original promoter. (Established 1911; formerly called "Zona.")

DAYTONA BEACH (Volusia): For Mathias Day, who established the place in 1870. Named "Daytona" in 1872; became Daytona Beach in 1926, when Seabreeze, Daytona Beach, and Daytona were consolidated. DAYTONA CREST and DAYTONA SHORES are offspring.

DENAUD (Hendry): For Pierre DeNeau or Denaud, who owned land there.

DENNETT (Madison): For Dennett H. Mays, prominent citizen and large-scale planter and property owner (1904).

DESTIN (Okaloosa): For Captain Leonard Destin, who came from New England and founded it more than a century ago.

DICKERT (Suwannee): For Judge C. P. Dickert, former owner of the farm for which the sidetrack and station were established.

DOCTOR PHILLIPS (Orange): For Dr. Phillips, large-scale citrus grower.

DOCTOR'S ARM (Monroe): For a Dr. J. V. Harris who first owned the property, old-timers say. This place is a cove on Big Pine Key where a point of land sticks out like a sheltering arm. Thus the name is both a commemorative and a descriptive one.

DOWDELL (Hillsborough): For son-in-law of Captain Davis who founded the town of Wimauma in the same county.

DOWLING PARK (Suwannee): For one-time owners Thomas and Robert L. Dowling, who ran a turpentine camp there.

DUDLEY (Jackson): For a pioneer family (ca. 1890).

DUMMITT CREEK (Brevard): For a pioneer settler and citrus grower (late nineteenth century).

DUPONT (Flagler): For Abraham DuPont, founder (ca. 1835).

DURANT (Hillsborough): For a resident.

DURBIN (St. Johns): For a family named Durbin who settled the area. (Formerly the "Heights of Durbin.")

EARNESTVILLE (Escambia): For W. T. Earnest, mill owner. (Formerly "Bay Springs"; post office still "Bay Springs.")

EDDY (Baker): For one Washington Eddy (ca. 1885).

EDGE (Glades): For a man named Edge, by his turpentine company partner named McCormack.

ELDRIDGE (Volusia): For a local family. (Established ca. 1876; originally known as "Astor Junction"; post office known as "Bishopville," q.v.)

ELLIS (Jackson): For a pioneer family (ca. 1875).

ELLZEY (Levy): By and for Rev. R. H. Ellzey (1876).

EMERSON (Suwannee): For a Mr. Emerson who owned a sawmill there.

ENSLEY (Escambia): For Fred B. Ensley. (Once called "Fig City" because of the fig production; established about 1912.)

ESTO (Holmes): For an early settler.

FAIRBANKS (Alachua): For Samuel Fairbanks, who established it in 1823, five years before the railroad station was built.

FATIO (Volusia): For Francisco Philippe Fatio, a Swiss who acquired the land in a grant from England in 1772. (Established in 1851 by John W. Starke of South Carolina.) See "Switzerland" in "Names Commemorating Places in Other Lands," and "Fleming" in "Names Commemorating People," this Appendix.

FELDA (Hendry): For the oldest settlers, Mr. and Mrs. F. L. Taylor—the F and L from his initials and the E, D, and A from her maiden name, now unknown.

FELLSMERE (Indian River): For E. Nelson Fell, who in 1910 acquired about 144 square miles of land in what is now Indian River County. (*Mere* means "lake" or "pond.")

FENTRESS (Santa Rosa): For Calvin Fentress. (Established about 1912; post office formerly called "Red Rock.")

FERRELL STILL (St. Johns): For Clarence Ferrell, who owned a turpentine still there.

FLEMING (Clay): For the Fleming family, who received the island on which it is located as a Spanish land grant in 1790. See "Hibernia" in "Names Commemorating Places in Other Lands," this Appendix. (George Fleming had married into the Fatio family, *q.v.*)

FOLEY (Taylor): For J. S. Foley, general manager of the Brooks-Scanlon Lumber Company in 1929 when the company built the town to house employees of the sawmill it located there.

FOOTMAN (Brevard): By and for Joe Footman. (Was a boat landing and post office on Merritt Island, now only a place.)

FULFORD (Dade): For an early settler.

FULLERS (Orange): For a man who settled there (1905).

FULLERTON (Volusia): By and for George I. Fullerton (1925).

GAINER (Bay): For an early settler.

GAINSBORO (Orange): For a Colonel Gaines (1880).

GIBSONTON (Hillsborough): For a pioneer family.

GLASS (Jackson): For one Mr. Glass.

GLENCOE (Volusia): Named in 1878 for William H. Coe, who settled there in 1875 and whose son, W. A. Coe, was postmaster when the post office was established. (*Glen* means "secluded valley.")

GOETHE (Bay): For George Goethe, one of the first men who operated a sawmill in this section of Florida.

GOODNO (Glades): For E. E. Goodno, prominent cattleman from Kansas, who imported Brahma bulls from India in the 1860s to improve Florida beef stock.

GOULDING (Escambia): For H. M. and W. J. Goulding of Dublin, Ireland, who owned the Goulding Fertilizer Company, now the American Agriculture Chemical Company (1889).

GRANT (Brevard): For an early settler in the area (named for him in 1890 by Mrs. Edwin Nelson).

GRASSY (Monroe): For a pioneer settler whose name was Grassy. (Or so they say!)

GREENSBORO (Gadsden): For J. W. Green, who in 1895 bought 160 acres near his birthplace and secured a post office called *Green's*. In 1907, when the Apalachicola Northern Railway was built, a depot was located on the Green farm, which was then platted as a town and named *Greensboro*.

GREER (Pasco): For the Greer family from Georgia, owners of a large sawmill at this place.

HAILE (Alachua): For the Haile family, pioneer settlers (1880–84).

HALL CITY (Glades): For a Chicago doctor.

HAMPTON (Bradford): For Hampton Terry, ten-year-old son of a farm family around whose farm the community grew (1882).

HAMPTON SPRINGS (Taylor): For early settler Joe Hampton, who is said to have been directed to the place by Indians, who believed in the healing power of the springs, and whose wife was believed to have been cured of rheumatism by the waters.

HARDEETOWN (Levy): For a prominent family who lived there (1917).

HARP (Santa Rosa): For a pioneer, F. A. Harp (ca. 1900).

HARWOOD (Volusia): For N. B. Harwood, who established it as a sugar plantation (1840).

HASTINGS (St. Johns): For the H. G. Hastings Seed Company, Atlanta, Georgia (which, presumably, sold the seed potatoes for this famous potato community).

HAWTHORNE (Alachua): For James H. Hawthorne, early owner of the town site (1881). By order of the United States Geographic Board, the post office name is spelled without the final e, but the town name defiantly retains it.

HAYWOOD (Jackson): For Francis P. Haywood, who established it in 1869. (Originally "Haywood's Landing.")

HIGGINS (Gulf): For a former large-scale property owner in that section.

HIGLEY (Lake): For E. E. Higley, who established it in 1833.

HILDRETH (Suwannee): For C. M. Hildreth, Sr., who owned a turpentine camp there.

HILLIARD (Nassau): For the Hilliard of Hilliard and Bailey, lumber manufacturers, who established it as a trading post in 1881.

HINSON (Gadsden): For a family of that name.

HODGSON (Levy): For Thomas Hodgson (1890).

HOLDER (Citrus): For the Holder family, former owners of the old Globe Mine, a hard rock phosphate mine, now mined out. (The railroad station there was named "Ladonia" by the railroad and still retains that name, though the post office is Holder.)

HOLLEY (Santa Rosa): For the Reverend W. D. Holley, Baptist minister (ca. 1903).

HOLMES BEACH (Manatee): For Jack E. Holmes, builder and developer.

HOPKINS (Brevard): For G. R. Hopkins, who started the place in 1921 as a lumber mill town.

HORNSBY SPRING (Alachua): For a Hornsby who lived there.

HOUSTON (Suwannee): For an early settler.

HOWEY-IN-THE-HILLS (Lake): For W. J. Howey, the founder (incorporated in 1926).

JACOBS (Jackson): For the persons who owned the land (1810). Also called "Jacob."

JENNINGS (Hamilton): For Robert Jennings, who settled there in 1860, operating a farm and general store—or, according to another report, by and for George Jennings, a northerner who came there on a raft by way of the Alapahah River in 1884.

JOHNSON (Putnam): For the Johnson family, prominent when the place was established (1861).

JUDSON (Levy): For Judson Carter, who opened a store and operated a sawmill there (ca. 1880).

KELSAY CITY (Palm Beach): For Harry S. Kelsey.

KEMP CHANNEL (Monroe): For an early homesteader in the Keys.

KENDALL (Dade): For Major Kendall, vice-president of the British Land Company, who owned extensive orange groves there (ca. 1900).

KEUKA (Putnam): For William L. Keuka, pioneer settler of Putnam County.

KINGSTON (Volusia): By and for George W. Kingston of El Paso, Illinois, a settler (1875). (Now a part of Daytona Beach.)

KIRKLAND (Suwannee): For a local farm family.

KNABBS SPUR (Baker): For a local family (1900).

KNIGHTS (Hillsborough): For William Knight, father of Jesse Knight, a settler.

KNOWLES (Hillsborough): Renamed about 1910 for H. H. Knowles, the founder. (Originally "Oaklawn.")

KYNESVILLE (Jackson): For the landowner (1875).

LAKE ALDRED (Lake): For Aldred Abrams.

LAKE ALFRED (Polk): A large lake named for Alfred Parslow, an early settler who had acquired the original franchise for the railroad and had built up an estate there. There is also LAKE ALFRED (Polk), a town named for the lake (1913).

LAKE CHILDS (Highlands): For an early surveyor.

LAKE GRIFFITH (Lake): For an early settler.

LAKE KERR (Marion): For a Scottish settler.

LAKE PICKETT (Orange): Town named for a family of pioneer cattlemen who settled there in the late 1880s.

LAKE STEARNS (Highlands): For an early surveyor.

LAKE WALES (Polk): For the lake, which in turn honors the name of a family who once lived near there. *Waels* was the original spelling; *Wales* appeared with the platting of the town in about 1911. Also, WEST LAKE WALES (Polk).

LAKE WEIR (Marion): A lake named for Dr. Weir (or Ware), whose home was near the lake. Also in Marion County are the towns LAKE WEIR (1874) and WEIRSDALE, and in Lake County SOUTH LAKE WEIR—all named for the lake.

LAKE WILLIS (Lake): For Willis T. Jackson.

LAKE WOODWARD (Lake): For two Woodward brothers.

LANEPARK (Lake): For Captain A. J. Lane, who planned a town that did not develop because of a freeze that blighted the citrus industry.

LANIER (Osceola): For a family there.

LAWTEY (Bradford): For William Lawtey, son-in-law of Colonel V. J. Shipman, leader of the group that established the town (1877).

LEESBURG (Lake): For Calvin and Evander Lee, who established the place in 1863—or if another report is true, for the Lee family of New York, who founded the town in 1856. There is also NORTH LEESBURG (Lake).

LELLMAN (Pinellas): For a man named Lellman who owned land in the vicinity.

LILLIBRIDGE (Hillsborough): For Morton M. Lillibridge, who came from Texas. (Established in the early 1880s.)

LINDSEYS (Holmes): For Ben Lindsey, who owned a turpentine still there.

LINTON (Palm Beach): For W. S. Linton, congressman from Michigan, who established the place.

LLOYD (Jefferson): For W. J. Lloyd, in 1857. It had formerly been known as *Bailey's Mills.*

LOCKHART (Orange): By and for David Lockhart, who built a sawmill there (1870).

LOVETT (Madison): For Hezekiah Lovett, who established it during the 1890s.

LUKENS (Levy): For the owner of the cypress mill formerly located there.

LYNN HAVEN (Bay): For W. H. Lynn, who came there in 1911 from New York state and subsequently influenced the commander of the Grand Army of the Republic to locate a colony of GAR men there.

MacCLENNY (Baker): Renamed in 1885 for H. C. MacClenny, founder and large-scale landowner (1860).

McCULLOUGHS CREEK (St. Johns): For the McCullough family, homesteaders.

McDAVID (Escambia): By Joel McDavid, for the pioneer McDavid family. (Established as a station and post office in 1883.) There is also McDAVID CREEK.

McDONALD (Orange): For a pioneer (1887).

McINTOSH (Marion): For a squatter named McIntosh who set up a sugar mill there and was later scalped by Indians.

McKINNONVILLE (Escambia): For the Robert McKinnon family (1910).

McLANES (Orange): For the McLane family, settlers (1887).

McLELLAN (Santa Rosa): For the McLellans, pioneers (1903).

MAJETTE (Bay): For the Majette family, engaged in turpentine and naval stores operations in that vicinity.

MALONE (Jackson): For John W. Malone, developer (1911).

MANNS SPUR (Baker): For the Mann family (about 1905).

MARKHAM (Lake): For Marcellus Markham, who operated a turpentine still there (1873).

MARSHALL CREEK (Jackson): For a pioneer family of the mid-nineteenth century.

MAYO (Lafayette): For a Colonel Mayo (1874).

MAYSLAND (Madison): For the Mays family, large-scale landowners, who settled here in 1835.

MAYTOWN (Volusia): For May Cook, lifelong resident. (Named in 1890.)

MEDLEY (Dade): For Sylvester Medley, who settled there in 1905.

MERCER (Suwannee): For J. T. Mercer, who owned a plantation there.

MIMS (Brevard): For B. J., C. N., and Robert E. Mims, brothers who established the place in about 1894. Also in Brevard is EAST MIMS.

MINORVILLE (Orange): For the Minor family, large-scale landowners and farmers, who established the place in about 1900.

MONTBROOK (Levy): For a man named Montbrook—or, some say, Mont Brooks—a landowner. (Established about 1896; formerly "Phoenix.")

MOORE HAVEN (Glades): For its founder, James A. Moore.

MOSELEY HALL (Madison): For Lewis M. Moseley (ca. 1825).

MUNSON (Santa Rosa): Named for Captain Charles Munson, manager of a lumber company there (about 1909).

MURPHEE (Bay): For a pioneer family—sometimes spelled *Murfee*.

MUSE (Glades): For the son of an early settler.

NEWLAND SPRINGS (Suwannee): For the Newland family, who owned it.

NILES CHANNEL (Monroe): For an early homesteader in the Keys.

NOWATNEY (Hillsborough): For an early settler, W. W. Nowatney (1890s).

NUTALL RISE (Taylor): For John Nutall, first settler near this "rise," or place where the Aucilla River reappears after flowing underground for a while.

OSTEEN (Volusia): For H. E. Osteen, early cattleman in the area (1856). First known as "Saulsville" for another resident, George Sauls.

PABOR LAKE (Highlands): For and by C. W. Pabor.

PACE and PACE JUNCTION (Santa Rosa): For Jim Pace, important Florida lumberman (1909).

PARAMORE (Jackson): For the Paramore family.

PARKER (Bay): For W. H. Parker, early settler.

PARKER (Escambia): For the Parker family (1910).

PARKLAND (De Soto): For L. H. Parkland (1880s).

PARRISH (Manatee): For the original settler.

PAYNE'S PRAIRIE (Alachua): Possibly for a Dr. Payne who had large land holdings south of the prairie, and who lived in Micanopy during the nineteenth century. Dr. Payne attempted to improve the orange stock by grafting the buds of sweet seedlings onto the wild orange stock. Another possibility is that Payne's Prairie was named for the Indian "King Payne" (see chapter 3). King Payne is more often given as the man commemorated by the prairie's name—perhaps because he seems a more romantic figure.

PELLICERS CREEK (St. Johns): For the Pellicer family, landowners.

PERKINS (Franklin): For a Tallahassee family (1860).

PETERS (Dade): By and for Tom Peters, "tomato king," who made enough money on his tomatoes in one season to buy the Halcyon Hotel in Miami—or so it is said. (Established in early 1900s.)

PHILLIPS (Duval): For the Phillips family, who established it before the Civil War.

PICKETT LAKE (Orange): Lake named for a family of pioneers.

PIERSON (Volusia): For Nela Pierson and family, who established it in 1876.

PITTMAN (Lake): For George T. Pittman, one of its founders (1883).

PITTMAN CREEK (Holmes): For "Old Wash" Pittman and "Uncle Billy" Pittman.

PLUMMERS COVE (Duval): For Daniel Plummer, who took the property in 1802. (Settlement established first in 1792.)

POPE (Baker): For a prominent family of lawyers.

PORT SEWELL (Martin): For Captain Henry E. Sewell, pioneer resident.

RAIFORD (Union): For an early settler, H. W. Raiford, who came in 1900 and established a turpentine still, post office, and commissary.

REDINGTON BEACH and NORTH REDINGTON BEACH (Pinellas): For Charles E. Redington, developer.

REMINGTON (Clay): For prominent early settlers. (Established by English colonists.)

RHODES SPUR (Leon): Probably for G. W. Rhodes, owner of nearby RHODES SPRINGS. (Established 1860.)

RICHMOND (Dade): For a Dr. Richmond, who lived in the area about 1895.

RIXFORD (Suwannee): For George C. Rixford, who founded it in 1873.

ROBERTS (Escambia): For the Roberts family, settlers.

ROEVILLE (Santa Rosa): For Hannibal Roe, pioneer farmer (1920).

ROGERS (Volusia): By and for Sherman Rogers (1890).

RUSS CREEK (Jackson): For a prominent family (ca. 1860).

RUTLAND (Sumter): For the Rutland family (1884).

SADLER (Taylor): For C. J. Sadler (1902).

SAPP (Baker): For a member of the Sapp family—perhaps M. A. Sapp, father of the "rabbit-eye" blueberry industry in northwest Florida.

SAUNDERS (Bay): For the Saunders family, prominent early settlers.

SCANLON (Taylor): For the Brooks-Scanlon Lumber Company there. (Established 1920.)

SCOTTS FERRY (Calhoun): For Lieutenant G. W. Scott, whose party was massacred by Indians in 1816 during the turbulent years immediately before Florida became a United States territory.

SCOTTSMOORE (Brevard): For two men from Vermont named Scott and Moore. (Established during the land boom in 1925.)

SELLERS LAKE (Lake): For the Sellers family, who established it around 1848–49.

SHARPES (Brevard): For a family who settled there.

SHELTON (Dixie): For a local family.

SIMSVILLE (Jackson): For Josiah Sims, former owner of the land.

SIRMANS (Madison): For John P. Sirmans, who operated the first store there during the 1840s.

SMITH CREEK (Wakulla): For an esteemed citizen. (Established in 1845 by James Kees and settlers mostly from Georgia and South Carolina.)

SNEADS (Jackson): For a pioneer dentist of the town.

SPEER LAKE (Orange): For owners of the surrounding land, the Speer Dairy Company.

STANTON (Marion): For E. Stanton Perrin, who established it in 1881.

STOCKTONIA (St. Johns): For the Stockton family, first settlers.

STUART (Martin): For Samuel C. Stuart, first telegraph operator and station agent when the Florida East Coast Railway was built across the St. Lucie River in 1893.

SULLIVAN (Santa Rosa): For the Sullivan Milling Company (1920).

TAYLOR (Baker): For a Florida family.

TENILE (Escambia): For the Tenile family from South Carolina, who settled there.

THAGGARD (Hamilton): For J. F. Thaggard, who operated a farm there (1885).

THOMPSON (Monroe): For a Key West family. (Post office established 1884; now defunct.)

TICE (Lee): For Chauncey O. Tice, who owned orange groves and a packinghouse at the site (early 1900s).

TILDENVILLE (Orange): For a pioneer resident named Tilden (1900).

TOWNSEND (Lafayette): For a prominent family (1895).

TRAPNELL (Hillsborough): For the Trapnell family, pioneer residents (1854).

TROUT CREEK (St. Johns): For the Trout family, who owned land near there. There are at least six *Trout Creeks* in the state. It seems far more likely that for most of them the name was given for the fish in the streams than that it commemorated a human family name, but the latter is what "they say" in the case of the St. Johns County Trout Creek.

TURNER (Highlands): For a resident named Turner.

VICKSBURG (Bay): For a Mr. Vickers, who was joint owner of a turpentine still there. His partner, Mr. R. L. McKenzie, is said to have cooperated with Vickers in naming the place; Vickers used part of his own name and McKenzie added the "burg."

WALDO (Alachua): For Dr. Benjamin Waldo, practicing physician in the county and later a state legislator (ca. 1856).

WALLACE (Santa Rosa): For the Wallace family (1912).

WALSINGHAM (Pinellas): For a prominent nearby citrus grower.

WELCHTON (Jackson): For Columbus Welch, large-scale property owner and prominent resident.

WELLBORN (Suwannee): For L. W. Wellborn, who laid out the town.

WEST FARM (Madison): For the West brothers, who established it in 1882.

WEST LAKE (Hamilton): For E. J. West, who settled there in 1870.

WHIDDON CORNERS (Hendry): For the prominent Whiddon family (1875).

WHITTIER (Osceola): For a Florida family (before 1875).

WILBUR-BY-THE-SEA (Volusia): By and for J. W. Wilbur, who established the place in about 1920.

WILEY (Brevard): For a Dr. Wiley, who named it "Wiley Avenue" in 1893.

WILLISTON (Levy): For J. H. Willis, who established it sometime before 1885.

WILSON (Brevard): By and for the homesteader, James Wilson (1910 or 1912).

WILTON MANOR (Broward): For E. J. Willingham, who developed the area during the 1920s.

WINDLYS ISLAND (Monroe): For an old settler.

WOODALL (Dade): For an early settler.

WOODS (Liberty): For the Woods family (1905).

YELVINGTON (St. Johns): For the Yelvington family, early settlers.

YOUNGSTOWN (Bay): For the first settler, T. B. Young of Georgia, who distilled turpentine and manufactured rosin there.

ZELLWOOD (Orange): For Colonel T. Elwood Zell, who established the place in the 1870s and built his winter home there.

ZUBER (Marion): For the Zuber family.

❀ NAMES COMMEMORATING PLACES ❀
IN OTHER STATES

Alabama

ALABAMA HOLLOW (Santa Rosa): A stream.

ALABAMA JUNCTION (Manatee)

AUBURN (Bay): For the town where Alabama Polytechnic Institute is located. The founder, a Mr. Raffield, attended that university, they say.

California

BERKELEY (Polk)

CORONADO BEACH (Volusia)

HOLLYWOOD (Broward): Established in 1921 and called "Hollywood-by-the-Sea" by Joseph W. Young of California, who planned to establish here a moving picture colony like that in Hollywood, California.

PALO ALTO KEY (Monroe)

PASADENA (Pasco)

PASADENA (Pinellas)

PETALUMA (Dade)

SAN DIEGO RIVER (St. Johns)

SHASTA (Levy)

Colorado

DENVER (Putnam)

Connecticut

BRANFORD (Suwannee): Named by pioneer citizen Robert A. Ivey, close friend of Henry B. Plant, for Plant's former home, Branford, Connecticut. (Plant's rail business was closely linked with that of the river steamers that plied the Suwannee here in the nineteenth century.)

NORWALK (Putnam)

ONECO (Manatee)

WATERBURY (Manatee)

Delaware

DOVER (Hillsborough)

Georgia

LaGRANGE (Brevard)

MARIETTA (Duval)

MAXVILLE (Duval)

MUSCOGEE (Escambia): Established in 1870, and named for Muscogee County.

Illinois

PEORIA (Clay)

Indiana

VALPARAISO (Okaloosa): Named by John Perrine, who came here from Valparaiso, Indiana, about 1918. NEW VALPARAISO and VALPARAISO BAY are also in Okaloosa County.

Iowa

IOWA CITY (Seminole)

Kansas

GRAND RIDGE (Jackson)

Kentucky

BOWLING GREEN (Hardee): Named by a number of farmers from Bowling Green, Kentucky, who settled here in the 1880s. (Formerly "Utica.")
CYNTHIANA (Lake)

Louisiana

TULANE (Duval)
TULANE (Highlands)

Massachusetts

AUBURNDALE (Polk): By citizens from Auburndale, Massachusetts.
BLAKE (Volusia): For a settlement near Boston.
BUNKER HILL (Collier)
BUNKER HILL (Leon)
HARVARD (Gilchrist)
LONGWOOD (Seminole): For a district of Boston.
LOWELL (Marion)
LYNNE (Marion)
MOUNT PLYMOUTH (Lake)

Michigan

GRAND RAPIDS (Highlands)

KALAMAZOO (Volusia)
LANSING (De Soto)
NILES (Gulf)

Minnesota

MINNEOLA (Lake)

Missouri

MISSOURI KEY (Monroe): Named by a homesick worker on Flagler's overseas railroad.

Nebraska

NEBRASKA (Hillsborough)

New Hampshire

NASHUA (Putnam)

New Jersey

MONTCLAIR (Lake)
PRINCETON (Dade): Named by Gaston Drake and a group of Princeton University alumni, 1905.

New York

BUFFALO (Manatee)
CASSADAGA (Volusia)
ELMIRA (Gadsden)
HARLEM (Putnam)
LAKE BROOKLYN (Clay)
LAKE PLACID (Highlands)
MANHATTAN BEACH (Duval)
MURRAY HILL (Duval)
TARRYTOWN (Sumter)
WATERTOWN (Columbia)

North Carolina

GREENWOOD (Jackson)
PIEDMONT (Orange)
RALEIGH (Levy)

Ohio

OHIO KEY (Monroe): Named by a homesick worker on Flagler's overseas railroad.

TOLEDO (Indian River)

Oregon

UMATILLA (Lake)

Pennsylvania

ALTOONA (Lake)

ARIEL (Volusia): For Lake Ariel, Pennsylvania.

EMPORIA (Volusia): For Emporium, Pennsylvania, the origin of most of its early settlers.

ERIE (Manatee)

KEYSTONE HEIGHTS (Clay): Named in 1922 by J. J. Lawrence of Pittsburgh, for the "Keystone State." Originally called Brooklyn.

KEYSTONE PARK (Pasco)

MOHAWK (Lake): Some claim the village was named for the Mohawk River in New York.

South Carolina

GREENVILLE (Madison)

HAMBURG (Madison): Named by founder Samuel S. Hinton in 1840 for his former home in South Carolina.

NEWBERRY (Alachua)

Tennessee

CONASAUGA (Manatee): Possibly named from the river in Georgia instead.

HERMITAGE (Gadsden): For Andrew Jackson's home in Tennessee.

OCOEE (Orange)

TRENTON (Gilchrist): Renamed by Ben Boyd, a Confederate veteran, after his Tennessee home. Formerly called "Joppa." Gainesville's *Weekly Bee* (Gainesville was then in the same county) reported the new name on July 21, 1883, after it was changed to Trenton in April.

Texas

DALLAS (Marion)
WACO (Madison)

Vermont

VERMONT HEIGHTS (St. Johns)

Virginia

ARLINGTON (Duval): For the home of Robert E. Lee. (Established in 1868.)

LYNCHBURG (Polk)

MONTICELLO (Jefferson): For Thomas Jefferson's home in Virginia. This city, appropriately enough, is the county seat of Jefferson County. It sprang up during the first decade of American rule, apparently for the express purpose of serving as county seat. Jefferson's home, Monticello, served as model for the county courthouse. There is also a MONTICELLO JUNCTION in Jefferson County.

RICHMOND (Lake)

VERNON (Washington): For George Washington's home, Mount Vernon. (This village was once the county seat of Washington County.)

VIRGINIA KEY (Dade)

Washington

TACOMA (Alachua)

Wisconsin

WISCON (Hernando): A clipped version of "Wisconsin."

Uncertain Origins (and American "Stock" Names)

AUGUSTA (Hernando)

BRISTOL (Liberty): Nobody seems to know why the name of this county seat was changed to Bristol in 1859. (The post office had originally been called "Ridleysville" after the first postmaster, appointed in 1852.) It seems likely that it was named for the Bristol that straddles the Virginia-Tennessee line, for many settlers in the Liberty County area were from that mountain region.

CAIRO (Bay)

COLLEGE PARK (St. Johns)

CUMBERLAND SOUND (Nassau): Rather than commemorating another place, this name may be for William Augustus, duke of Cumberland, son of George II, who was a popular English hero before his death in 1765. The sound is in an area extensively named by the English.

DECATUR (Leon)

ENGLEWOOD (Sarasota)

HIWASSEE (Orange): This was the name of several extinct Cherokee settlements and possibly was transferred from Tennessee.

KEEWAYDIN KEYS (Collier): Assumed to be named either for the territory in Canada named *Keewatin,* or a village named *Keewaydin* in Pennsylvania. There is also a *Kewadin* (pronounced "Keewaydin") in Michigan.

LEXINGTON (Alachua)

SEDALIA (Gadsden)

SPRINGFIELD (Bay)

 NAMES COMMEMORATING PLACES
IN OTHER LANDS

British Colonies

GOLDSBORO (Seminole): For the African Gold Coast. (This is a Negro quarter, established in 1900.)

GRENADA (Hillsborough): Apparently for the colony in the British West Indies.

MALABAR (Brevard): Named in 1875 for the district in British India. CAPE MALABAR is also in Brevard County.

MELBOURNE (Brevard): Named by John Hector Cornwaith, an early settler and former resident of the Australian city. He wanted to name the place for Park Ridge, the Illinois home of a local girl he admired (or so the story goes), but she persuaded him to settle the matter by drawing straws; and she won. The town was established about 1878. Another story is that it was so named by the sea captain who was the town's first postmaster, because Melbourne, Australia, was the last port he had visited. There is also a MELBOURNE BEACH in Brevard.

NASSAU, NASSAU RIVER, NASSAU SOUND, NASSAUVILLE (all in Nassau County): For the capital of the Bahamas. This naming started with that of the Nassau River during the English period, for the area was settled by emigrants from the Bahamas.

TASMANIA (Glades): For the island off the coast of Australia.

TORONTO (Orange): Settled by Canadians and named for the capital of the province of Ontario.

TRINIDAD (Marion): For the island in the British West Indies.

England

ALBION (Levy): This is the poetic name for England.

AVON PARK (Highlands): For Stratford-on-Avon. Founded in 1885 by Oliver M. Crosby of New York and Mr. and Mrs. William King of England.

BRIGHTON (Highlands)

DEVON (Levy)

KENT (Nassau)

OXFORD (Sumter)

PLYMOUTH (Orange): Established by English people in 1925.

RUNNYMEDE (Osceola): Named for a hotel built here by an Englishman in the 1880s.

RYE (Manatee)

UPCO or UPCO HALL (Lee): Corrupted from "Upton Hall," the name of the home of its founder, William Pearde of England (1896).

WINDERMERE (Orange): For a town and lake in England's lake country, by John Dawe from England (1887). Orange County also has a WINDERMERE JUNCTION.

France

ALSACE (Manatee): For the French province.

BOULOGNE (Nassau): For the French city.

CHAMPAIGN (Madison): Said to be named for the Champagne region in France, despite the wrong spelling.

CLERMONT (Lake): For the birthplace of A. F. Wrotniski, general manager and treasurer of the company which established the town (ca. 1884). SOUTH CLERMONT, also in Lake County, is an offspring.

RIVIERA BEACH (Palm Beach): For the French Riviera because

a visitor remarked, "This is the Riviera of America." (Formerly called "Oak Lawn.")

ROCHELLE (Alachua): Presumably named (in 1884) for La Rochelle, in France, though no reason is known. One wonders if the abundance of limerock in the vicinity might be the answer. (French *roche* means "rock.") When established in 1850 by Madison Starke Perry, later governor of Florida, and others, the town had been given another French-flavored name, "Gruelle."

ST. CLOUD (Osceola): For the town in southern France which was the former residence of French monarchs.

Germany

BERLIN (Marion)

GOTHA (Orange): For the German city where H. A. Hempel, the founder, was born. (Established in 1878.)

MUNICH (Union)

NEW BERLIN (Duval): Named by Dr. von Balsom during the Civil War, for his home in Germany.

Ireland

CORK (Hillsborough)

DUBLIN (Lake)

DUBLIN (Taylor)

HIBERNIA (Clay): Settled by the Flemings of Ireland as a cotton plantation (1790). *Hibernia* is the poetic name for Ireland. (See "Fleming" in "Names Commemorating Men," this Appendix.)

IRELAND (Collier)

KILLARNEY (Orange): For the Killarney Lakes in Ireland (1878).

Italy

GENOA (Hamilton): Presumably for the birthplace of Columbus.

ITALIA (Nassau): Presumably for Italy because of the name's romantic appeal. Settled in 1881 by Colonel William MacWilliams, postmaster and brick manufacturer.

LAKE COMO (Putnam): For Lake Como in Lombardy, Italy, for romantic appeal.

NAPLES (Collier): For Naples, Italy, because of the similarity of the two areas. NORTH NAPLES is also in Collier.

RIALTO (Lee): For Venice's Rialto.

SALERNO (Martin): For the Italian seaport.

VENICE (Sarasota): For the Italian city because of topographical resemblance. VENICE INLET, also in Sarasota County, is an offspring.

VERO BEACH (Indian River): Said to be a shortened version of the name of Verona, Italy, though some say the name is somehow connected with Latin *veritas*, meaning "truth." It was originally called *Vero*. (Founded 1880.)

Portugal

LISBON (Lake): Established in 1854 by W. J. Alsobrook.

MADEIRA BEACH (Pinellas): Named by A. B. (Bert) Archibald, early Gulf Beach developer.

Russia

MOSCOW (Hillsborough): For the home of Russian Dr. F. N. Weightnovel, who served as mayor.

ST. PETERSBURG (Pinellas): For the home of Peter Demons (originally Demonschoff), president of the Orange Belt Railway and an associate of the founder. Demons is said to have won the privilege of naming the place by drawing straws with the founder, General John C. Williams (1875). There are also ST. PETERSBURG BEACH and ST. PETERSBURG WHARF.

Scotland

ABERDEEN (Jackson): For the chief city of North Scotland.

ARGYLE (Walton): For Argyll County in West Scotland. A Miss McDonald was postmaster the year the place was established (1883).

DUNDEE (Polk): For the town in Scotland.

DUNEDIN (Pinellas): For the Gaelic name of Edinburgh, Scotland, home of J. O. Douglass and James Somerville, who petitioned the government for a change of name at the time the post office was established there in 1878. (Formerly "Jonesboro" when it was established in the 1850s.)

INVERNESS (Citrus): For Inverness, Scotland, by an early Scottish settler.

IONA (Lee): For the historic island off the coast of Scotland by John and Donald Bain of Scotland, who established the place.

LANARK (Franklin): For a resort hotel built there in the 1890s and apparently named for Lanark, Scotland.

MELROSE (Alachua): Renamed for Melrose, Scotland, by a Scottish resident in 1882. (Previously called "Shakerag" for the pony-racing activity which characterized it; the starter waved a white cloth to get the ponies started.)

PAISLEY (Lake): Known earlier as "Lightwood," but renamed for Paisley in Scotland (ca. 1886).

PAISLEY (Marion)

SCOTLAND (Gadsden)

Spain

ANDALUSIA (Flagler): For the old division of southern Spain.

BISCAYNE BAY (Dade): Named by Spanish explorers for the Bay of Biscay, north of Spain, or else, as Fontaneda says, for a man called *El Biscaino* ("the Biscayan," from the Spanish province of Biscaya); in any case it commemorates a Spanish place. BISCAYNE, KEY BISCAYNE, and BISCAYNE KEY, all also in Dade, are variations.

CORDOVA (Pasco)

EBRO (Washington): For the river in Spain.

OVIEDO (Seminole): For the city in Spain. The name was selected in 1879 for its pleasant sound (though the Florida pronunciation—"O-veé-da"—does not preserve the Spanish "O-vyáy-do") and for its harmony with Florida's heritage.

PONTE VEDRA (St. Johns): Renamed for Pontevedra, Spain, in 1932, when a name was sought which would have a connection with the historic past. It was formerly "Mineral City," owned and developed by the National Lead Company. Not only is the name written differently from the original Spanish name (as if it were two words rather than one), but as one would expect, the pronunciation has suffered a change. Instead of "pōne-tay-váy-dra," as the Spaniards say it, Floridians say "pŏnta-veedra."

Switzerland

GENEVA (Clay), on LAKE GENEVA: For the Swiss city and lake.

GENEVA (Seminole): For the Swiss city because of its similar situation on a lake.

LUCERNE (Polk): For the Swiss city.

SWITZERLAND (St. Johns): For his native country by Francisco Philippe Fatio, settler, who had received a British land grant in 1772 and remained in Florida after the Spanish returned in 1784. He called his St. Johns River plantation "New Switzerland."

Miscellaneous Foreign Places

BELGIUM (De Soto)

BOHEMIA (Escambia): For the native home of a pioneer settler, Josephine Kapman Hyer.

DANIA (Broward): After their own country, by Danes from Wisconsin. The place was incorporated with this name in 1927, but was originally called *Modello* after the Florida East Coast Railroad's Model Land Company, which founded the community.

DANZIG (Walton)

FORMOSA (Orange)

HAVANA (Gadsden): For the Cuban city. The cultivation of Little Cuban Sun tobacco began in this area in 1829, and the town is said to have been named by an old schoolmaster because of it.

MEXICO (Pasco)

NATAL (Hernando)

NEW SMYRNA (Volusia): Named by Dr. Andrew Turnbull, who in 1767 obtained a grant from the British crown and established an unsuccessful colony of Greeks and Minorcans on this site. The name is for Smyrna, his wife's former home in Asia Minor.

NEW UPSALA (Seminole): For Uppsala, in Sweden, by General Henry S. Sanford, who brought 150 Swedes over to farm his land and settled them there (1872).

ORIENT PARK (Hillsborough): For the area east of the Mediterranean, of like climate.

OSLO (Indian River): For the capital of Norway.

PANAMA CITY (Bay): For the Canal Zone city because this place is on a direct line between Chicago and Panama City, Canal Zone, by George W. West, original developer. The present city is a 1925 consolidation of St. Andrew, Millville, and Panama City.

ROUMANIA (Glades)

SLAVIA (Seminole): For Yugoslavia by the Slavia Colony Company, which purchased the land and settled Yugoslavs upon it (1915).

SOUDAN (Polk): For the region in Africa, because this was a Negro settlement.

YAMATO (Palm Beach): For the province where the Empire of Japan was first begun and whose name is often applied by the Japanese to all Japan. This settlement was begun by fifty Japanese as an experiment in colonization.

ZANTE (Orange): This is the name of an Ionian island in the Mediterranean Sea.

Appendix B

Additional Descriptive Names

 ✿ FLORA ✿

Citrus Trees

CITRUS CENTER (Glades)

CITRUS PARK (Hillsborough)

FRUITVILLE and FRUITVILLE JUNCTION (Sarasota)

GROVE (Bay)

GROVE CITY (Charlotte)

GROVE PARK VISTA (Pinellas)

LEMON ISLAND (Marion)

MAMMOTH GROVE (Polk)

ORANGE (Liberty)

ORANGE (Manatee)

ORANGE AVENUE (Marion)

ORANGE BEND (Lake): Named because of wild orange groves and its location on a bend of Lake Griffin.

ORANGE CITY (Volusia): Originally known as "Wisconsin Settlement" for the settlers, but changed (1880) because of extensive orange groves. ORANGE CITY JUNCTION is also in Volusia County.

ORANGE DALE (St. Johns)

ORANGE HAMMOCK (Flagler)

ORANGE LAKE (Marion): A village situated on ORANGE LAKE.

ORANGE SPRINGS (Marion)

PORT ORANGE (Volusia)

SATSUMA HEIGHTS (Putnam)

TEMPLE TERRACE JUNCTION (Hillsborough): See TEMPLE TERRACE, chapter 4.

The Cypress Tree

BIG CYPRESS (Pasco)

BIG CYPRESS SWAMP (Collier)

BLUE CYPRESS CREEK (Indian River)

CYPRESS (Jackson)

CYPRESS CREEK (Calhoun)

CYPRESS GATE (Marion)

The Oak

EIGHT OAKS (Orange): For eight large oaks that grew there (1885).

GLENOAK (Pinellas)

GROVE PARK (Alachua): Surrounded by beautiful oak trees, which gave rise to the name (1883).

HARBOR OAKS (Volusia): On the coast and shaded by oaks. Also known as HARBOR POINT.

LONEOAK (Franklin)

OAK (Marion)

OAKDALE (Jackson)

OAKGROVE (Okaloosa)

OAK HILL (Alachua)

OAK HILL (Volusia): For the oak growing on a shell mound near the home of the first settler (1866).

OAKHURST (Pinellas)

OAK KNOLL (Manatee)

OAKLAND (Orange)

OAKLAND PARK (Broward)

OAKS (Polk)

OAKTON (Putnam)

OAK VEGETABLE (Marion)

OAKWOOD (Flagler)

SHADY GROVE (Taylor)

TWIN OAKS (Volusia): For the twin oaks in the garden of an early settler.

The Palm

COCOANUT BLUFF (Calhoun)
COCOANUT KEY (Monroe)
PALM (Hillsborough)
PALMA SOLA BAY (Manatee)
PALM BAY (Brevard)
PALM BEACH, PALM BEACH HARBOR, WEST PALM BEACH, WEST PALM BEACH CANAL (Palm Beach)
PALM COAST (Flagler): A gigantic planned community now under construction, slated for completion by the year 2000—one of those Florida developments always dear to the hearts of promoters and profiteers, but increasingly disturbing to lovers of the Florida environment. A hundred thousand acres of virgin land is being cleared of its growth to accommodate this project and some Floridians are not certain that the days of pirates are over.
PALMDALE (Glades)
PALMETTO BEACH (Escambia)
PALMETTO JUNCTION (Manatee)
PALMGROVE (Taylor)
PALM HARBOR (Pinellas)
PALM RIVER (Hillsborough)
PALM SPRINGS (Seminole)
PALM VALLEY (St. Johns)
PALMVIEW (Manatee)
PALM VILLA (Seminole)
ROYAL PALM PARK (Collier)

The Pine

BIG PINE ISLAND (Dixie)
BIG PINE KEY (Monroe): The only one of the Florida Keys to be heavily forested with pine trees. Pines on other Keys were long ago drowned out by saltwater from hurricane tides, but Big Pine is on higher ground. There is also LITTLE PINE KEY.
GULF PINE (Pasco)
INWOOD (Jackson): This place is in the midst of a pine forest.
OLD PINE LEVEL (De Soto)
PINE (Escambia)
PINE (Marion)

PINE BARREN, PINE BARREN CREEK, and LITTLE PINE BARREN
CREEK (Escambia)
PINE CITY (Pinellas)
PINE CREEK (Calhoun)
PINE FOREST (Escambia)
PINEHURST (St. Johns)
PINE ISLAND, PINE ISLAND SOUND, and LITTLE PINE ISLAND (Lee)
PINE ISLANDS (Monroe)
PINE KEY (Pinellas)
PINELAND (Lee)
PINELAND (Taylor)
PINE LEVEL (Manatee)
PINELLAS, PINELLAS PARK, and POINT PINELLAS (Pinellas)
PINE LOG (Bay) and PINE LOG CREEK (Bay and Washington)
PINE LOG CREEK (Okaloosa and Walton)
PINEMOUNT (Suwannee)
PINEVILLE (Escambia)
PINEWOOD (Santa Rosa)
PINEY POINT (Manatee)

Miscellaneous Plants and Trees

AGRICOLA (Polk): The Latin word for "agriculturist," or
"farmer."

ALAFIA (Hillsborough): There is convincing evidence that this
name is from the Creek *Thlafi* ("hunting"), with the locative
prefix "A," the whole being a near equivalent of the English
"Hunting Place." But one authority on Florida place-names of
Indian origin doubts that the name is of Indian derivation at
all. He says it is possibly from the Spanish word *alafia*, designating members of the dogbane family, the oleander and
periwinkle, which grow profusely in Florida. The Federal
Writers' Project, too, equates the name with "Sp., Oleander."
Alafia also means "grace" or "pardon" in Spanish. The town
is named from the ALAFIA RIVER (Polk and Hillsborough
counties).

ALAQUA CREEK (Walton): A corruption of the Seminole-Creek
hilukwa, "sweet gum." (The sweet gum is a tree growing
abundantly in this and other sections of Florida.) There is
also LITTLE ALAQUA CREEK in this county.

ALVA (Lee): For a small white flower which the Danish founder
saw growing there (1884).

ANONA (Pinellas): For *Annona reticulata*, the custard apple, fruit of a small West Indian tree growing in Pinellas County, along the Florida west coast, and in the Everglades.

BAMBOO KEY (Monroe)

BAY HILL (Sumter)

BAY RIDGE (Orange)

BAYWOOD (Putnam)

BUCKEYE and BUCKEYE CREEK (Escambia)

BUCK HORN (Gulf): For a tree near it in the river that resembles the horns of a deer.

CASSIA (Lake): Probably for the Chinese cinnamon or cassia bark tree, which resembles the camphor tree, conspicuous in Florida.

CATAWBA (Santa Rosa): For the Catawba grapes cultivated in this section.

CHASSAHOWITZKA (Citrus): A village, a short broad stream, and a bay. See CHASSAHOWITZKA, chapter 4.

CHERRY LAKE and CHERRY LAKE FARMS (Madison)

CITRONELLE (Citrus): For the citrons cultivated here.

CORN BLUFF (Calhoun)

COTTON BLUFF (Calhoun)

COTTONDALE (Jackson)

DELLWOOD (Jackson)

ELDERBERRY (Glades)

ELMWOOD (Marion)

FARMTON (Volusia)

FERNCLIFF (Palm Beach)

FERNDALE (Lake)

FORESTERS POINT (Putnam)

FORT KISSIMMEE (Okeechobee): See KISSIMMEE, chapter 4, for an explanation of this name and those of KISSIMMEE LAKE (Osceola), KISSIMMEE RIVER (Osceola, Highlands, Okeechobee, and Glades), and KISSIMMEE PARK (Osceola).

GLENWOOD (Volusia)

GLENWOOD TERRACE (Highlands)

GREENACRES CITY (Palm Beach)

GREEN COVE SPRINGS (Clay): The St. Johns River forms a curve at this point, sheltered by trees. In addition there are sulphur springs located here.

GREEN CREEK (Clay)

GREENFIELD (Pasco)

GREENHEAD (Washington)

GREEN POND (Polk)

GUM CREEK (Bradford, Holmes, Jefferson, Okaloosa, Putnam, Walton, Washington): For the sweet gum tree, which grows extensively in northern and central Florida.

HICKORIA (Highlands): Also spelled HICORIA.

HOMOSASSA (Citrus): From the Seminole-Creek *homo* ("pepper") and *sasi* ("is there"), designating a place where wild pepper grows. Also HOMOSASSA RIVER and HOMOSASSA SPRINGS (Citrus).

ISLAND GROVE (Alachua)

ITCHEPUCKESASSA RIVER (Hillsborough): From Creek *hichi* ("tobacco"), plus *pakpaki* ("blossoms"), plus *sasi* ("to be there"), thus "where there are tobacco blossoms."

JUNIPER CREEK, EAST and WEST (Okaloosa)

LAKE FERN (Hillsborough)

LAKE GRASSY (Highlands)

LAKE GROVE (Gulf)

LAUREL HILL (Okaloosa)

MAPLE CREEK (Hillsborough)

NUT (Calhoun)

OCHOPEE (Collier): Possibly Seminole-Creek for "hickory tree" (*ochi-api*), but uncertain. May be from Seminole-Creek *chapofa* ("field"). Postmaster Sidney H. Brown understands it to mean "Big Farm," while others have said it means "Big Field." The town sprang up in the early 1930s and at the time it secured a post office, in 1932, was the largest settlement in Collier County. Now it is distinguished for having the smallest post office building in the nation—a former tool shed 7'3" x 8'4", with room for only one customer at a time.

PEACH ORCHARD (Alachua)

PECAN (Putnam)

PLANTATION and PLANTATION KEY (Monroe)

PLEASANT GROVE (Escambia)

POPLAR DELL (Escambia)

PUMPKIN KEY (Monroe)

RED BAY (Walton)

REEDY BRANCH (Santa Rosa, Escambia, Liberty, and Washington)

REEDY CREEK (Walton, Holmes, Okaloosa, Santa Rosa, Polk, Calhoun, Bay, Escambia)

RICE CREEK (Putnam): Rice is thought to have been grown there by the Indians.

SAWGRASS LAKE (Brevard)

SEAGROVE (Walton)

SHADY (Marion)

SOUTH MULBERRY (Polk)

SPRUCEBLUFF (St. Lucie)

SUGARLOAF (Monroe): On SUGARLOAF KEY, named for the sugar-loaf pineapples once cultivated there.

SUMATRA (Gadsden): For the Sumatra tobacco grown there.

SUMATRA (Liberty)

SYCAMORE (Gadsden)

SYLVAN LAKE (Seminole)

TALUGA RIVER (Liberty): Possibly shortened and corrupted from Seminole *talaka chapco* ("cow peas"). Seems related to TELOGIA, below.

TELOGIA (Liberty): According to one authority, this name is probably a corruption of TALUGA, above; but according to another it is composed of Creek *tala* ("palm") and *chee* ("little"). Gadsden County has a TELOGIA CREEK.

THISTLE (Manatee)

TITIE CREEK (Okaloosa): For the titie flower.

VEGETABLE (Manatee)

VINELAND (Charlotte)

WILLOW (Manatee)

WILLOW ISLAND (Osceola)

WONDERWOOD (Duval)

WOODLAND (St. Johns)

WOODMERE (Sarasota)

❁ FAUNA ❁

Reptiles, Insects, and Animals

Bear

BEAR BAY BRANCH (Walton)

BEAR BAY CREEK (Washington)

BEAR BRANCH (Okaloosa, Santa Rosa, Liberty, Walton, and De Soto)

BEAR CREEK (Bay, Franklin, Gadsden, Okaloosa, Pasco, Santa Rosa, Seminole, Walton)

BEAR GULLEY CREEK (Seminole)
BEAR HEAD (Walton)
BEAR ISLAND (Flagler)
BEARS CUT (Dade)
BEAR TREE (Marion)
LOKOSEE (Osceola): From the Seminole *lokose* ("bear"), derived from the Creek *nokose* ("bear").
NARCOOSSEE (Osceola): From the Creek *nokose* ("bear"). Named by a railroad official.

Beaver

ECHASHOTEE RIVER (Pasco): From Seminole-Creek *echas* ("beaver"), plus *hute* ("house" or "den").

Bee

BEE BRANCH (Hardee, Holmes, Hendry, Okaloosa, Walton)

Cats

CAT ISLAND (Dixie)
KOSTA or TIGER LAKE (Polk): *Kosta* is of Seminole-Creek derivation, from *kacha*, meaning "panther."
TIGER BAY (Polk)
TIGER TAIL HAMMOCK (Wakulla)

Cow

BOVINE (Brevard)
COW BRANCH (Putnam, Pinellas)
COW CREEK (Franklin, Jefferson, Levy, Volusia, Wakulla)
COWHAM (Citrus)
COWHEAD CREEK (Duval)
COWHIDE CREEK (Escambia)
COW LOG BRANCH (Indian River)
COW PEN BRANCH (Okaloosa)
COW PEN SLOUGH (Sarasota)
WACASASSA RIVER (Levy): From Seminole *wacca* ("cow" or "cattle"), plus *sasi* ("there are")—thus "Where there are cattle" or "cattle range."

Deer

BUCK (Escambia)
BUCKHORN CREEK (Wakulla)
BUCK KEY (Monroe)
DEER CREEK (Nassau)
DEERFIELD BEACH (Broward)
DEER ISLAND (Levy)
DEER LAKE (Hillsborough)
DEERLAND (Okaloosa)
DEER PARK (Hillsborough)
DEER PRAIRIE SLOUGH (Sarasota)
DEERS ISLAND (Pasco)
DEERS RUN (Putnam)
NORTH DEERFIELD (Palm Beach)

Fox

CHULUOTA (Seminole): Probably from Seminole *chula* ("fox"), plus *huti* ("den"), though there is some feeling that Creek *chule* ("pine"), plus *eto* ("tree"), or *ote* ("island"), may be the source of the compound.
FOX POINT (Franklin)

Manatee

EAST MANATEE (Manatee)
LITTLE MANATEE (Manatee)
LITTLE MANATEE RIVER (Hillsborough)
MANATEE (Manatee)
MANATEE RIVER (Manatee)

Otter

OTTER BRANCH (Walton)
OTTER CREEK (Bay, Calhoun, Citrus, Holmes, Lafayette, Wakulla)
OTTER ISLAND (Manatee)

Rabbit

CUBEE SWAMP (Jefferson): Possibly derived from the Creek *chufa* ("rabbit").

RABBIT ISLAND (Osceola)
RABBIT KEY (Monroe)

Raccoon

RACCOON KEY (Monroe)

Turtle (Land and Sea)

GOPHER RIDGE (St. Johns)
LOCHAPOPKA LAKE (Polk): From Seminole-Creek *locha* ("turtle"), plus *papka* ("eating place").
LOCHLOOSA (Alachua): Possibly from Choctaw *luksi* ("terrapin"), plus *lusa* ("black"), giving "black terrapin." But because of early spellings there is some doubt of this. The town is named for the nearby LOCHLOOSA LAKE.
LOGGERHEAD KEY (Monroe): For the loggerhead turtles found there.
LOXAHATCHEE (Palm Beach): A river and a town, the name from Seminole-Creek *locha* ("turtle"), and *hachi* or *hatchee* ("river").

Wolf

WOLF BRANCH (Walton, Liberty, and Lake)
WOLF CREEK (Osceola): Once called by the Indian name *Ya-ha Hatchee*, which means in Creek "Wolf Creek" or "Wolf River." There are other WOLF CREEKS in Florida also—in Walton, Brevard, Jefferson, and Santa Rosa counties.
WOLF SINK (Levy)
WOLF TRAP BRANCH (Santa Rosa)
YEEHAW (Indian River): From Seminole-Creek *yaha* ("wolf").

Birds

CUCKOO POINT (St. Johns)
CURLEW (Pinellas)
DOVE KEY (Monroe)
DUCK KEY and LITTLE DUCK KEY (Monroe)
EAGLE BAY (Okeechobee)
EAGLE KEY (Monroe)
EAGLE LAKE (Polk)

FLAMINGO (Orange): For the gorgeously plumed aquatic bird which is not native to Florida but has been brought here from tropical islands similar in climate to parts of Florida.

GULL POINT (Escambia)

HILOLO (Okeechobee): From the Seminole-Creek *alola* ("long-billed curlew").

LAKE BIRD (Taylor)

OPAL (Okeechobee): Said to be derived from the Creek *opa* ("owl").

ORTEGA CREEK (Duval): See ORTEGA, chapter 4.

OSOWAW and OSOWAW JUNCTION (Okeechobee): From Seminole-Creek *osahwa* ("crow").

OSPREY (Sarasota)

PARROT CREEK (Holmes)

PELICAN (Palm Beach): Also called PELICAN POINT.

PELICAN ISLAND (Volusia)

PELICAN KEY (Monroe)

PELICAN LAKE (Palm Beach)

PENNAWA CREEK (Osceola): From the Creek *pinwa* ("turkey").

PENNICHAW (Volusia): Possibly from Seminole-Creek *pinhachi* ("turkey tail").

PIGEON KEY (Monroe)

TOTOSAHATCHEE CREEK (Orange): From Seminole-Creek *totolosi* ("chicken"), plus *hachi* ("creek").

TURKEY CREEK (Baker, Brevard, Hillsborough, Liberty, Marion, Okaloosa, Orange, Santa Rosa, Seminole, Union, Walton)

TURKEY HEN CREEK (Okaloosa)

TURKEY LAKE (Orange)

TURKEY SLOUGH (Okeechobee)

Fishes

BOGIE CHANNEL (Monroe): Between Big Pine Key and No Name Key; said to be named for a fish common in the West Indies which early settlers in the area caught. No present-day fishermen have ever heard of bogies, though they may still be catching the fish under a different name.

CHARLIE APOPKA CREEK (Hardee): A corruption (or folk etymology) of Seminole-Creek *tsala apopka* or *chalo papka* ("trout eating place"). Note other *apopka* names and see discussion of APOPKA in chapter 4. TSALA APOPKA LAKE (Citrus) has the same derivation and meaning as CHARLIE APOPKA CREEK. It has been shown on early maps as *Lake Charley Apopka.*

CLAMBAR (Manatee)

FISHEATING CREEK (Highlands and Glade): A translation from the Seminole-Creek name, which was another *apopka* example, *Thlath-to-popka-hatchee.*

FISHWEIR CREEK (St. Johns)

MULLET KEY (Manatee)

MUSCLE CREEK (Marion): Probably a misspelling of *mussel,* designating a freshwater clam.

OYSTER BAY (Monroe)

PEPPERFISH KEYS (Dixie)

SEAHORSE KEY (Levy)

SOUTH POMPANO (Broward): See POMPANO BEACH, chapter 4.

TARPON and TARPON JUNCTION (Hillsborough)

TARPON BAY (Lee)

TARPON SPRINGS (Pinellas): There is a fresh-water spring bayou in the heart of this town, which is situated on the Gulf of Mexico, whose warm waters are hospitable to the tarpon fish.

TROUT (Palm Beach)

TROUT CREEK (Charlotte, Franklin, Hillsborough, Lee, Walton)

TROUT LAKE (Highlands)

TROUT RIVER (Duval)

 OTHER DESCRIPTIVE PLACE-NAMES

Saltwater Names

ATLANTIC BEACH HEIGHTS (Brevard)

BAHIA (Brevard): The Spanish word for "bay."

BAYBORO (Pinellas)

BAY HARBOR (Bay)

BAY HARBOR ISLANDS (Dade)

BAYHEAD (Bay)

BAYOU (Santa Rosa)

BAYPORT (Hernando)

BAYSHORE (Lee)

BAY SPRINGS (Escambia)

BAYVIEW (Lee)

BAYVIEW (Pinellas)

BEACON BEACH (Bay)

BRIDGEPORT (Pinellas)

CAYO AGUA KEY (Monroe): *Cayo Agua* means, in Spanish, "water key."

EAST BAHIA HONDA KEY and WEST BAHIA HONDA KEY (Monroe): See BAHIA HONDA, chapter 4.

ESTERO BAY, ESTERO ISLAND, and ESTERO RIVER (Lee): Named from the Spanish word for "inlet" or "estuary."

GULF BEACH (Escambia)

GULF COAST JUNCTION (Hillsborough)

HARBOR VIEW (Charlotte)

HARBOR VIEW (Pinellas)

INLET BEACH (Bay)

INTERBAY (Hillsborough): Meaning "between bays."

LIGHTHOUSE POINT (Franklin)

NEW FOUND HARBOR KEYS (Monroe)

OCEAN RIDGE (Palm Beach)

PILOT TOWN (Duval)

PORTLAND (Walton)

SALINE (Charlotte): Meaning "salty."

SALT SPRINGS (Pasco)

SHOREACRES (Pinellas)

SOUTHPORT (Bay)

SURFSIDE (Dade)

WAVELAND (Martin)

WAVELAND (St. Lucie)

WEST HARBOR KEY (Monroe)

Freshwater Names

BIG RED WATER LAKE (Highlands)

BLACKWATER CREEK (Hillsborough, Lake)

BLACKWATER RIVER (Santa Rosa)

BLUE CREEK JUNCTION (Taylor)

BLUE POND (Clay)

BLUE RUN (Marion)

BLUE SPRINGS (Marion)

BOILING CREEK (Santa Rosa)

BRIDGEND (Seminole)

BROADBRANCH (Calhoun)

CANAL BASIN, CANAL CROSS, and CANAL POINT (Palm Beach)

CAUSEWAY COMMUNITY (Hillsborough)

CLEARWATER HARBOR, CLEARWATER KEYS, and LITTLE CLEAR-WATER PASS (Pinellas)

COLDWATER (Santa Rosa): On COLDWATER RIVER, for which the town was named. Also in Santa Rosa are EAST FORK COLD-WATER CREEK and WEST FORK COLDWATER CREEK.

CROOKED CREEK (Bay)

CRYSTAL BEACH (Pinellas)

CRYSTAL LAKE (Washington)

CRYSTAL RIVER (Citrus): A town on CRYSTAL RIVER from which it takes its name. CRYSTAL BAY is also in Citrus County.

CRYSTAL SPRINGS (Pasco)

DEEP BOTTOM CREEK (Duval)

DEEP BRANCH (Wakulla)

DEEP CREEK (Columbia, Nassau, Putnam, St. Johns, Volusia)

DEEP HEAD BRANCH (Walton)

DEEP LAKE (Collier)

EASTLAKE (Marion)

ECONFINA (Bay): Near the ECONFINA RIVER, which rises in Jackson County and flows through Washington and Bay counties. The name is from the Creek *ekana* ("earth") and *feno* ("bridge") and may be translated as "Natural Bridge." ECONFINA SPRINGS is also in Bay County.

ECONFINA (Taylor): On a Taylor County ECONFINA RIVER (name translated above).

ECONLOCKHATCHEE RIVER (Orange): From Creek *ekana* ("earth"), plus *laiki* ("mound"), plus *hatchee* ("creek")—"Earth Mound Creek." There is also LITTLE ECONLOCKHATCHEE CREEK (Seminole).

EDGEWATER (Escambia, Hernando, Volusia) and EDGEWATER JUNCTION (Volusia)

EQUALOXIE CREEK (Liberty): Believed to be the same as *Wepolokse*, a Seminole word derived from Creek *wewa* ("water") and *polokse* ("round") and meaning "round water" or "pond."

FAHKAHATCHEE (Collier): The name of a bay, a swamp, and a river in this county, formed from Creek *fakka* ("clay" or "mud") and *hatchee* ("creek"), giving "Mud Creek." FAHKA-HATCHEOCHEE RIVER, also in Collier, has the ending *ochee*, making the diminutive of FAHKAHATCHEE, "Little Mud Creek."

LAKE CITY JUNCTION (Columbia)

LAKEMONT (Orange)

LAKE OF THE HILLS (Polk)

LAKE PARK (Lake)

LAKE PARK (Palm Beach)

LAKE PORT (Glades): Also spelled LAKEPORT.

LAKESIDE (Hendry)

LAKEWOOD (Walton)

LAKE VIEW (Broward)

LAKE VIEW (Hillsborough)

LAKE VILLA (Pinellas): Also written LAKEVILLA.

LAND O' LAKES (Pasco)

MIOMI LAKE (Sumter): Possibly a corruption from Seminole *Wyoma*, meaning "bitter water," or "whiskey."

NATURAL BRIDGE (Leon)

OCHLOCKONEE (Gadsden, Liberty, Leon, Wakulla, and Franklin): This is the name of a river, of two or three settlements, and of the bay into which the river flows (in Franklin County). The name means "Yellow Water" and is from Hitchiti *oki* ("water") and *lakni* ("yellow"). Despite its official spelling, the name is locally pronounced "Oh-clock-ny," omitting notice of the third *o*.

OKALOACOOCHEE SLOUGH (Hendry and Collier): Meaning "Little Bad Water." From Hitchiti *oki* ("water"), plus Creek *holwaki* ("bad"), plus *uchi* ("little"). Probably an appropriate name for the stagnant water of a slough.

OKHAKONKONHEE LAKE (Polk): From Hitchiti *oki* ("water"), plus Creek *ekan* ("land"), plus Creek *kunke* ("crooked")—thus "Crooked Land Water."

POND CREEK (Santa Rosa)

POND CREEK (Walton)

RED BEACH LAKE (Highlands): For the red clay forming part of its shore.

RIO (Martin): Spanish for "river."

RIVER (Wakulla)

RIVER BRIDGE (Indian River)

RIVERDALE (St. Johns)

RIVERLAND (Hernando)

RIVERSIDE (Calhoun, Dade, Putnam, Washington)

RIVERVIEW (Hillsborough)

SHOAL RIVER CREEK (Okaloosa)

SHOALS (Walton)

SHOALS RIVER (Walton and Okaloosa)

SILVER RIVER (Marion)

SILVER SPRINGS (Marion)

SPRING CREEK (Jackson)

SPRING CREEK (Lee)

SPRINGDALE (Taylor)

SPRING GARDEN (Volusia)

SPRING GLEN (Duval)

SPRING HILL (Clay)

SPRING HILL (Hernando)

SPRINGHILL (Leon)

SPRING LAKE (Clay and Hernando)

SPRING PARK (Marion)

SPRINGSIDE (Putnam)

SWEETWATER (Dade, De Soto, Hardee)

SWEETWATER BRANCH (Alachua, Flagler, Okeechobee, Walton)

SWEETWATER CREEK (Bay, Calhoun, Duval, Flagler, Hillsborough, Leon, Liberty, Putnam, Santa Rosa, Seminole, St. Johns)

SWIFT CREEK (Union)

WECHYAKAPKA LAKE (Polk): From Creek *we* ("water") and *ayakapeta* ("to walk in")—hence "Lake Walk-in-the-Water."

WEEKIWACHEE RIVER (Hernando): From *wekiwa* (see WEKIVA) for "spring" and *chi*, meaning "little"—thus "Little Spring."

WEKIVA: The name of a tributary of the St. Johns on the boundary between Seminole and Lake counties; of a lake near Orlando (Orange); of a settlement in Orange County; of a spring in Orange County; and of a spring and stream in Levy County. Sometimes spelled WEKIWA, which is the Creek for "spring of water."

WELAUNEE CREEK (Jefferson): From Creek *we* ("water") and *lane* ("yellow") or "Yellow Water."

WETAPPO CREEK (Gulf): From Creek *we* ("water"), plus *tapho* ("broad"), giving "Broad Water."

WETUMPKA (Gadsden): From Creek *we* ("water"), plus *tamka* ("sounding"), meaning "Sounding Water." (It should be noted here that this name may be an imported one, for it is not truly descriptive of the community to which it is applied in Gadsden County. A city in Elmore County, Alabama, near the falls of the Cousa River, bears the same name.)

WEWAHITCHKA (Gulf): A name given with the idea that it means "water eyes," because a pair of eyes is formed of two oblong lakes along the town's edges. It actually derives from Creek *wewa* ("water"), plus *ahechka* ("view" or "prospect") and thus means "water view."

WHITEWATER BAY and WHITEWATER LAKE (Monroe): From an Indian name of the same meaning.

YELLOW WATER CREEK (Clay)

Natural Beauties and Climatic Advantages

BONITA SPRINGS (Lee): The diminutive of Spanish *bueno* ("good"), signifying "pretty."

BUENA VISTA (Dade): Spanish for "good view" or "beautiful view."

CHARM (Seminole)

CONTENT KEY (Monroe)

FAIRMOUNT (Citrus)

FAIRVILLA (Orange): Also called FAIRYVILLA.

FROSTPROOF and WEST FROSTPROOF (Polk)

GRAND VIEW (Lake)

HIALEAH (Dade): Of Seminole-Creek origin, from *haiyakpo* ("prairie"), plus *hili* ("pretty")—thus "pretty prairie," says one source. Another notes that the name appears to be an extended version of Miccosukee *Hiatlee* ("prairie").

MANALAPAN (Palm Beach): Said to be an Indian word meaning "good bread" or "good country."

MOUNT PLEASANT (Gadsden)

MOUNT PLEASANT CREEK (Duval)

OASIS (Polk)

OZONA (Pinellas): Connoting fresh, pure air.

PARADISE (Alachua): This name of approbation, while doubtless expressing the vision of those who selected it, is not truly descriptive of the rather drab little settlement which it designated, though the natural features necessary for the establishment of a paradise were all about. The community itself is hardly noticeable now since superhighways have been built through and around it.

PLEASANT HILL (Osceola)

RICHLAND (Pasco)

RICHLOAM (Hernando)

SALVISTA (Lee): This name is reported to mean "healthy view" (from Spanish *salud*, meaning "healthy," and *vista*, meaning "view"), but it should be noted that it could well mean "salt view" or "salty view," from equally good derivations ("salt" in Spanish is *sal*). The spelling SALIVISTA, sometimes used, rather confirms the latter interpretation.

SCENIC HIGHLANDS and SCENIC HIGHWAY (Polk and Highlands)

SHEEN LAKE (Orange)

SUMMER HAVEN (St. Johns)

SUPERIOR (Marion)

TREASURE ISLAND (Pinellas)

VILLA RICA (Palm Beach): Spanish for "rich town."

WEST SUMMERLAND KEY (Monroe)

Location Names

CENTER PARK (Duval)

CENTRAL (Gilchrist)

CENTRAL CITY (Liberty)

COUNTY LINE (Jackson)

EAST BAY and WEST BAY (Bay)

EAST BAY (Franklin, Santa Rosa)

EAST PASS and WEST PASS (Franklin)

EASTPOINT (Franklin)

EAST RIVER (Santa Rosa and Okaloosa)

EAST RIVER (Wakulla)

EXCELSIOR PARK (Polk): The place is on the ridge, or elevated section, of Florida.

MIDDLEBURG (Clay)

MIDDLE CAPE and NORTH WEST CAPE (Monroe)

MIDDLE CREEK (Broward)

MIDLAND (Polk)

NORTH BAY (Bay)

NORTH BAY (Dade)

NORTH BEACH and SOUTH BEACH (St. Johns): The latter is south of St. Augustine.

NORTH KEY (Levy)

NORTH RIVER (St. Johns): Because it is north of St. Augustine.

NORTHWEST CHANNEL (Monroe)

SIX MILE CREEK (St. Johns): Supposed to be six miles from St. Augustine.

SOUTH BAY (Palm Beach)

SOUTHBORO (Palm Beach)

SOUTH CAPE (Franklin)

SOUTH FORT (De Soto)

SOUTH NEW RIVER CANAL (Broward)

SOUTHSIDE (Dade): The first post office was on the south side of the river. This place is now part of Miami.

SOUTHSIDE (Marion)

SOUTHWEST CAPE (Franklin)

TEN MILE CREEK (Holmes): One claim is that it is ten miles from Bonifay, but like other "mile" creeks, of which there are many in Florida, it does not justify its name in any clear way.

WEST GATE (Palm Beach): At the western entrance to West Palm Beach.

And Still Others

ACLINE (Charlotte): Signifying "without inclination," thus a flat place.

ALACHUA, EAST ALACHUA, and WEST ALACHUA (Alachua): See ALACHUA COUNTY, chapter 2.

ALTURAS (Polk): Spanish for "heights."

BARE BEACH (Palm Beach)

BIG BAYOU (Pinellas)

BIG SLOUGH CREEK (Sarasota)

BLACK CREEK (Liberty, Walton)

BLACKCREEK (Leon)

BLACK POINT (Dade, Duval, Flagler, Okaloosa): The name of the Duval County "Black Point" is translated from the Spanish name for the place: *Punta Negra*.

BLIND CREEK (Hernando)

BLOODY BLUFF (Franklin)

BLUFF (Putnam)

BLUFF CREEK (Union)

BLUFF SPRINGS (Escambia)

BOCA GRANDE, SOUTH (Lee): See BOCA GRANDE, chapter 4.

BOCA RATON, NORTH (Palm Beach): See BOCA RATON, chapter 4.

BOCILLA PASS (Charlotte): Obviously related to BOCILLA ISLAND, discussed in chapter 4.

BOGGY (Escambia)

BOGGY BRANCH (Duval, Clay, Highlands, Hillsborough, Liberty, Okeechobee, Polk, Santa Rosa, Walton)

BOGGY CREEK (Bay, Escambia, Hillsborough, Manatee, Nassau, Orange, Osceola, Taylor)

BOGGY HOLLOW CREEK (Okaloosa)

BOGGY POINT (Okaloosa)

BRANDY CREEK (Nassau)

BROAD CREEK (Monroe)

CAPE BLANCO (Lee): *Blanco* means "white" in Spanish.

CAYO COSTA (Lee): Spanish for "coast key."

CHIPOLA (Calhoun): Named for the CHIPOLA RIVER. The meaning is uncertain; it is said by some to mean "upstream" but others say it is from the Chatot dialect (now lost) and compare it to Choctaw *champuli*, meaning "sweet"; CHIPOLA LANDING is an offspring.

CHOKOLOSKEE (Collier): From Seminole-Creek *chuko* ("house"), plus *liski* ("old").

CHUCCOCHARTS HAMMOCK (Hernando): From Seminole-Creek *chuko* ("house"), plus *chati* ("red"), the name of the hammock being taken from that of an Indian town, in which the houses were daubed with red clay.

COMPASS LAKE (Jackson): A settlement named for LAKE COMPASS, which is round like a compass. Also, NORTH COMPASS LAKE is in Jackson.

CORKSCREW RIVER (Monroe)

COTTAGE HILL (Escambia)

CRESCENT BEACH (St. Johns): For the shape of the beach.

CRESCENT CITY (Putnam): For the shape of a nearby lake.

CRESTVIEW (Okaloosa): On top of a hill.

CROOKED CREEK (Gadsden)

CROOKED ISLAND (Bay)

CROOKED RIVER (Franklin)

CROSS CITY (Dixie): Two public roads crossed at this point—one from Perry to Old Archer and the other from Branford to Horseshoe. W. H. Matthis conferred the name.

CROWN POINT (Orange): Because the land forms a point into Lake Apopka here.

DELRAY, NORTH (Palm Beach): An offspring of DELRAY BEACH, chapter 4.

DOUBLESINK (Levy): So named because there are two natural "sinks" (sinkholes) there.

DRY CREEK (Jackson): So named because it went dry in dry seasons.

EVERGLADES (Collier): A town at the western edge of the EVER-GLADES, which term is discussed in chapter 2 under GLADES

COUNTY. There are also PORT EVERGLADES and PORT EVER-GLADES JUNCTION (Broward), GLADECREST (Palm Beach), GLADES (Dade), and GLADEVIEW (Palm Beach).

FALLING CREEK (Columbia)

FLAT CREEK (Gadsden)

FLINT ROCK (Jefferson)

FORT BARRANCAS (Escambia): Derived from the Spanish "broken ground."

GLENDALE (Walton)

GRAND ISLAND (Lake): Not really an island, but so named because the village was almost surrounded by water (it was between Lake Yale and Lake Eustis) at the time it was established.

GUANO CREEK (St. Johns)

GULLY BRANCH (Franklin, Gadsden, Hillsborough, Leon, Liberty, Okaloosa)

GULLY CREEK (Liberty)

HALF WAY HOUSE (Escambia): Halfway between Pensacola and the Navy Yard.

HAMMOCK (Hernando)

HAMMOCK (Seminole)

HAMMOCK CREEK (Pasco)

HAMMOCK GROVE (Osceola)

HAMMOCK RIDGE (Alachua)

HICPOCHEE LAKE (Glades): From Seminole-Creek *haiyakpo* ("prairie"), and *chi* ("little").

HIGHLAND (Clay): So named because its altitude is considerably higher than that of adjacent villages.

HIGHLAND CITY and HIGHLAND PARK (Polk)

HILLCREST HEIGHTS (Polk)

HILLSIDE (Citrus)

HINTERLAND (Okeechobee)

HOMELAND (Polk)

HOMESTEAD (Dade): When the twentieth century was new, this area was known as "the homestead country" because the pineland was owned by the federal government and open to homesteaders.

HURRICANE CREEK (Holmes): Because it is a turbulent creek.

HYPOLUXO (Palm Beach): From Seminole *hapo* ("mound"), plus *poloksi* ("round").

INDIAN FORD (Santa Rosa): Where the railroad crosses a branch of Sweetwater Creek.

INDIAN PASS (Gulf): A pass or lagoon between the mainland and St. Vincent's Island.

INDIAN ROCKS BEACH (Pinellas): Because of large red rocks along the shore.

INDIAN SPRINGS (Volusia)

ITABO (Citrus): Probably a corruption of Creek *italwa*, meaning "town" or "tribe."

ITCHETUCKNEE SPRINGS (Columbia): Interpreted by one authority as "blistered tobacco," but by another as "beaver pond." The latter source believes the name to be composed of Creek *we* ("water"), *echas* ("beaver"), and *toka* or *tomeka* ("because of" or "made by"). Early spellings include "Weechatooka" and similar renderings.

JUNGLES (Pinellas)

KEY LARGO (Monroe): Longest of the reef islands (Spanish *largo* means "long").

KEYS (Dade)

LARGE MOUND EDGE (Glades)

LARGO (Pinellas): Named for nearby LAKE LARGO, which received the name (*largo* is Spanish for "long") from one of the nineteenth-century developers in preference to the less interesting "Big Lake" by which it had formerly been known.

LIGHTWOOD CREEK (Santa Rosa): For the pine or "lightwood" in the area.

LIMEDALE (Marion)

LIMEROCK (Jackson)

LIMESTONE (Hardee)

LITTLE BLACK CREEK and SOUTH FORK BLACK CREEK (Clay)

LITTLE BOILING CREEK (Santa Rosa)

LITTLE BULLFROG CREEK (Hillsborough)

LITTLE CREEK (Holmes, Gulf Lake, Orange, Osceola, Walton)

LITTLE CROOKED CREEK (Bay)

LITTLE RIVER (Dade, Gadsden, Suwannee)

LONG BEACH (Manatee)

LONG BEACH COLONY (Palm Beach)

LONG BRANCH (Bay, Clay, Duval, Liberty, Manatee, Orange, Okaloosa, Santa Rosa, Walton)

LONG BRANCH BLACK CREEK (Clay)

LONG CREEK (Walton and Okaloosa)

LONG ISLAND (Monroe, Pinellas)

LONG KEY (Manatee, Monroe)

LONG POINT KEY (Monroe)

LONGVIEW (Charlotte)

MAGNESIA SPRING (Lake)

MARTYRS (Monroe): A group of islands, forming a part of the Keys, called *Los Martires* by Ponce de León because they resembled suffering men.

MIAMI BEACH, MIAMI RIVER, MIAMI SPRINGS, NORTH MIAMI, SOUTH MIAMI, and NORTH MIAMI BEACH (Dade): See MIAMI, discussed in chapter 4.

MONTEVISTA (Lake): An American combination of Spanish words, intended for "mountain view" because of the view of the Thlauhatka Hills from the site.

MOUND KEY (Lee): Named for the prehistoric Indian burial mounds here. Florida's *Archives and History News* for November and December of 1970 reported that there is strong documentary evidence that this site was the location of the principal Calusa town of Colos [*sic*], visited by Pedro Menéndez de Avilés in 1565. It has recently been added to the National Register of Historic Places.

MOUNTAIN CITY (Okaloosa)

MOUNTAIN LAKE (Polk): Florida is not mountainous anywhere, but she has hilly areas, and her "mountain" names refer to these hills.

MUCKWAY (Glades): Named for the rich black muck soil of the Everglades area.

MUD KEY (Monroe)

MULAT (Santa Rosa): Named for BAY MULAT ("yellow bay"), *mulat* being from the Spanish *mulato* ("yellow" or "tawny").

MYAKKA RIVER (Manatee and Sarasota), MYAKKA CITY (Manatee), MYAKKA LAKE (Manatee), MIAKKA (Sarasota), EAST MYAKKA (Manatee), and PORT MAYACA (Martin): All related to MIAMI, discussed in chapter 4.

NEW RIVER (Broward, Liberty, Bradford): The one in Broward County is a nine-mile-long river running through Ft. Lauderdale—said to be the deepest in the world for its length and width. Indian legend says the river appeared overnight.

NEWTON (Levy): First called *Newtown*.

OBSERVATION ISLAND (Palm Beach)

OKLAWAHA (Marion): A place named for the OCKLAWAHA RIVER (Marion, Sumter, and Putnam), a corruption of Creek *aklowahe*, meaning "muddy."

OJUS (Dade): The Seminole word for "plenty." Said to have been named in about 1897 by Mr. Albert Fitch, who told an Indian he hoped to raise many pineapples and asked what he should name the place. The Indian suggested *Ojus*, meaning "much," "abundant," or "plenty."

OKEFENOKEE SWAMP (Southeastern Georgia and Northeastern Florida): From Hitchiti *oki* ("water") and Creek *fenoke* ("trembling")—thus "trembling water." Another name has been *E-cun-fino-cau*, from Creek *ekan* ("land") and *fenoke* ("trembling")—thus "trembling earth." The swamp is an area of mystery and quicksands.

OLD TOWN (Dixie): A name referring to the fact that the place was an old Indian settlement.

OLUSTEE (Baker): A name which may be from Creek *oklusti* ("blackish"), or from Hitchiti *oki* ("water") combined with Creek *luste* ("black"). There is also OLUSTEE CREEK (Columbia and Union), meaning "Black Water Creek."

OLUSTEE BATTLEFIELD (Columbia): The major engagement of the Civil War in Florida was fought here on February 20, 1865. It has recently been added to the National Register of Historic Places. The battlefield is two miles west of the town, across a county line. See OLUSTEE, above.

OSKIN (Okaloosa): A name of recent application said to have been derived from the Seminole-Creek *oski*, meaning "rain."

PALATLAKAHA CREEK (Lake): A corruption of *Pilaklikaha*, meaning "big swamp site," from *opilwa* ("swamp"), plus *lako* ("big"), plus *laiki* ("site").

PANASOFFKEE (Sumter): The name of a village and a lake, derived from Seminole *pani* ("valley") and *sufki* ("deep")—hence "deep valley."

PARK (Martin)

PARK RIDGE (Polk)

PARKTON (Manatee)

PASSAGE KEY and PASSAGE KEY INLET (Manatee)

PEBBLEDALE (Polk)

PENINSULA (Volusia)

PENINSULA POINT (Franklin)

PILHUENA ISLAND (Marion): This name is of unknown origin, but it seems probable that the first element is from Creek *opilwa* ("swamp") or *pilo* ("boat").

PLAINS (Highlands)

POINT LA VISTA (Duval): A point of land on the St. Johns River, *la vista* being "the view" in Spanish.

PRAIRIE and PRAIRIE JUNCTION (Polk)

PRAIRIE CREEK (Charlotte, DeSoto)

PRAIRIE RIDGE (Okeechobee)

PROSPECT BLUFF (Franklin): Translated from *Achackweithle*, corrupted from Creek *ahechka* ("view" or "prospect"), plus *huethle* ("standing (up)"), applied to an acclivity.

PUNTA GORDA (Charlotte): Renamed in 1888 for a point of land near the town which the Spaniards had called *Punta Gorda*, meaning "wide point." PUNTA GORDA BAY and PUNTA GORDA WHARF are in the same county.

PUNTA RASA JUNCTION (Lee): An offspring of PUNTA RASA, discussed in chapter 4.

RAINBOW SPRINGS (Marion): For the many-colored appearance of the water when the sun is high.

RED BLUFF CREEK (Escambia)

REDHEAD (Washington): For a red clay hill.

REDLAND (Dade): For the red soil of the "redlands district," where it is located.

RED LEVEL (Citrus): For the reddish tinge of the soil and the level terrain.

RED ROCK (Santa Rosa)

RIDGE (Highlands)

RIDGETOP (Jackson)

RIDGEWOOD and RIDGEWOOD JUNCTION (Polk)

ROCK BLUFF (Liberty): For a rock bluff or embankment there. Also called ROCK BLUFF STILL (for a turpentine still).

ROCK CREEK (Charlotte, Jackson, Liberty, Okaloosa, Wakulla)

ROCKDALE (Dade): For a large rock quarry there.

ROCK HARBOR and ROCK HARBOR KEY (Monroe)

ROCKHILL (Hernando)

ROCKLEDGE (Brevard): For the ledges of coquina rock along the shore.

ROCK SPRINGS (Marion)

ROCK SPRINGS RUN (Orange)

ROCKY (Levy)

ROCKY BRANCH (Escambia and Polk)

ROCKY COMFORT CREEK (Gadsden)

ROCKY CREEK (Escambia, Hillsborough, Jackson, Levy, Okaloosa, Santa Rosa, Suwannee, Taylor, Walton)

ROCKY CREEK RUN (Levy)

ROCKY POINT (Alachua): For the abundance of natural lime-rock. Mrs. Ida McDonald, daughter of area pioneers, reports in a historical paper, "The first rock road in the state was built by the men of Rocky Point over which to haul their truck to the freight depot."

ROCKY POINT (Hillsborough)

ROUND LAKE (Jackson): For the circular lake near it.

RURAL (Hernando)

SADDLE BUNCH KEY (Monroe): Said to be in the shape of a saddle.

SHELL BLUFF (Flagler): For a hill of snail shells left by Indians. Also known as ANDALUSIA POST OFFICE.

SHELL CREEK and SHELL CREEK MANOR (Charlotte)

SHELL POINT (Wakulla)

SINK CREEK (Jackson): Also called SINK CREEK POST OFFICE. Named for a nearby creek that sinks underground and re-appears a quarter of a mile away.

SISTERS CREEK (Duval): Named for two small islands close together and alike.

SOUTHLAND (Charlotte)

SOUTH TAMPA, TAMPA BAY, TAMPA DOWNS, TAMPA NORTHERN JUNCTION, EAST TAMPA, PORT TAMPA, PORT TAMPA CITY, and WEST TAMPA (Hillsborough): All offsprings of TAMPA, chapter 4. There is also TAMPA SHORES (Pinellas), formerly called OLDSMAR (see chapter 3).

STEEL BRIDGE (Calhoun)

STEEPHEAD (Gadsden): Also spelled "Steaphead."

SULPHUR POINT (Bay)

SULPHUR SPRING (Citrus, Pasco)

SULPHUR SPRINGS (Hillsborough)

SUNNYSIDE (Clay)

SWAMP CREEK (Gadsden)

TALOFA (Putnam): The Creek word meaning "town."

TEN THOUSAND ISLANDS (Collier): It is said that "ten thousand" is no exaggeration, but is rather an underestimate of the number of these islands off the coast of Collier County.

THONOTOSASSA (Hillsborough): The name of a town on THONO-TOSASSA LAKE. It derives from Seminole-Creek *lonoto* or *thlonoto* ("flint"), plus *sasse* ("is there")—thus "flint is there." There are several aboriginal flint quarries in the vicinity of the lake, where flint was quarried for arrow and spear heads. THONOTOSASSA JUNCTION (Hillsborough) is an offspring.

TOHOPEKALIGA (Osceola): The name of two lakes, one called EAST TOHOPEKALIGA. The name is from the Seminole-Creek *tohopki* ("fort"), plus *a-laika* ("site")—thus "site of the fort."

TOHOPKEE (Osceola): Derived from the Seminole-Creek *tohopki*, meaning "fort."

TROPIC (Brevard)

VALLE (Holmes): Believed to be a shortened version of "valley"; it is at the head of Euchee Valley.

VIEW (Highlands)

VISTA (Levy): Spanish for "view."

WALL SPRINGS (Pinellas): For a walled-in spring and swimming pool.

WESTVILLE (Holmes)

WHITE SPRINGS (Hamilton): From the white sulphur spring there. WHITE SULPHUR SPRINGS (Hamilton) is the spring from which the town of WHITE SPRINGS got its name.

WHITEHOUSE (Duval)

WILDERNESS (Clay)

WILDMERE LAKE (Seminole)

YELLOW RIVER (Okaloosa)

ZOLFO SPRINGS (Hardee): *Zolfo* is Italian for "sulphur" and was applied by Italian laborers in the vicinity.

Bibliography

NOTE: Maps referred to in the book have for the most part been printed in sources listed below, and thus have not been listed separately. In addition we have relied constantly upon the Sectional Map of Florida issued by the State Department of Agriculture, 1958 and 1963, and Florida maps furnished us by Rand McNally & Co. from 1893, 1903, 1913, 1923, and 1933 publications. Encyclopediae and other reference books have also been omitted from the bibliography, though they have been helpful, as has the Authorized Version of the Holy Bible.

ARTICLES AND BOOKS

"Alachua County Takes Name from Big Sinkhole—Histories of Towns, Settlements Recalled." *Gainesville Daily Sun*. Gainesville, Fla., July 30, 1958.
American Name Society Bulletin 14 (April 1969)—Note on name change of Cape Canaveral; 10 (April 1968)—Note on Jonathan Dickinson; 14 (April 1969)—Note on Rattlesnake, Fla.
"Azalea Garden Enthusiast Dies." *Gainesville Sun*. Gainesville, Fla., January 21, 1966.
Bartram, William. *Travels Through North and South Carolina, Georgia, and East and West Florida. . . .* Philadelphia, 1791. Reprinted as *The Travels of William Bartram*. Edited by Mark Van Doren. New York: Dover Publications, 1928.
Beeler, M. S. "America—The Story of a Name." *Names* 1 (March 1953):1–14.
Bennett, Charles E. *Settlement of Florida*. Gainesville: University of Florida Press, 1968.
Bickel, Karl A. *The Mangrove Coast*. New York: Coward-McCann, 1942.
Boone, Lalla. "Florida: The Land of Epithets." *Southern Folklore Quarterly* 22 (June 1958):86–92.
Bresee, Felice. "Brooksville—Hernando County." In "A Gallery of Florida Towns." *All Florida and TV Week Magazine*. October 28, 1962.
———. "Marianna—Jackson County." In "A Gallery of Florida Towns." *All Florida and TV Week Magazine*. October 7, 1962.
Brevard, Caroline Mays. *A History of Florida from the Treaty of 1763 to Our Own Times*. DeLand, Fla.: The Florida State Historical Society, 1924–25.

Bridges, Stacey. "Palm Coast, More Growing Pains for Florida." *Gainesville Sun*, Gainesville, Fla., August 1, 1971.

Buchholz, F. W. *History of Alachua County*. St. Augustine, Fla.: The Record Company, 1929.

Campbell, Richard L. *Historical Sketches of Colonial Florida*. Cleveland, Ohio: The Williams Publishing Co., 1892.

"Cape Is Canaveral Again." *Gainesville Sun*. Gainesville, Fla., October 10, 1973.

"Cape Kennedy Bill Dead This Year." *Gainesville Sun*. Gainesville, Fla., December 30, 1970.

"Cape Renamed After Kennedy." *Gainesville Sun*. Gainesville, Fla., November 29, 1963.

Carter, Clarence Edwin, ed. *Territorial Papers of the United States, Vol. XXII, Florida Territory, 1821–1824*. Washington: U.S. Government Printing Office, 1956.

Cassidy, F. G. Review of George R. Stewart's *American Place-Names*. In *Names* (June 1972): 141–46.

Chun, Diane. "Windsor's Dreams Were Frozen in 1895." *Gainesville Sun*. Gainesville, Fla., August 6, 1972.

Copeland, Leeila S., and Dovell, J. E. *La Florida*. Austin, Tex.: The Steck Company, 1957.

Corse, Carita Doggett. *The Key to the Golden Islands*. Chapel Hill: The University of North Carolina Press, 1931.

DeBrahm, John Gerar William. *The Atlantic Pilot*. London: Printed for the Author by T. Spilsbury, and sold by S. Leacroft, 1772.

DeLand, Helen Parce. *Story of DeLand and Lake Helen, Florida*. Louis H. Walden, 1928.

Dodd, Dorothy. *Florida: The Land of Romance*. Tallahassee, Fla.: Department of Agriculture, 1956.

Dunn, Hampton. *Re-Discover Florida*. Miami: Hurricane House Publishers, 1969.

Ellerbe, Helen Cubberly. "Garbled Railroad History." In "Voice of the People." *Gainesville Sun*. Gainesville, Fla., October 3, 1971.

Fairbanks, George Rainsford. *Florida, Its History and Its Romance*. Jacksonville, Fla.: H. & W. B. Drew Co., 1904.

Federal Writers' Project. *Florida: A Guide to the Southernmost State*. New York: Oxford University Press, 1939.

Federal Writers' Project of the Works Projects Administration. "Florida Place-Names." Unpublished manuscript.

Fitzgerald, T. E. *Historical Highlights of Volusia County*. Daytona Beach, Fla.: The Observer Press, 1939.

Florida Board of Conservation, Division of Water Resources and Conservation. *Gazetteer of Florida Streams*. Tallahassee, Fla., 1966.

Florida Department of Agriculture. *Know Florida*. Tallahassee, Fla., 1958.

Fontaneda, Hernando de Escalante. *Letter of Hernando de Soto, and Memoir of Hernando de Escalante Fontaneda Respecting Florida. Written in Spain, About the year 1575*. Translated by Buckingham Smith. Washington, 1854.

Ford, Norman D. *Norman Ford's Florida*. 14th ed. Greenlawn, N.Y.: Harian Publications, 1970.

Fryman, Frank B., Jr. "Fort Cooper Site Excavated." *Archives & History News* (January–February 1971): 1.

Gannett, Henry. *The Origin of Certain Place Names in the United States*. Washington: U.S. Government Printing Office, 1902.

Gold, Pleasant Daniel. *History of Duval County, Florida*. St. Augustine, Fla.: The Record Company, 1928.

———. *History of Volusia County, Florida.* DeLand, Fla.: The E. O. Painter Printing Co., 1927.

"Good Old Fort Lonesome." *Gainesville Sun.* Gainesville, Fla., June 27, 1970.

Gore, E. H. *From Florida Sand to "The City Beautiful."* Privately published, n.d.

Hamilton, John W. "A Simplified List of Spanish Place-Names in Florida." Unpublished manuscript. University of Florida, 1946.

Hanna, Alfred Jackson, and Hanna, Kathryn Abbey. *Florida's Golden Sands.* Indianapolis and New York: The Bobbs-Merrill Co., 1950.

———. *Lake Okeechobee.* Indianapolis: The Bobbs-Merrill Co., 1948.

Hanna, Kathryn Abbey. *Florida: Land of Change.* Chapel Hill: The University of North Carolina Press, 1941.

"How Did Keys Get Names?" *The Key West Citizen.* Key West, Fla., November 15, 1964.

Jahoda, Gloria. *The Other Florida.* New York: Charles Scribner's Sons, 1967.

Kennedy, Stetson. *Palmetto Country.* New York: Duell, Sloan & Pearce, 1942.

LaCoe, Norm. "Her Wild Days Are Over." *Gainesville Sun.* Gainesville, Fla., March 19, 1967.

Lanier, Sidney. *Florida: Its Scenery, Climate, and History.* Philadelphia: J. B. Lippincott & Co., 1876.

Life and Speeches of Henry Clay. Vol. 1. New York: James B. Swain, 1842.

Lorant, Stefan, ed. *The New World.* New York: Duell, Sloan & Pearce, 1946.

Lowery, Woodbury. *The Spanish Settlements Within the Present Limits of the United States. Florida, 1562-1574.* New York: Russell & Russell, 1959.

McDonald, Ida. "A Manuscript Reminiscence of Payne's Prairie." Unpublished manuscript, n.d.

McMullen, Edwin Wallace, Jr. *English Topographic Terms in Florida, 1563-1874.* Gainesville: University of Florida Press, 1953.

Mixson, Buzz. "From the Area Desk." *Gainesville Sun.* Gainesville, Fla., April 19, 1969.

Moore-Willson, Minnie. *The Seminoles of Florida.* Kissimmee, Fla., 1928.

Morris, Allen. *The Florida Handbook 1947-48.* Tallahassee, Fla.: The Peninsular Publishing Company, 1946.

———. *The Florida Handbook 1949-50.* Tallahassee, Fla.: The Peninsular Publishing Company, 1949.

———. *The Florida Handbook.* 3d ed. Tallahassee, Fla.: The Peninsular Publishing Company, 1952.

———. *The Florida Handbook.* 4th ed. Tallahassee, Fla.: The Peninsular Publishing Company, 1953.

———. *The Florida Handbook.* 5th ed. Tallahassee, Fla.: The Peninsular Publishing Company, 1955.

Morse, Jedediah. *The American Gazetteer.* Charlestown, Mass.: Printed by and for Samuel Etheridge, and for Thomas and Andrews, Boston, 1804.

Mullin, John M. *Facts to Know Florida.* Jacksonville, Fla.: Mullen Feature Syndicate, 1938.

"Names Sound Odd to Others but Familiar to Home Folk." *Florida Times-Union.* Jacksonville, Fla., September 20, 1953.

Oppel, Rich. "Czechs in Fla. . . ." *Gainesville Sun.* Gainesville, Fla., July 25, 1968.

"Osceola's 'Bones' in Marion County." *Gainesville Sun.* Gainesville, Fla., October 2, 1976.

Pap, Leo. "The Portuguese Adstratum in North American Place-Names." *Names* (June 1972): 111-30.

Patrick, Rembert Wallace. *Florida under Five Flags.* Gainesville: University of Florida Press, 1955.

Plowden, Jean. *History of Hardee County*. Wauchula, Fla.: Printed by the *Florida Advocate*, 1929.

Ramsay, Robert L. *Our Storehouse of Missouri Place Names*. (Missouri Handbook Number Two, *The University of Missouri Bulletin*.) Columbia: University of Missouri Press, 1952.

Read, William A. *Florida Place-Names of Indian Origin and Seminole Personal Names*. Baton Rouge: Louisiana State University Press, 1934.

Rhodes, Harrison Garfield, and Dumont, Mary Wolfe. *A Guide to Florida for Tourists, Sportsmen and Settlers*. New York: Dodd, Mead & Co., 1912.

Romans, Bernard. *A Concise Natural History of East and West Florida*. Vol. 1. New York, 1775.

Simpson, J. Clarence. *A Provisional Gazetteer of Florida Place-Names of Indian Derivation Either Obsolescent or Retained Together with Others of Recent Application*. Tallahassee, Fla.: Florida Geological Survey, Special Publication No. 1, 1956.

Sixth Report. U.S. Geographic Board. Washington, D.C.: U.S. Government Printing Office, 1933. Republished by Gale Research Company, Book Tower, Detroit, 1967.

Solís de Merás, Gonzalo. *Pedro Menéndez de Avilés, Adelantado Governor and Captain-General of Florida, Memorial by Gonzalo Solís de Merás*. Translated from the Spanish with Notes by Jeannette Thurber Conner. Deland, Fla.: The Florida State Historical Society, 1923.

Stewart, George R. *Names on the Land*. New York: Random House, 1945.

Utley, George B. "Origin of the County Names in Florida." *The Florida Historical Quarterly* 1(October 1908): 29–35.

Vignoles, Charles. *Observations Upon the Floridas*. New York: E. Bliss & E. White, 1823.

Warnke, James R. *Ghost Towns of Florida*. Boynton Beach, Fla.: Star Publishing Co., 1971.

Wattenbarger, James. "Passing Panorama." Unpublished manuscript. University of Florida, 1942.

"Yes, There Really Was a Hogtown." In "Old Gainesville Album." *Gainesville Sun*. Gainesville, Fla., October 25, 1970.

INTERVIEWS, TELEPHONE CONSULTATIONS, AND CORRESPONDENCE

Alachua County Abstract Company.

Betty Carver, Secretary to Fred W. Maley, Village Manager, Bal Harbour, Florida.

Mrs. J. C. Dunn, Gainesville, Florida.

Barbara Foster, *Gainesville Sun* Librarian, Gainesville, Florida.

Office of Don Fuqua, U.S. Representative.

Miss Marion Futch, Montgomery, Alabama.

W. Lansing Gleason, Eau Gallie, Florida.

Edward J. Gurney, U.S. Senator.

Faculty Members of the University of Florida College of Agriculture and College of Arts and Sciences.

Librarians at the University of Florida Library, the P. K. Yonge Library of Florida History, and the Gainesville Public Library, Gainesville, Florida.

Duane C. Moxon, Superintendent, United States Department of the Interior, Bureau of Indian Affairs, Seminole Agency.

Ocala (Florida) Chamber of Commerce.

Moody Pearce, Clerk of the Circuit Court, Crawfordville, Florida.

Postmasters at Eau Gallie, Florida; Eau Galle, Wisconsin; Bristol, Florida; and Bal Harbour, Florida.

Mrs. Carolyn Lewis Prowse, Orlando, Florida.

Dr. Thomas Pyles, University of Florida and Northwestern University.
Ralph Turlington, Alachua County Representative in the Florida Legislature.
Wisconsin State Historical Society
And many, many others whose knowledge of Florida history and folklore we have
absorbed from childhood onward.